Foreword

With explosive growth in house-church numbers in the developing world today, and in church planting in general, the publishing of "The Christian Compass" resource handbook is very timely indeed. Rev. Les Wheeldon has produced a wonderful easy to read, study manual that will be of enormous encouragement and help to those in pioneering evangelism, in church planting and in leadership. While there is much excitement and activity in the developing world relating to the church planting movement phenomena today, and in turn the growth of Christianity, if there is cause for concern it is based around the lack of Biblical knowledge and of training for those thrust into church leadership. The Christian Compass is a very practical and useful resource tool of sound Biblical teaching, where both mature believers and those new to the Christian faith, can benefit from in their personal walk with the Lord, in their study of the Word, and in the preparation of messages to make disciples for Jesus Christ.

Rev. John Elliott
International Director
World Outreach International

Copyright © 2010 Leslie John Wheeldon

All rights reserved.

All scripture quotations, unless otherwise indicated, are taken from the New King James Version®. Copyright © 1982 by Thomas Nelson, Inc. Used by permission. All rights reserved.
Scripture quotations marked KJV are from the King James Version of the Bible.

Re-print with study notes Copyright © 2012

Cover photograph by Nick Allsopp

Preface

Since beginning my ministry in 1979 I have been privileged to get to know thousands of faithful servants of God in over sixty countries. I have been touched by their willingness to suffer hardship and sometimes persecution as they have faithfully taught God's word, sometimes despite having little access to libraries or teaching materials. This little book is dedicated to them.
I am most grateful to ICM Singapore and especially Richard Toh for asking me to write this book. I also must thank my dear wife Vicki for her patience and dedication in preparing and arranging the material; also Rob and Carol Betts for their expertise in editing the final draft.

Les Wheeldon
January 2011

CONTENTS:

1: WHO IS GOD? — 1
- How do we know God? — 2
- What are the unique characteristics of God? — 4
- The Trinity: Who is the Father? — 10
- The Trinity: Who is the Son? — 14
- Jesus is both the Son of God and God the Son — 15
- The Trinity: Who is the Holy Spirit? — 17

2: THE PLAN OF SALVATION — 19
- Mankind is a special creation but with a fallen nature — 19
- God's Solution — 34
- Our necessary response to obtain assurance of eternal life — 38

3: THE BIBLE – THE WORD OF GOD — 42
- The need of the hour: to hear God speak — 42
- Why is the Bible so important? — 43
- The spiritual art of reading the Bible — 48

4: WATER BAPTISM AND ITS MEANING — 57
- What the Bible teaches about water baptism — 57
- Water Baptism: a picture of death and resurrection — 59
- Some important questions about baptism — 60

5: THE PERSON AND WORK OF THE HOLY SPIRIT — 63
- Who is the Holy Spirit? — 63
- What does the Holy Spirit do? — 66
- How do I receive the Holy Spirit? — 70
- Eight Biblical types of baptism in the Holy Spirit — 74
- The Gifts of the Spirit — 81

6: THE PRICE AND POWER OF DISCIPLESHIP — 88
- The Great Commission to make Disciples — 88
- The example of Jesus — 89
- Characteristics of true disciples — 90

THE CHRISTIAN'S COMPASS

7: THE MINISTRY OF PRAYER AND INTERCESSION — 101
- What is prayer? — 101
- The teaching of Jesus on prayer — 102
- The Example of Jesus in Prayer — 111
- An Example of Prayer in the Old Testament — 117
- An Example of Prayer in the New Testament — 118
- The teaching of Paul on prayer — 119
- Examples of prayer in history — 120
- Practical helps to follow God's order in prayer — 123

8: DIVINE HEALING AND DELIVERANCE — 124
- Divine healing — 124
- Deliverance: who is Satan? — 133
- How do people become troubled by evil spirits? — 137
- Biblical deliverance –the Gadarene demoniac — 142
- Summary of the Main Steps in deliverance — 144

9: THE CHALLENGE OF LEADERSHIP — 151
- Principles of leadership in the New Testament — 151
- How did Jesus form leaders and how is this relevant to us today? 156
- Paul's teaching on apostles'/leaders' attitude — 162
- Leadership in Israel — 166
- church leadership in the New Testament — 168
- The role of leaders — 170
- The Role of deacons — 173
- Qualifications for leadership/eldership — 174

10: THE PREACHING MINISTRY — 176
- The need to declare God's truth — 176
- Essential foundations of the preaching ministry — 177
- The snares of the preaching ministry — 182
- Five spiritual keys for preachers — 185

Ten practical keys --- 188

11: CHURCH PLANTING AND EVANGELISM ---------------------- 191

Methods, principles and passion! ----------------------------------- 191

Ten principles of spiritual life for the Church planter -------------- 192

Methods in Church planting -- 200

Conclusion --- 207

12: CHURCH GROWTH --- 208

Growth with God's approval -- 208

Keys to obtaining outpouring of the Holy Spirit -------------------- 209

Promoting growth in older Churches -------------------------------- 218

The seven Churches of Asia -- 220

Key methods that can be used to grow the Church ----------------- 224

Identifying false methods of Church growth ----------------------- 225

Snares of Church growth -- 227

What is success? --- 229

13: A GLORIOUS CHURCH IN A GLORIOUS KINGDOM --------- 231

The keys of the kingdom and the New Testament Church -------- 231

What are the keys of the kingdom? --------------------------------- 234

The King and the Kingdom -- 238

Parables of the kingdom and the Church --------------------------- 239

Keys to a healthy Church in the book of Acts ---------------------- 242

Attacks on the early Church -- 242

Causes and cures of divisions in the Church ----------------------- 246

The signs of Saul's carnality: -------------------------------------- 250

The marks of David's spirituality: ---------------------------------- 251

Ephesians - God's blueprint for a glorious Church ----------------- 252

Solomon's Temple – a type of the Church -------------------------- 254

Ezra – the Temple rebuilt – a type of the Church rediscovered --- 255

14: THE FUTURE -- 258

Four main methods of interpreting Revelation --------------------- 258

The Prophetic Timetable --- 261

THE CHRISTIAN'S COMPASS

An overview of the book of Revelation -------------------------- 270

The Millennium -- 272

The Day of Judgment -- 274

The new heaven and the new earth -------------------------------- 277

The Purpose of teaching about the End Times --------------------- 278

The Christian's Compass study guide. --------------------------- **280**

1

WHO IS GOD?

Long ago there was a king who wanted to know who God is. He asked all his wise men to show him God. The wise men protested that there was no ruler who had ever asked such a thing. But the king insisted, and finally commanded his wise men to leave his presence, travel the world, and not to return until they had found God.

Some months later a shepherd heard of the king's desire to see God. He sent the king a message saying: "Please let the King meet me in my village square at noon on a certain day and I will show him God"

This caused quite a stir, and the king himself became very excited. Now it was a very hot country, in the days before there were cars or air conditioning; so the king was carried in a sedan chair, with curtains to protect him from the sun. At last they reached the village, and at midday the shepherd came striding down from the hills and walked into the square. The king slowly stepped out of his chair, and approached the shepherd.

"So shepherd, are you able to show me where God is?"
"Yes", said the shepherd, "look, there He is!", and he pointed straight up in the sky at the midday sun. The king looked up but instantly turned his eyes away. In pain and despair the king cried out, "I cannot look at the sun! It would blind me!" "Indeed", said the shepherd. "You want to see God, and yet you cannot even look upon one of the little things He has made!"

The Christian's Compass

HOW DO WE KNOW GOD?

1. People Have a Thirst to Know God

Human beings are born not knowing God because there is a veil of sin on our hearts. The Bible says that only a fool would say there is no God [Psalm 14:1]. It also says that every person knows, from the order and beauty of creation, that God is powerful and that He exists [Romans 1:20]. But the Bible also says that God is unknowable unless He reveals Himself [1 Timothy 6:16 and John 1:18]. Throughout the world people have tried to understand God, and in their ignorance they have built up false religions which present God as distant, cold and unloving. Many religions portray God as a dragon, or a strange and fearful animal [Romans 1:23]. In Athens, Paul found an altar to the unknown God [Acts 17:23]. We cannot work out from philosophy who God is or what He is like.

2. God has Revealed Himself

There are several stages in the self-revelation of God:

(a) The Natural World Declares God's Glory and Power

> If a person walking on a beach found a computer, he would immediately ask the question: who made it? He would not assume that the computer was the random product of wave action!! If he found a computer with radio links to hundreds of other computers, and cameras, microphones, and communication skills, he would ask where this 'conscious mind' came from. Creation points to a thinking, intelligent, and powerful being who created the world we see around us. [Psalm 19:1-4]

> Romans 1:19-20 informs us that several essential characteristics of God are known by all people through the creation, in particular His eternal power and Godhead.

At the beginning of the 19th century, surgeons were beginning to understand the complexity of the human body by performing autopsies and examining the way the body functions. One atheist boldly claimed that he could demonstrate the function of every part of the human body in purely physical terms. A human being was a mechanical machine, a collection of chemicals, and nothing more. However, a Christian surgeon hearing these words pointed the atheist to a piano and issued the challenge: take it to pieces and tell me when you find the music!

The point is of the utmost importance since the piano was made for the purpose of producing music. Music has no physical substance, even though it is produced by physical means. It begins in the human soul. The piano is meaningless unless there is music. So too the physical world, and mankind itself, has no meaning without the Creator's plan and purpose, which is that people should live a beautiful life to God, full of the music of love and kindness.

(b) Human Conscience has an Awareness of God [Romans 2:14-15]

Human beings are aware of right and wrong, and we are also aware that things are not well with humanity. The awareness of right and wrong is present in everyone. This indicates that it is the stamp of the Creator. Paul says in Romans 1:32 that we know the righteous judgment of God. It is because of this knowledge that God will hold us guilty before Him.

This general revelation is common to all mankind to some degree or other and it is the basis for the order of society with standards imposed by governments through the police and the justice system. It is this common understanding that makes us respond to the gospel since it awakens the longing for righteousness which is in everyone.

We can know right and wrong through our conscience, but the way of salvation is only known through the scripture and the work of the Holy Spirit. It cannot be deduced from the natural light of reason or observing creation.

(c) God has Revealed Himself through the Bible

The Bible is God's word spoken to God's servants, and is the key to all we know about God. Without the Bible we would be forced to speculate about God, to work out who He is by logic and philosophy. This would be only guesswork. But God has spoken and revealed Himself and His plans for the human race.

(d) God has Revealed Himself through the Incarnation

Jesus is the exact image of God. He shows the heart of God and shows exactly how God feels, reacts, and thinks. The Law shows God's moral attributes, and Creation shows His wisdom and power; but in order to show God as a person, God sent His Son.

WHAT ARE THE UNIQUE CHARACTERISTICS OF GOD?

This question is of huge importance, since it is only as we have a correct perspective on God that we fully realise the power of His being, in comparison with other beings such as the devil and humans. There is only one God and this means that there is no rival to Him. There is no being that comes close to even resembling God. Mankind is made in the image of God, but there is a vast difference between what God has created and the Creator Himself. Mankind can never be God.

There were once some scientists who got into conversation with God and explained that they now had the power to create a human life in the laboratory. God was very interested to see how they would do this, and so looked on in wonder. They reached out to take some clay to shape a human form, but God stopped them and said: "That is my clay, make your own!"

---

1. God is God! [Deuteronomy 4:35; Isaiah 43:10-13, 44:6-8]

This is the greatest concept that the human mind can ever think about. It is difficult even to begin to think of a being that is dependent on no other person or power. God does not breathe to live! He *is*. He does not come from any source, since He is the source of all.

One common question asked by unbelievers is, *"Who made God?"* This question reveals the weakness of the human mind to imagine a being without cause. God is the origin of all things. Ezekiel 47:1-12 and Revelation 22:1 describe the Temple and the throne of God with a river flowing from them. The obvious question is, *"Where does the water come from?"* It is not a trickle but a mighty flood as great as Niagara. It waters the whole earth, and beyond this fact is the truth that the whole universe is created and upheld by Almighty God. The river reveals the immensity of the fact of God. He flows with ceaseless supply, with resources that come from within His being. He can create as much or as little as He wishes. He can create a thousand universes as easily as one, or a million!

How big is God? The question is impossible to answer, since God's being is not to be measured by size. His being is defined rather by His unity of consciousness: He is a Person! The Bible declares that He is one [Deuteronomy 6:4]. His size is irrelevant since the greatest fact is that He is God. Such a being is High and incapable of being reduced to a symbol or an image. Idolatry in all its forms dishonours God and must be renounced, even in Christian forms. Pictures of Jesus can never convey a true sense of who He is.

Who is God?

2. Omnipresent - God is Everywhere

The French philosopher Voltaire once observed a child learning his catechism in an orchard on a beautiful sunny day. "Young man," said Voltaire, "I will give you all the apples in the orchard if you can tell me where God is."

"Really sir?" said the young man. "And can you tell me then where He is not?"

Jeremiah describes God seeing all things, including things done in secret [Jeremiah 23:23-24]. David describes the impossibility of escaping the presence of God [Psalm 139: 7-12]. This means that He is a witness of the sins of the human race, but also near at hand to save whoever calls upon Him. Acts 17:24-28 describes how even the heathen live in the compass of God's being. They do not know Him and are not inwardly in fellowship with Him, but they are surrounded by Him and sustained in their being by His merciful power that enfolds the whole universe. This does not contradict the fact that the Bible also reveals a personal manifestation of His presence in certain places and at certain times. God is freely revealed in heaven [Revelation 4]. God was manifested on earth through His Son and also now through His Church.

God is the sustainer of all things [Hebrews 1:3]. But God does not indwell everything. He sustains nature but He does not indwell trees, mountains and animals.

Canon Holmes, a missionary to India, saw Hindus tapping on trees and stones and asking, "Are you there?"

The Christian answers both yes and no: yes, God is all around us, sustaining all things, and within the reach of every person; but no, He is not confined to trees and stones, but is free in the universe and not bound by the things He has created.

Jesus taught us to pray that God would be glorified and that His kingdom would come on earth as it is in heaven. This means that although God is everywhere, He is able to come to His people in a way that may be felt and experienced. In times of great revivals or outpourings of the Holy Spirit, men and women fall down at the presence of God. The

Christian takes great comfort from the fact that God will never leave or forsake him, but will be with him always [Hebrews 13:5-6 and Matthew 28:20]. We as Christians are to rejoice when God's presence is powerfully felt, but we are also to take great comfort from the fact that even when we do not feel God's presence, He is still there with us.

3. Infinite

God cannot be measured by any human means. He is beyond all our attempts to contain or grasp Him. There is no other being that is remotely close to God in His infinite dimensions. True, people are partakers of eternity through the gift of God; also angels and fallen angels partake of this eternal existence. But even so, mankind and angels have a beginning. They were created. God has no beginning or end, either in time or space. Thus He is infinitely greater than the devil or all the powers of humanity and demons together.

God has more power in a whisper than all the combined powers that oppose Him. In the battle for the human soul, it is not a question of how strong we can become, but whether we will be on God's side or the devil's. As soon as it is clear where we stand, the conflict is brought to a conclusion, and the devil is defeated. The devil cannot stand against God in a believer: *"You are of God little children, and have overcome them, because He who is in you is greater than he who is in the world."* [1 John 4:4]

4. Eternal

God is *"from everlasting to everlasting"* [Psalm 90:2]. The word in the Hebrew here means 'to the farthest point of human sight, to the vanishing point in the distance'. As far as the human mind can stretch to the past or into the future, that is only the smallest beginning of this vast endless Being. He is different from mankind in that He has no beginning. God has neither beginning nor ending [Hebrews 7:3].

The everlasting quality of God's life is the bedrock of all the Christian concepts of righteousness, love, heaven and hell. Our finite human understanding is frail in the face of everlasting life. But it is the fact of a last judgment, with eternal consequences, which underlies the great urgency of the Bible.

5. All-knowing

God's knowledge is comprehensive. He knows the end from the beginning [Isaiah 46:10]. God knows all things from the past, present and the future. God's knowledge is perfect [Job 37:16]. God looks on the heart, not merely on outward things. He understands fully and immediately everything that is in the heart; it doesn't need to be explained to Him [1 Samuel 16:7 and 1 Chronicles 28:9].

The fact that God knows all things does not mean that He has predetermined what every person will do. The foreknowledge of God does not mean that He overrules our choices at every moment, or else we could never be held responsible for any action. No, God knows all things by virtue of His infinite being. He has given to us the power of moral choice by His infinite sovereign will.

6. All-powerful

"With God all things are possible" [Matthew 19:26]. God does whatever pleases Him; no power can override His will. Why, then, is Satan allowed to be active in the universe? God has decided that this will lead to the fulfilment of His plan to bring the human race to the desired goal of union with Himself. This fact of the Omnipotence of God is what underlies the Christian's boldness to pray for God to act and intervene on his behalf. There is nothing too big or too small to ask and nothing too hard for God to do. Because of this, faith alone is the key - not natural processes. It is as easy for God to give a person a million dollars, as it is for Him to give one dollar. God honours faith. Therefore, our view of God must be accurate or we will limit God's activity in our lives [Psalm 78:41].

Is there anything that God cannot do?
Yes, the Bible reveals that God cannot deny Himself [2 Timothy 2:13], He cannot lie [Titus 1:2], nor can He sin [1 John 3:5-6]. God can do anything, but He cannot cease to be perfect and loving.

7. Holy

God's holiness points to the fact that He is different from humans. His ways are higher and nobler.

> " *'For My thoughts are not your thoughts, nor are your ways My ways', says the LORD, 'For as the heavens are higher than the earth, so are My ways higher than your ways, and My thoughts than your thoughts.'* " [Isaiah 55: 8-9]

God's purity is not like the mere moral strictness some people seek to attain to. God's being is filled with a majesty and a glory which sets His holiness apart from all others. The effect of God's holiness is to produce godly fear in the heart of the person who approaches Him. Thus Moses approached the burning bush, but as he drew near, he was commanded to remove his sandals since the ground he stood on was holy. Moses then covered his face at the sight of God [Exodus 3:5-6].

God's love may make us think that God is one of us, since He comes down to our level; but despite His humility, He does not become base like us, rather He remains glorious. The disciples became so familiar with Jesus that on occasions they spoke to Him as if He were a mere man. Peter rebuked Jesus in Matthew 16:22. But only a few days later, he, James and John were on their faces before Him, blinded by the unspeakable glory of His being that was unveiled before them [Matthew 17:6].

God demands more than external moral conformity to His law. He requires truth in the inward parts [Psalm 51:6 and Matthew 5:8]. God is unapproachable in holiness, as revealed by the innermost chamber of the Tabernacle, which was out of bounds to unregenerate man [Hebrews 9:8]. Mankind in his sinful state cannot have fellowship with a holy God. The presence of God would mean death to him. The gulf between God and mankind is so huge, that it could only be spanned by the death of Christ [Hebrews 10:19].

8. Unchanging

"I am the Lord, I do not change." [Malachi 3:6]. God does not change in character, in nature, or in His thoughts and words. His promises cannot be broken nor His word changed. This means that when God speaks, an event takes place. People can speak and nothing changes. But when God speaks, it happens. So, when Christ said, *"It is finished"*, He was not describing something that He was observing; instead, He was declaring what He was doing by the force of His word.

9. Loving

Throughout the Bible, God is revealed as a God of love. God loved the guilty couple Adam and Eve even in the moment that they fell. God's instinct was not to condemn but to give hope and promise. He promised them salvation through the seed of the woman (thus giving a promise of the virgin birth from the dawn of human existence). He clothed them with animal skins before driving them out of paradise. The New Testament confirms this implicit love by great statements such as John 3:16, declaring that: *"God so loved the world that He gave His only begotten Son."*

God's great dilemma that is revealed in the cross is that He can neither cease to love nor cease to be holy and righteous. If God merely forgave people without demanding punishment, then He would cease to be righteous and holy. If He condemned the whole human race to hell, He would be holy but not loving. The cross shows God's answer to this, in that on the cross He remained both loving and righteous.

A certain ancient kingdom was being torn apart by the spread of adultery, and the resulting destruction of families. The nation was filled with misery and children were suffering terrible inward hurts and distress as they saw their parents hating each other. The king tried many methods to change this terrible slide into anarchy, but nothing seemed to work. At last he found a solution which was very harsh but worked instantly. He commanded that if any man were found to have committed adultery, he must be punished by having his eyes put out. The decree was passed, and through the fear of the king, adultery stopped in the kingdom.

Several years went by and the nation slowly emerged from the confusion and misery of those years. Then one day, his servants brought to him a man who had been caught in the act of adultery. His servants were distressed, and the king soon realised why. The man they had caught was the king's own son! The king thought long and hard. If he forgave his son then he would break his own law, but how could he punish his own son whom he loved? At last the king made his fearful decision. Two eyes would be blinded, not those of his son, but the eyes of the king himself. The deed was done, and the son was broken by the father's love. The nation was not weakened by this terrible and wonderful deed of love and righteousness, but was rather strengthened. The son too was filled with a deep resolve never to break his father's word again.

The cross fulfils God's love and righteousness in one great act. When God gave His Son Jesus, it was like allowing His own eyes to be put out, because of the great love with which He loves His Son.

---

10. Merciful

God's mercy indicates the fact that He is moved by the plight of the human race. It is by His mercies that mankind is allowed to continue to exist [Lamentations 3:22]. Mercy is the one point of appeal that God is unable to resist. Whoever appeals for mercy will find it, but only if it is passed on in merciful attitudes by the one who finds mercy. *"Blessed are the merciful for they shall obtain mercy."* [Matthew 5:7]

His mercy is revealed in His longsuffering towards disobedient sinners. God does not quickly punish us, but waits so that we may repent and He may have mercy on us.

11. Faithful

God is declared to be faithful on many occasions [for example, Deuteronomy 7:9; 1 Corinthians 1:9; 1 John 1:9]. This is the simple fact that God is worthy of our faith, since He will never deny Himself or fail on any promise [2 Timothy 2:13]. As the sun rises and sets in a perfectly predictable manner because of the laws of nature set in place by God, so God will never swerve from His promises. He can be relied upon and believed. There is nothing erratic or strange about Him or His ways. He is the never-changing One and whoever trusts in Him will not be disappointed.

12. Personal

Of all God's attributes, this is an essential revelation of the Bible. God is not an impersonal force in nature; He is a person, with feelings and a character. He has a unity of conscious thought and personality. We humans, who are made in the image of God, have character and feelings like our Maker. It is for this reason that we can, for example, perceive God's sense of humour in the way He created monkeys and parrots.

The Bible says that God can laugh [Psalm 2:4], rejoice [Zephaniah 3:17], weep [John 11:35], and many other things that are expressive of personality and character. God loves the human race and cares for us with deep love and compassion. The sum of all these things is that God is good.

THE TRINITY: WHO IS THE FATHER?

1. There is One God

The teaching of the Trinity of Father, Son and Holy Spirit is fundamental to the Christian gospel. This teaching affirms that God is One, a truth that resounds through the Old and New Testaments.

"Hear O Israel: The LORD our God, the LORD is one" [Deuteronomy 6:4]. This declaration of the One True God was made twice a day by the people of God. It was quoted by Jesus in Mark 12:29. Jesus also addressed His Father as *"the only true God"* in John 17:3. Other verses affirm the same great foundational truth: *"Besides Me, there is no god"* [Isaiah 44:6]. *"There is one God"*, declares Paul in Romans 3:30, 1 Corinthians 8:6 and 1 Timothy 2:5; as does James in James 2:19.

2. There are Three Persons in the One God

This is the affirmation that although there is perfect unity between the three in one, yet there is also a distinction. In other words, the Father is not the Son and the Son is not the Holy Spirit. This is expressed so perfectly in John 1:1, where it is written that the Word (Christ) is both God Himself and also with God. Jesus prays to the Father and speaks of the life and glory they shared from eternity [John 17:24]. Jesus is the mediator between the Father and sinners [1Timothy 2:5]. He is our Advocate before the Father [1 John 2:1]. The Holy Spirit prays for us to the Father [Romans 8:27].

The Trinity can be likened to a pool of water fed by three underground springs. The person drinking the water is drinking all three, and cannot distinguish the three as he looks at the pool. But as he enters the water he will realise that there are three currents swirling around and, at different points in the pool, will feel the influence and power of one of the underground springs as distinct from the other two.

Thus a believer may not easily sense a distinction between the three persons, since they are truly one. Nevertheless, we will sense the ministry of the Redeemer – Christ, bringing the sinner back to God the Father, and being washed and renewed through the Holy Spirit.

---

3. The Old Testament and the Trinity

The fact of the Trinity is contained in the Old Testament but is not fully developed. So, in Genesis 1:1, the Bible says '*Elohim*' (which is the plural of 'El' or God) '*created*', which is in the singular. This is like saying *"We am happy!"* This is reaffirmed when God says, *"Let Us make man in our image"* [Genesis 1:26]. Trinity is written into the three-dimensional physical universe. The Trinity is revealed at various moments in the Old Testament account, such as when Nebuchadnezzar saw the form of the Son of God in the fiery furnace in Daniel 3:25. God appeared to Abraham in the form of three persons: [Genesis 18:1-2].

The Trinity is present in the Old Testament, but neither the Fatherhood of God, nor His Sonship, nor the details of the work of the Holy Spirit are elaborated in detail. Some have said that the Father is revealed in the Old Testament, the Son in the Gospels and the Spirit in the book of Acts. However, this is not true:

- God was revealed as Father in the Old Testament [Deuteronomy 32:6; Isaiah 63:16 and 64:8; Malachi 1:6 and 2:10].

- God was revealed as Son in the Old Testament [Psalm 2:7; Psalm 72:1; Proverbs 30:4; Daniel 3:25].

- The Holy Spirit was revealed in the Old Testament [Genesis 1:2; Psalm 51:11; Joel 2:28].

The key point is that God in the Old Testament was not intimately known. There was a veil between the people and God, which was represented by the veils in the Tabernacle that prevented people from approaching God.

It is Jesus who brings the clear knowledge of the God of the Old Testament and thus brings the key to unlock these passages [Luke 24:44 and John 1:18]. It is Jesus who brings the clear revelation of the Father and the Son, and finally, in the upper room, of the Person and work of the Holy Spirit in John 14:16-17. Mankind is so ignorant of God. But even the disciples did not fully understand what Jesus taught [John 14:9].

It was through the work of the cross that the veil was torn and the way was prepared for us to know God intimately [Matthew 27:51]. It is the Holy Spirit who reveals the mystery of God hidden from the foundation of the world. It is from the Day of Pentecost onwards that the full understanding of Father, Son and Holy Spirit is given.

4. God the Father

The Father is revealed as 'greater than Jesus' in John 14:28, and as the central focal point of the Godhead. All things are for Him and through Him [Hebrews 2:10]. Jesus worships Him as His God and His Father [John 20:17]. The Father is the Source from whom the Spirit flows [John 15:26]. Jesus rules through His death and resurrection, but in the climax of the ages, He will then submit all things to the Father, so that the Father is all in all [1 Corinthians 15:28].

The great fact of the Father is that he is not merely a Father in title but a tender-loving Father in character. This is revealed in the parable of the prodigal son in Luke 15, where the Father is seen loving his sons, both the wasteful one who wanders far from him and misuses his love, and the quiet one who is faithful in conduct but bitter and resentful in heart. God is seen as a loving Father who keeps constant watch for the return of his son; he opens his arms to embrace the returning prodigal. He also is tender and kind to the son who remains in the house.

Who is God?

Some have suggested that Jesus died on the cross to satisfy the Father's wrath. This is not true. While it is true that God's wrath is on the sinner [Ephesians 2:3], it is the wrath of God the **Father, Son and Holy Spirit**. God is one. The Bible also reveals that it was the Father's love that initiated the plan of redemption that climaxed in the cross. John 3:16 declares that it was God the Father who so loved the world that He gave His only begotten Son for the sins of the world. God is a tender, loving and sacrificial Father.

The greatest fact about the Father is His love, which is focused primarily on His Son. The Father loves the Son and has committed all things into His hands [John 3:35], so that He might judge the world [John 5:22]. God has made His beloved Son the cornerstone of the ages. Every person will stand or fall according to what they do with His beloved Son [1 Peter 2:6-8].

There was once a rich man, who owned a large house. He had one son, but his wife died in childbirth and so he brought up the son on his own. The rich man's household had many servants, including a gardener who often played with the son as he was growing up. They became very attached to each other with the passage of time, as the boy enjoyed talking and working with him in the garden. The rich man loved his son, and as he had a gift as a painter, he poured out his love by painting a portrait of his son. The picture was a very good likeness, but what particularly shone through was the affection of the Father. Then tragedy stuck, as the son fell ill and died. The father was heartbroken and it was only a few years later that he too passed away.

The father's funeral was a lavish event, and hundreds of relatives appeared who had never visited him while he was alive. The reason that so many came was because there were no near relatives left alive to inherit the large family fortune. Many hoped that they might get something - if only a little. After the funeral the relatives gathered in the rich man's home to hear the reading of the will. The lawyer cleared his throat and opened the leather-bound document. He looked over his glasses and said: "Before we proceed any further, I need to ask if there is anyone here who would like to have this portrait of the son?"

The relatives were offended at this apparent interruption of the reading of the will and some were openly angry. But the lawyer insisted, until at last the gardener, who was at the back of the room, timidly raised his voice: "Excuse me, although I am not related to the family, I did so love that boy, and would be so grateful if I could have that painting." The relatives breathed a sigh of relief that the matter was settled. "Give it to him quickly and get on with the will!", someone shouted.

"Actually, that settles the matter", said the lawyer. There were gasps of confusion until he explained. "The father has indicated his clear instruction that whoever loved his son and desired to have this painting, inherits everything else with it, including the house and all the money." There were protests and arguments which went on for many hours, but the matter was settled.

The greatest fact about the Father is that He loves Jesus, not least for His love and submission to the Father's will, as he obeyed the Father even to death on the cross.

THE TRINITY: WHO IS THE SON?

The central question of the whole Bible revolves around the identity of Jesus Christ. The early apostles preached that He was the Messiah - the fulfilment of the Old Testament hopes and dreams of One who would redeem the nation of Israel and rule over it. Jesus asked the question of the apostles *"Who do men say that I, the Son of Man, am?"* [Matthew 16:13]. They answered that the people were saying He was the reincarnation of one of the great Old Testament prophets or perhaps of John the Baptist. Jesus then pressed further, asking them to speak out their own conclusions. Whether it was a sudden flash of inspiration, or a rising conviction in his heart, Peter blurted out the great confession: *"You are the Christ, the Son of the living God."* [Matthew 16:16].

This confession goes to the very heart of the person and the mission of Christ. If Jesus Christ were simply a good man then His words would be important, but if He is God then His words are perfect and all-important. If He is God then His death becomes the most terrible crime committed by the human race. But it also means that we must understand why He died, and listen to God's word about the meaning of His death and also the wonder of His resurrection.

JESUS IS BOTH THE SON OF GOD AND GOD THE SON
Looking at the evidence:

1. The Prophecies

There are two kinds of prophecy of Christ. The first is simple and direct. The second is hidden, through types and figures and historical events.

(a) The Direct Prophecies

The main direct prophecies include:

- Genesis 3:15: The 'seed of the woman' prophesies the virgin birth and the cross, with its victory over Satan, in one concise phrase.
- Genesis 49:10-11: Here Messiah is foretold as coming from the tribe of Judah, and here also is mentioned the cleansing power of the blood of the cross.
- Deuteronomy 18:15-19: The prophet like Moses, who will be the essential key person for the covenant, replacing Moses.
- 2 Samuel 7:16: The often-repeated promise that Christ will be of David's line, and sit on David's throne for ever.
- Psalm 16:10: The resurrection foretold.
- Psalm 22: The crucifixion described.
- Psalm 34:20: None of Messiah's bones will be broken.
- Psalm 41:9: The betrayal of Judas foretold.
- Psalm 68:18: Messiah's ascension.
- Psalm 69:21: The gall and the vinegar of the cross foretold.
- Psalm 72: The glorious reign of the resurrected Messiah foretold, and the gathering in of the Gentiles.
- Psalm 110: Messiah will be priest and king.
- Psalm 118:22: Messiah will be rejected.
- Isaiah 7:13-14: The virgin birth; Messiah will be God with us.
- Isaiah 9:1-2: Messiah's ministry in Galilee.
- Isaiah 9:6-7: Messiah is God.
- Isaiah 35:5-6: Miracles of Messiah foretold.
- Isaiah 50:6: Messiah will be struck and spat upon.
- Isaiah 52:13-53:12: Messiah's sufferings to take away sin, by a substitutionary death.
- Jeremiah 31:15: Massacre of the baby boys in Bethlehem and the surrounding area foretold.
- Daniel 9:24-27: The year of Christ's anointing and death foretold.
- Hosea 11:1: The flight into Egypt foretold.
- Micah 5:2-5: Messiah's birthplace foretold.
- Zechariah 9:9: Messiah's entry into Jerusalem on a donkey.

- Zechariah 11:12-13: Messiah sold for 30 pieces of silver, and the money thrown to the potter.
- Zechariah 12:10: Messiah's piercing foretold.
- Zechariah 13:7: The disciples will forsake Jesus.

(b) The Types and Figures

There are many types and figures of Christ in the Old Testament. Here are a few:

- Genesis 22: Abraham offers Isaac, prefiguring the cross.
- Genesis 37-50: The life of Joseph, betrayed by his brothers, the sons of Israel, brought to the lowest prison and raised to the highest throne, to save the world from famine.
- The life of Moses prefigures the life of Christ.
- Exodus 12-13: The Passover lamb prefigures the death of Jesus, the Lamb of God, bringing deliverance from spiritual bondage.
- Leviticus 16: The Day of Atonement describes in a picture the work of Christ on the cross and the blood presented in heaven to reconcile sinners to God.
- Numbers 21:6-9: The serpent lifted up in the wilderness is a picture of the cross, with Christ lifted up for the salvation of sinners.
- The book of Jonah foretells the death and resurrection of Jesus Christ, with three days between the two events. This book also foretells the preaching of the gospel to the whole world and the gathering in of the Gentiles following these events.

2. The Miracles Jesus Did and Still Does Today

There are countless miracles performed by Jesus in the Gospel accounts, and Christians can give abundant witness to this ongoing miraculous ministry of Christ. There are many testimonies to the miracle power of Jesus today. Ask believers you know whether they have experienced the miracle power of Jesus.

Franklin Graham was flying a small plane across America when the instruments went dead, resulting in the loss of the radio and lights also. There was a small airport at a town called Jackson, called Thompson airport. It was so small that that evening no lights were on and the runway was closed. He suddenly saw a green light in the control tower which guided him and assured him it was safe to land. Then the runway lights went on, enabling him to land safely, but they were abruptly switched off again before he reached the end of the runway.

Only later did he learn that that evening Sydney McCall was showing a Baptist minister and his wife around the airport. He told them about the meaning of showing lights from the control tower, which would guide a plane in. He had then held a green light out of the window of the control tower as a demonstration of how to guide a plane in. He then demonstrated the runway lights by switching them on for half a minute and then off again. God's hand directed the events perfectly!

3. Biblical Evidence for Jesus' Pre-existence

John 1:1 states that Jesus was with God at the beginning of eternity. John 17:24 affirms that Jesus was loved by the Father and partook of the Father's glory before the foundation of the world. Jesus said in John 8:58 that He existed before Abraham. Philippians 2:6-8 explains that His birth was an advent, not a beginning.

4. Biblical Evidence that Jesus is God and Man

John 1:1 states that He is **with** God and is Himself God. Hebrews 1:6 declares that all angels worship Jesus. John 9:38 states that a man worshipped Jesus without being corrected. Hebrews 1:8 affirms that the Father calls Jesus God. Colossians 1:16 explains that He is the Creator.

THE TRINITY: WHO IS THE HOLY SPIRIT?

- **He is HOLY.** This is a uniquely divine quality, and refers to His 'otherness' or the difference between the human and the divine. God is holy, pure, clean and in a different dimension.
- **He is SPIRIT** - uncreated, non-material.
- **He is INVISIBLE.** Unbelievers do not know of His existence [1 Corinthians 2:14, John 14:17]. Some believers do not even notice Him [Acts 19:2]! He is content to be invisible, as He loves the glory of Jesus.
- **He is DOVE-LIKE** [Matthew 3:16]. He is gentle, and easily driven away, yet never fearful or offended. Doves are clean, not scavengers.
- **He is the THIRD PERSON OF THE TRINITY,** and is God. Many of the attributes of the Spirit are attributes of God alone:
    - Eternal [Hebrews 9:14]
    - Omnipresent [Psalm 139:7-10]
    - All-powerful [Luke 1:35]

- All-knowing [1 Corinthians 2:10-11]
- The author and inspirer of the Bible, the Word of God [2 Samuel 23:2-3]
- Life-giving [John 6:63 and Genesis 2:7]

♦ **He is EQUAL WITH GOD and has a distinct personality,** as the following verses show:
- "In the name of the Father, and of the Son and of the Holy Spirit" [Matthew 28:19].
- The Holy Spirit comes to take the place of Jesus [John 16:7].

♦ **He is the SERVANT,** executing the will of the Father:
- He is sent by the Father [John 15:26].
- He speaks words that He is given to speak [John 16:13].

♦ **He is LINKED WITH THE CROSS** – since He cannot live in a carnal, sinful heart. He is gentle and submissive. He would never be able to function in an uncrucified heart [Acts 7:51].

♦ **He is a PERSON,** and in many verses personal pronouns are used such as He, Himself etc. [John 15:26; 16:7-8]. Various aspects of personality are attributed to Him, such as:
- Mind [Romans 8:27]
- Love [Romans 15:30]
- Grief [Ephesians 4:30]
- Will [1 Corinthians 12:11]
- He cries out [Romans 8:26]
- He intercedes [Romans 8:26]
- He instructs/teaches [Nehemiah 9:20; John 14:26]
- He leads/guides [Acts 16:6-7]
- He can be lied to [Acts 5:3]

He has MANY TITLES – for example:
- The Spirit of the living God [2 Corinthians 3:3]
- The Spirit of life [Romans 8:2]
- The Spirit of wisdom and understanding, counsel and might, knowledge and the fear of the Lord [Isaiah 11:2]
- The Spirit of grace [Hebrews 10:29]
- The Spirit of glory [1 Peter 4:14]
- The Spirit of promise [Ephesians 1:13]
- The Spirit of judgment and burning [Isaiah 4:4]
- The Spirit of holiness [Romans 1:4]

♦ **He is ACTIVE IN CREATION** [Genesis 1:2; Job 33:4].
♦ **The Holy Spirit is ACTIVE** and involved in the work of salvation.

See Chapter 2: The Plan of Salvation.

2

THE PLAN OF SALVATION

MANKIND IS A SPECIAL CREATION BUT WITH A FALLEN NATURE

1. Mankind's Origin

In the beginning, human beings were not sinners. They were created in the image of God by the very hand of God and given a soul by the Breath of God [Genesis 1:26; 2:7]. Mankind was created.

Evolutionists propose the THEORY that mankind is descended from the apes; which in turn evolved from primitive creatures. The fossil record, however, has innumerable gaps showing there is no evidence of life evolving from one species to another. How life could have started from non-living matter is also an impossibility. Nowhere has this been observed in the earth. Scientists have tried to create life artificially by introducing electrical charges into mixtures of basic chemicals. These experiments have resulted in such total failure, that many scientists have speculated that life must have evolved on another planet in different and therefore better conditions, and maybe this primitive life was brought here by a comet, or a meteorite.

Such a hypothesis begs more questions than it answers and is patently improbable to the nth degree! How could life survive the extreme temperatures of outer space, including the fierce heat produced when a meteorite enters earth's atmosphere? How could life survive without water and oxygen for thousands of years, travelling from one planet/solar system to another. This might even involve thousands of years of interstellar travel! Nevertheless people are more willing to believe these myths than to give any credence to the Bible accounts.

Other missing links include the huge gap between mankind and the apes. There are huge problems with the theory of evolution, such as how so many varied, interdependent forms of life could have arisen. Which came first - the chicken or the egg? This question can be repeated a thousand-fold. Which came first - the bee or the flower? male or female? the chrysalis, the caterpillar or the butterfly? fish gills or fish lungs?

The point is that it is entirely reasonable to conclude that mankind is a special creation of God. There are more believers among scientists as a proportion of the population than among any other groups. It is not unscientific to state that God created the world.

2. Three Ways in which We Are in the Image of God

(a) We are Moral Beings with the Power of Choice

At the Creation, the first man and woman were placed in the garden and given a moral command, implying the power of moral choice [Genesis 2:17]. This was not a purely negative command. It was a positive exhortation to enjoy all the fruits of the garden, except for one. Mankind could not escape the demands of moral choice, and neither can we now. Everyone must realise that they are responsible for the choices they make. They can wash their hands as Pilate did, but there is no way of escaping this responsibility.

This means that everyone will be held to account for how they handle the instinctive knowledge of the Creator in their hearts [Romans 1:19-20]. All will have to answer for the moral conscience that is common to all of us [Romans 2:15]. This moral stature is an indication of the huge distance between mankind and the animals. The humanist develops a materialistic view of the universe, which holds that there is no such thing as right and wrong, only opinions about these things. This is clearly untrue, since the world is infected with evil, which brings misery and death to millions. Men and women are moral beings.

The second truth relating to mankind's moral power is that **there are moral consequences of our moral choices**. Where there is sin and disobedience, there are results, and we must reap the reward of our sin, in personal misery and shame. To grow in moral character and stature, we must deny ourselves. But moral collapse will bring a harvest of misery and shame that will be reaped for the rest of our lives. There are even physical results of moral failure:

- An unforgiving heart will produce a bitter spirit, which will produce a stressed, unhappy soul.
- Envy and jealousy produce constant misery with our lot. They make us always covetous of what others have. The resulte is depression.
- Sexual immorality will result in venereal diseases, from syphilis to AIDS. Unwanted pregnancies bring the dilemma and trauma of abortion.
- Heart attacks, ulcers and cancers have been linked by doctors to soul states that produce the stressful conditions in which these diseases thrive.
- The end result of moral failure will be seen in the final reckoning of the human race on the Day of Judgment. Our moral dimension of being, only has any meaning if there is also a day of reckoning. If not, then the evil-doers of the world escape while enjoying the pleasures of sin. Hitler must be judged for his deeds; otherwise he lived a life of evil only to escape at the last minute. There is no escape. God created humans as moral beings and so every person will be held to account.

Finally, it is God's compassion for the sinner that made Him identify with us in the death of His Son. The cross is God's offer of righteous escape through the sinless, perfect sacrifice of Jesus. The cross meets the moral demands of the Creator for absolute righteousness.

(b) We Have the Power of Loving Affection in Our Nature

Human beings were created to be in fellowship with God and with our fellow human beings. We were created as part of a family and given the nature and image of God, who is love. This passionate commitment of love is both a wonderful and a terrible attribute of the human race. When it is manifested, there is an astounding power in love.

A story is told of some farm workers in Scotland during the 19th century. All the workers and their wives were in the fields for harvest. One woman had brought her baby and laid it in the hay while she worked. Suddenly an eagle descended and snatched up the baby by its tightly bound clothes, and then flew to its nest, high up on a cliff face.

The men considered frantically the impossibility and danger of attempting a rescue, and discussed at length the best and safest plan. They were shocked and surprised when someone noticed the distant figure of the fearless mother scrambling already halfway up the cliff, not resting till she had rescued her infant.

Love is a tremendous power for good, and motivates heroic sacrifice of the highest order. Men and women have laid down their lives in acts of great devotion to one another. We are made in the image of God and have the instinct of love in our hearts.

However, this instinct is destructive when it is directed through sin to selfish indulgence and self-fulfilment. Lust is the negative of love, and it is overpowering in its destructive surge. Men and women will lie, kill, steal and destroy in order to obtain their selfish desires. The absence of true love creates a vacuum in the human heart. Vacuums do not actually occur in nature; if a vacuum is made, there will be pressure exerted till it is either filled, or the container is horribly twisted or implodes. So in the human heart there is a power of lust that will direct the life to terrible acts of self-fulfilment which twist and deform the human character.

The only pure basis of human life is therefore love for God. Sin, by definition, is the redirection of that love to lower, unworthy objects. Only if God is loved is there the spiritual power available to enable human beings to fulfil their high and noble calling.

(c) *We Have a Spirit, a Unified Consciousness, an Inner Mind*

The Tabernacle in the Old Testament had three main areas or 'rooms' – the outer court, the Holy Place and the Holy of Holies or Most Holy Place. These can be seen as symbolising several truths, one of which is that human beings are made up of three key aspects – body, soul and spirit. The Most Holy Place pictures the fact that there is an inner, deeper level of a person's being that is not physical, and not merely intellectual. It is like a room which is the centre not just of thought but also of personality. Our inner life has several characteristics:

- ♦ We have **unique personality**. Every human being is unique, just as there are no two flowers or snowflakes the same. Each person is a special and precious creation. Once this is lost to view, there are no limits to how deep mankind descends. Abortion is not a crime if we are just a random collection of chemicals. No human being can be discarded or disposed of as unimportant. In God's eyes all are special, wonderful and precious.

- We have the **power of thought**. We are self-aware, and can relate to our environment in a thoughtful way. We have the power to use this thought for high or low things. Mankind has invented wonderful machines, such as space rockets, televisions, and aircraft. But sadly such inventions can be turned to evil, and have been used in warfare to kill and destroy. Mankind has great power of thought, but this power is totally weak when facing the problem of sin. We cannot cure our own hearts, and we are also totally incapable of curing other people's.

- We have the capacity for **fellowship with God**. We can think of and worship God, and can identify with Him. We can at least grasp some idea of the concept of infinity. We have an inward sense of eternity we sense that we will live for ever, though we are not sure how this can be. Mankind is created between the dust and the stars. We can examine infinitely small things under a microscope, and lift our eyes and see stars billions of miles away in outer space. We are dust, and our bodies will return to the dust, but our spirits are eternal and will return to God who gave them [Ecclesiastes 12:7].

3. Mankind's Problem, Our Fallen Nature, Sin and the Curse

The first man, Adam, was created in the image of God and was sinless. He was given the work of guarding and cultivating the paradise which was created for him. He was to build a relationship with his wife and walk with God. He had freedom to enjoy all of creation, but he failed and sinned. Why?

The tempter Satan was allowed to tempt the man and his wife. He approached the pair through the woman. There is no evidence that the man was absent when the woman was tempted. The woman had not had the direct instruction from God not to eat of the tree, since she was created after the man. Eve had learned all that she knew from Adam.

The temptation and Fall occurred in the following stages [Genesis 3]:

The Christian's Compass

(a) Satan Attacks the Word of God

Satan opens his attack by speculating about the word of God. While questions are useful in our pursuit of truth, meaningless speculation is not profitable and will lead to unbelief and then to sin. Satan begins with, *"Has God said?"*. This is the same question that all who have doubted the Scripture have repeated. It may be right to seek to understand how the Bible was written, and why it is to be believed. But the arguments themselves will not convince unless finally we willingly submit and recognise that the Bible is the Word of God, that it is perfect and unchangeable. Doubt in the word of God is the origin of all evils that have beset the human race.

Other idle speculations include *"Is there a God?"* and *"Who created God?"* In the end, these questions cannot be answered. The point is that 'unbelief' may be innocent acceptance of what others have said, but in the end the truth of God is so clear that to reject God, human beings must disobey and rebel against Him. There must be willingness to believe the evidence, or no proof will ever satisfy the rebellious mind.

(b) Eve Talks with the Devil

Eve's mistake is to take the devil's words seriously, and to enter into discussion with him. We should not think that the devil appeared to her in the form of a slithering snake. The word for 'snake' in the Hebrew is *nahash,* meaning *'shining one'*. As Genesis is dealing with original things, it is not necessarily correct to think of the devil as a serpent like the snakes we know today. Hence it is possible that the devil appeared to the woman as a shining angel, with intelligence and reason.

(c) Eve Opens Her Mind to the Devil

Once Eve's mind is open to speculation, the devil speaks a blatant lie, contradicting the word of God: *"You will not surely die"* [Genesis 3:4]. This lie is in respect to the terrible consequences of disobedience. The devil asserts that sin will have no repercussions, even asserting that life will be better, fuller and on a higher plane because of sin. The devil says to the woman that her eyes will be opened and she will be like God - *"Elohim"*. Within this lie is a further lie, that God is seeking to withhold something from the human race by His laws and standards. This is a lie about the goodness of God. God does not mean to harm human joy by His word, but to increase it. God is good.

THE PLAN OF SALVATION

(d) Eve Believes the Lie

The woman believes the lie and is now considering in what way her life will be improved by sinning. Eve believes that there will be sensual pleasure (*"good for food"* v6); that it will bring stimulation to her brain and soul through the eyes (*"pleasant to the eyes"*); and that it will provide a short-cut to increased intelligence (*"a tree desirable to make one wise"*). These three aspects are summed up in 1 John 2:16: *"For all that is in the world - the lust of the flesh, the lust of the eyes, and the pride of life - is not of the Father but is of the world"*.

These verses sum up the motives of mankind, and describe the enthronement of lust above God. They are the basis of all temptation, including the temptations of Jesus in the wilderness. Temptation is always tailored by the devil to the person he is speaking to. Some he will tempt with pornography, others with sheer pride in their superior intelligence.

(e) Eve Sins

Eve is utterly convinced, and so the time of temptation gives way to an act of sin - first by Eve. The effect on her is immediate - she falls. The Bible never describes this sin as a 'fall' but it is clear that this is what happened. Eve fell from fellowship with God, into a lower form of life. On one level she probably experienced a deep, intense thrill as new, forbidden pleasures coursed through her soul, exciting her taste buds, her imagination and her sense of achievement and independence from God. But a cloud came between her and God, resulting in the immediate loss of peace and well being. Her conscience was troubled, and new emotions were flooding into her heart - feelings of fear, shame, guilt, failure. Truly, Eve fell.

(f) Adam Sins

Adam observes Eve's sin as a spectator. He sees the look of wild pleasure on his wife's face. Like a new drug addict drawn to the thrill of unknown feelings, he does not see the sense of lostness in her eyes, which was later to dominate her whole life. Whatever Adam saw, he wanted it; so, without the direct lies and deceptions of the devil, he chooses what Eve has experienced, and eats the fruit. It is no doubt the case that he was open to Eve in a way that he would not have been open to the devil. In the same way, many people would not go down a path of sin if they really knew where that path would lead.

Adam also falls, and all the same feelings of pleasure and excitement flood his being, along with all the pain and emptiness. Adam and Eve died indeed on the day they ate of the forbidden fruit. Their spirits died to God and they lost their connection to the one Source of perfect happiness and fulfilment.

(g) Adam and Eve Become Self-conscious

Adam and Eve instantly become conscious of themselves. They are conscious of their nakedness. It may have been that when they were created, their nakedness was covered with the glory of God, which they instantly lost when they sinned. Whether this is true or not, it is definitely true that they became conscious of themselves, and felt shame and fear.

(h) They Flee from God

The man and woman now flee from God. They hide from Him among the trees of paradise. So, too, many can hide their sinful hearts among religious practices. Pastors, worship leaders, Sunday school teachers must all be careful to come to the light when the convicting power of the Holy Spirit touches their hearts. We must not hide behind good things thinking they will give us good standing before God.

(j) God Calls to Adam

God calls the guilty man. God knows where he is, but wants him to hear His voice from afar. Adam was doubtless shocked to hear that God was not angry but deeply grieved. The Hebrew word for *"Where are you?"* sounds like a great cry of pain from the heart. The voice of love calling them would have made them bold to step forward and approach God.

(k) Adam Blames Eve

It is a tragic moment in the account that Adam does not confess his own sin but rather proceeds to excuse himself and to blame both the woman for offering him the fruit, and even God for giving him the woman!

(l) Eve Confesses Everything

Eve, to her credit, freely confesses that she was deceived and she sinned.

THE PLAN OF SALVATION

(m) God Changes the Environment of the Human Race

God proceeds to His corrective action, and addresses the devil, the man and the woman each in their turn:

- **God curses the devil**: God does not enter into conversation with the devil but simply reduces him to a lower order of being. Whatever Satan lost at this point is not clear. As the snake is without arms and legs, so Satan in spirit was reduced from his stature as a punishment for tempting the human race and leading them to sin. Satan emerges from the garden a seriously impaired being, with reduced agility. There is no doubt that the devil is limited both in space and time. He cannot be everywhere at the same time, neither does he know everything. Doubtless he can move freely geographically, and at considerable speed, but he is finite.

- **God promises salvation to mankind**: already here in the first reactions of God to the Fall, there is abundant mercy and promise. God now proceeds directly to promise the human race that He will put everything right that has gone wrong. This is love indeed, that God should react so mercifully to such disobedience. He will become angry if we persisted in sin, but God is slow to anger.
  Here is the first promise of Messiah and already there is the promise that the Saviour of the world will be born of a woman but not of a man. Messiah, from the woman's seed will bruise the serpent's head but will suffer greatly in the act of deliverance from the power of darkness.

- **Physical changes will happen for the woman**: now, as a result of the Fall, God introduces the experience of pain into childbirth. Sin's consequences cannot be avoided. Pain is a mystery, and all human beings experience a measure of it. The woman has her full share, and the history of the woman bringing children into the world has many sad chapters. However, this too is a picture of the sufferings of Messiah to bring the human race to new birth. The woman lays down her life in suffering for the birth of children. While we would rid the world of pain, we must trust that God knew why this was needful for the correcting of human waywardness. The woman will also suffer as a result of changes in the nature of the man, for he will no longer naturally use his strength to protect, but to dominate and rule her [Genesis 3:16].

- **God curses the ground and so mankind must toil**: note here that it is not the human race that is cursed, though they suffer the results of the curse. God curses the ground and from this moment mankind must labour and suffer pain in producing food and gaining prosperity. Note that there was no money, no markets, and no wealth then. Mankind would later invent money as a means of interchange of goods, but at this moment he had everything, with no need to own anything.

Included in this curse is all the strain and stress that comes on the human race in its fight for survival. Mankind's existence is finely balanced. He is not naturally wealthy, but must live between the fine balance of a hostile environment and the desire to be independent of God and have abundance. God has set these boundaries so that we might look to Him for blessing in our labours. Rich people accumulate money and easily forget God because they think they do not need Him. God could have given the human race an easier life, but it is in the conflict for survival that people turn to God [Proverbs 30:8-9].

- **God clothes the guilty pair with animal skins**: to do this, God has to shed blood, and the first animals died at His hands. He kills them to clothe His beloved, though lost, children. This is a picture of the cross in that God made Jesus, the Lamb of God; a sacrifice for sin so that He could clothe us with His righteousness. From the very beginning God showed His determination to save the human race. Though we cannot be certain that Adam and Eve were saved, yet this act of kindness may be an indication that they trusted in Him and were clothed with righteousness as a result.

- **God drives them out of paradise**: doubtless they did not want to go! Perhaps they could sense the hostility of the world outside. Perhaps there were cold winds (hence the need for animal skins to protect them). Perhaps they heard lions roaring, and other predators. They must have resisted the direction in which they were now forced to go, but there was no choice. They had sinned and they must now receive the full wages of their sin.

Winston Churchill said:
"Would you rise in the world? You must work while others amuse themselves. Are you desirous of a reputation for courage? You must risk your life. Would you be strong morally or physically? You must resist temptation. All this is paying in advance, that is, prospective finance. Observe the other side of the picture: the bad things are paid for afterwards."

4. Sin, its Scope and Power

THE PLAN OF SALVATION

(For this section, read John chapter 8.) John 8 is the reversal of the Fall, in that here a guilty woman is brought before her Judge, the Lord Jesus Christ. The onlookers are the crowds, and the accusers are the religious leaders using the Law of Moses to accuse the woman and to trap the Judge. The woman is accused by human beings, but forgiveness and power to sin no more are given to her by the Saviour. Here is redemption.

(a) Conviction of Sin

The first step in salvation is to be convicted of sin. It is our sin that makes us need a Saviour. The name Jesus was given in Matthew 1:21 because *"He will save His people from their sins"*. Conviction of sin is the opportunity for salvation but not the certainty. The Pharisees were convicted of sin in John 8:9 but they hardened their hearts and did not come to Jesus for forgiveness and cleansing. We must know that we have sinned and that we are lost for ever because of this. The woman was taken in her sin and doubtless felt guilt. Adam and Eve were taken in their sin too.

(b) The Human Reaction – Condemnation

Sinners are quick to condemn those who fail. This can be seen by the reactions of journalists when a politician falls into sin.

(c) The Divine Reaction – Mercy

Jesus reacts to the woman with mercy; this is God's automatic response to the problem of sin. He seeks a way to forgive and remove it.

(d) The Sinless One has the Right to Condemn

Only one was sinless. Christ alone had the right to condemn the woman, but instead He offers her forgiveness.

(e) All Have Sinned and Fall Short of the Glory of God *[Romans 3:23]*

All the accusers, from the oldest to the youngest, go out convicted by their own conscience.

The Pharisees condemned the woman because they did not understand that they were also sinners. They thought that sin was social and criminal. They knew that adultery and lying were sins against society, and that murder and stealing were criminal acts. They thought, however, that they were better than adulterers, murderers and liars and that therefore they were not sinners of the same kind. They thought that salvation was deserved by being morally good - they did not need help, because they were superior to these weak, useless sinners. They did not understand that sin is first a spiritual problem.

Jesus then teaches them what sin is, in John 8:

- **Sin is from beneath** [v23]. Sin causes humanity, at its best, to be earth-bound and worldly. Mankind is base and weak. His 'head may be of gold but his feet are of clay' [Daniel 2]. This means that we cannot escape the low order into which we are born.

- **Sin is slavery** [v31-35]. We may decide to commit a sin; for instance, someone may decide to start taking a drug. But the sin quickly takes control of them. We are slaves to sexual thoughts and lusts, and prisoners to habits and addictions which quickly begin to dominate our lives.

- **Sin is of the devil** [v44]. Jesus said that human beings are of their father the devil, and by sin mankind is bound to the evil of the power of darkness. There are depths to sin and darkness in the human heart, of which we are only dimly aware. This does not mean that the human race is possessed by the devil, but it does mean that we have an affinity with evil, and are connected to the power of darkness. The devil does not control the human race, but he does have influence over our hearts and minds to stir them to do evil. We do have some power to resist and choose what is right, but we cannot cut the connection between ourselves and the power of darkness.

- **Sin is enmity with God** [v41 and 59]. The Jews picked up stones to stone Jesus, because they felt that there was something about Him they hated. Sinners hate God with an irrational hatred, and this is what made the cross inevitable. Sinful mankind cannot live with God, the enmity is too strong; and so when God came to live in this sinful world, it was only a matter of time before the conflict climaxed in a confrontation that would lead to Christ's crucifixion.

Other chapters in the Bible teach us the following about sin:

- **Sin is like a wild animal**. Genesis 4.7 is the first mention in the Bible of the word 'sin'. Cain was already a sinner, of course, but here there is a new dimension to sin, a specific temptation to sin that is ready to pounce on him like a wild animal. God tells him that he has the power to resist this temptation, but if he does not he will be overpowered by it. This is the true nature of sin - a wild, lion-like creature that will overpower every person unless they steadfastly resist temptation.

- **Sin is like leprosy** [Matthew 8.1-3]. It is a disease of the spirit. As leprosy destroys the nerve endings so that a person can feel nothing physically, so also sin destroys the faculty of feeling in the heart, hardening it and removing all sensitivity to God and conscience.

- **Sin is neglecting to do what is right** [James 4:7-10]. We are often able to say what is wrong, but we must also be able to do what is right. It is possible for a person to believe all the right things, and to attend and enjoy Church, and yet be full of sin because of a selfish attitude to money, possessions, time, witnessing etc.

- **Sin is the opposite of faith** [Romans 14:23]. Sin is independence from God, and the intention to survive and live without God. Faith is the life of depending on God and centring all our life around Him. Therefore to live without faith is to live a life full of sin, no matter how moral and idealistic we may be.

- **Sin leads to death** [Romans 6:23]. Sin has terrible consequences, both in the short term and in the long term. If we are unaware of the consequences, we will dream our way into disaster. Sexual sin will produce unwanted pregnancies, abortion, sexually-transmitted diseases (STDs), including diseases that produce infertility. The worst form of STD is AIDS for which there is no known cure. Lies destroy relationships. Some sins can result in imprisonment.

- **Sin is separation from God** [Isaiah 59:2]. The worst thing about sin is that it cuts the soul off from God, which is spiritual death. The sinner still has a very vague awareness of God, but is blind, deaf and dead to spiritual things. There is nothing the sinner can do to change this. He needs a Saviour.

Apart from God's saving power, sin is the strongest power that we can know. We are unable to tame it and unable to overcome it with money, psychology, education, time or any human resources. We need a Saviour from sin.

5. Satan and Demons

Satan does not control the human race. It is clear that sin began in the heart of Lucifer (Satan is called this in Isaiah 14:12), and it was pride that was the original sin as Lucifer attempted to rise above the throne of God [Isaiah 14:12-14]. Lucifer conceived a selfish attitude of SELF-advancement, which is the very root and nature that infected him, and now infects the human race through him.

Demons are the third of the angels of heaven which followed Lucifer in his rebellion against God. Lucifer's defeat at the cross is described in Revelation 12, and there it speaks of *"his angels"* [v9] who suffer the same fate as Satan. These demons are active in the human race, speaking to tempt, to deceive, and to bind souls to evil. Their power over people is broken through salvation, but sometimes there is a need for more specific deliverance ministry. (See later chapter.)

Not all sinners are yielded to evil and not all know the depths of Satan [Revelation 2:24]. The human heart is darkened in sin, but if we cross over into forbidden areas, we will know terrible powers of evil unleashed upon our souls. The drug addict yields his will to drugs, and demons take control of his mind and imagination. He needs salvation and deliverance. People who indulge in pornography find that there are evil powers that take control of their imagination and pollute their minds and even their dreams. Such people need salvation and deliverance.

6. There is no salvation by any human-centred means

Two pastors named John Valentine and Norman Meeten visited a prison in Liverpool, England. As they tried to preach they were continually interrupted by one highly educated prisoner. At last one of the pastors issued a challenge to him: "I will ask you one question, and if you have the answer we will sit down and listen to you, but if not you must sit down and listen to us!"

The man accepted the challenge. The question was: "Do you have the answer to sin?" The man responded: "If I had the answer to sin, I would not be here in prison!" He sat down and listened.

A large part of most governments' budgets is spent on law enforcement, trying to control the problem of sin. Yet no amount of education or policing is able to break the cycle of evil. In the 20th century mankind arguably reached a higher level of existence in terms of technology and prosperity. But the 20th century was without doubt the century

THE PLAN OF SALVATION

of the most violent wars, and of the greatest number of deaths through starvation and disease because of a lack of willingness to share resources. Governments, educators, psychiatrists and law officers simply do not have the solution to sin.

In prisons there are people from all walks of life. There are educated and illiterate, rich and poor, male and female, healthy and sick. There is no pattern of life that people have found to save themselves. We are hopelessly lost, without an answer.

A man fell down a hole and was unable to get out. He cried out for help and at last a religious teacher came by who told him to try harder and he would be sure to get out given enough time. Then along came a psychiatrist who encouraged him to think of a peaceful scene by a river. But hunger and pain kept reminding the man of reality. A university professor came by who recommended a good correspondence course in self-improvement techniques.

At last Jesus came by. On hearing the man's cries he immediately jumped down into the hole, and showed the man how to climb up onto his back and shoulders and so escape from the hole. When the man reached the top, Jesus was already there to welcome him and teach him how not to get into the same mess again.

"Religion is a description of man's best efforts to reach up and find God. Christianity is a description of God coming down to lift man up to Himself." [Source unknown]

God's Solution

1. The Representative Man: Jesus Christ

God's first answer to mankind's problems was to send His Son to become a man. Because there was no-one good enough, and because all had sinned, there was nobody to show the human race the way of escape. Jesus shows the sinless life. Jesus is God, but as Philippians 2:7 explains, He: *"made Himself of no reputation, taking the form of a bondservant, and coming in the likeness of men."*

Jesus became one of us. He took on human form in order to show us how to live, minister, and walk with God. Jesus Christ is God's pattern for human beings. While we cannot attain to His way of life by self-effort, we are able to attain it through the gift of salvation and the power of the Holy Spirit. By a new birth, we begin life as He began His life in the manger. We may not have the power to be totally sinless, but we do have the power to be holy and to live day by day without sin.

When a believer is born again by the power of the Holy Spirit, he begins life again like Jesus in the manger in Bethlehem. We begin life at the cross but we are transported into a new beginning. If we walk with God we will go through different stages of His life: through waiting years, temptations, anointing with power, agonising prayer, and works of power. We are to be like Him; Jesus came first to show us how to live and then to give us His life. We are not to be like the disciples in the Gospels but like Christ; we are to be like the disciples in the book of Acts, who lived in victory.

2. The Cross, the Perfect Sacrifice:
  - its Scope and Power to Deliver from Sin

There was no sacrifice perfect enough to make mankind right with God. Hebrews teaches that the sacrifices of the Old Testament could never take away sin. It is the sacrifice of Jesus that alone has that power. The Bible teaches that the sacrifice of Jesus on the cross obtained our salvation because:

- ♦ **God laid all our sins on Him** [Isaiah 53:5-6]. God punished Jesus for our sins. The Bible teaches that *"the soul who sins shall die"* [Ezekiel 18:4]. God loves the world and yet must exact punishment on every sin. Every sin requires a sacrifice to remove it, otherwise God cannot forgive. So Jesus bore our punishment.

THE PLAN OF SALVATION

There were once two friends who grew up in the same village. They went to the same school and were so close they were inseparable. They studied together, fished in the local streams together, and rode their bikes for hours around the countryside. When they finished high school, one went to a famous university and studied law. Within 10 years he was a famous judge, renowned for his tough sentences, and severe application of the law of the land. The other got into bad habits and made bad friends. He became a salesman, but quickly saw opportunities to make extra money through dishonest trading. His life went downhill and he had all kinds of problems, especially with alcohol. Then one day he was caught by the police and taken to prison.

The judge at his trial was his boyhood friend. Many knew this and were curious to see if their former friendship would affect the judge's ruling. The judge listened carefully to all the crimes his friend was accused of. Slowly and deliberately he outlined his judgment. "The accused man has clearly made wrong choices and defrauded many people. It is therefore the judgment of the court that he pay the maximum fine of $150,000 and where possible that he refund all the money he has defrauded." There was a gasp from the court, and his friend bowed his head in shame. Then there was silence as the judge rose from his seat, walked down to the prisoner and handed him a cheque for the fine from his personal account.

In the same way, God must exact the full punishment for every sin committed by human beings. But the wonder of the cross is that this full punishment was laid on His own beloved Son, so that we might go free.

- Through Jesus's sacrifice we have **forgiveness**, and more than forgiveness, we have **justification**. This means that if we put our trust in Christ we are accepted as having all the moral perfections of Christ [Romans 3:24].

- Through the death of Christ, **the devil is destroyed** [Hebrews 2:14]. This does not mean that the devil has ceased to exist. If a television or a radio were dropped in a bath of water, it would be destroyed but it would not cease to exist. So also, by the death of the cross, Jesus took hold of the devil and destroyed his hold on the human race. The devil had the power of death, because he could point to the fact that every sinner was to die because of sin.

But on the cross Jesus took on Himself the punishment for sin and so removed the devil's right to accuse any person. There is no doubt that Jesus did more than just remove the devil's rights.

---

1 Samuel 17 describes how the Philistines had invaded the territory of Judah and the giant, Goliath, was challenging the armies of Israel. No-one was able to stand against him. But at last David appeared and, dressed as a mere shepherd, he challenged and attacked Goliath without a sword in his hand. He beheaded Goliath and led Israel in a tremendous victory.

This is a picture of the cross; it shows us what the cross looked like in the spirit. All the hosts of darkness were arrayed against the human race, and no human being was strong enough to fight the devil. But Jesus came and led the fight, absorbing all the power of evil into Himself, so destroying the devil in His mighty grip of love.

Jesus did not use the weapons of the flesh; He used the power of love to destroy the devil. The devil's power was broken and he suffered his worst defeat ever at the cross. Now the devil has no grounds to work in the human heart, and because of this, whoever believes in Jesus can experience immediate deliverance.

- ♦ On the cross, Jesus **destroyed the power of sin**. The name 'Jesus' was given to Him by the angel because, *"He will save His people from their sins"* [Matthew 1:21]. Hebrews 10:10 tells us that by the cross we have been made holy, (sanctified) or set free from the power of sin. This was something that the blood of bulls and goats could not do but the blood of Jesus can do [Hebrews 10:4].

- ♦ On the cross, Jesus also **destroyed death**. Because Jesus destroyed sin, he also took away the inevitable power of death. As sin was destroyed, we can have life, spiritual life, in fellowship with God. When Jesus said that whoever believes in Him shall never die [John 11:26] He was referring to the power of a restored relationship with God through Jesus's own blood. Anyone who believes in Jesus is free from spiritual separation from God. This means that physical death loses its sting [1 Corinthians 15:55]. The believer is also set free from eternal death, or the second death, which is the lake of fire [Revelation 20:14].

- ♦ On the cross, Jesus **destroyed the works of the devil** [1 John 3:8]. This means that all who call on His name can be healed and restored from all the various ills that have come on the human

THE PLAN OF SALVATION

race, including diseases, mental problems, demon possession, and sinful habits.

3. The Resurrection:
God's Seal that Salvation is Accepted by Him

When Jesus rose from the dead, it was more than just a mortal resurrection, as in the case of Jairus's daughter or Lazarus. They subsequently died. But Jesus was the first to rise from the dead and to die no more. He is the firstborn from the dead [Revelation 1:5]. His resurrection heralded the raising of the human race into a life and level far above anything ever known before. We experience this resurrection in two stages: firstly, by the baptism with the Spirit we are raised to sit in heavenly places in Christ [Ephesians 2:6]; secondly, we receive the bodily resurrection from the dead [1 Cor. 15:20-23].

The resurrection of Jesus Christ is the guarantee of God's promise that human beings can be restored to perfect holiness and eternal life with God. The baptism with the Spirit gives the inner assurance that we will be raised with Him to be with Him for ever [Ephesians 1:13-14]. The apostles preached the resurrection as the great hope of the gospel - that as Christ was raised from the dead physically to a new order of life, so too those who believe in Christ will have a level of healing and transformation that we can only guess at [1 Corinthians 15:42-44].

4. The Holy Spirit Poured Out in New Creation Power

Jesus had said that the apostles would not die until they had seen the Kingdom of God come with power, and this was fulfilled on the Day of Pentecost. The Holy Spirit was poured out on the Day of Pentecost to inaugurate more than just an anointing for the apostles' ministry. This was the inauguration of the Kingdom of God in human hearts.

The coming of the Holy Spirit brought the power of the cross in sanctification, washing and justification power [1 Corinthians 6:11]. Baptism with the Holy Spirit gave people the power of a new heart [Ezekiel 36:26-28 and Acts 15:8-9]. The first creation began with the creation of the earth and sky. It culminated in the creation of mankind. The new creation has begun with the creation of a new humanity through the cross, and will culminate with the creation of a new physical earth and sky for the new humanity to live in. On the Day of Pentecost a new humanity was brought into existence, with life on a different level, with the potential of living like Jesus, the Son of God. All who believe in Him are set on a course which will perfect them in the image of Jesus one day. [Romans 8:29-30].

Our necessary response to obtain assurance of eternal life

1. Repentance

Sinners cannot be saved merely by believing in Jesus, they must first repent of their sins.

Billy Graham's first great crusade was in Los Angeles in Sepembert 1949. Stuart Hamblen was a popular radio presenter, married to a dedicated Christian, but he himself was not converted. Stuart went at last to the crusade and offered to interview Billy on the radio in order to "fill the tent". This took place and Stuart often attended but struggled with his own position. He felt exposed by Graham's preaching. One night Billy Graham said, "There is a person here tonight who is a phoney!"

Hamblen stormed out of the tent, shaking his fist at Graham; but at 2am he phoned Graham at his hotel. Hamblen was drunk, so he got his wife to take him over. He asked Billy Graham to pray for him, but Billy refused. He said that he would only pray if he meant it with all his heart. He told the celebrity: "Go on back home. If you are not going to go all the way and let Jesus Christ be the actual Lord of every area of your life, don't ask me to pray with you and don't waste anybody else's time."

Hamblen struggled for hours but at last yielded in total surrender to Christ. He quit smoking, betting and drinking. He repented and believed with all his heart.

There are several key elements to true repentance:

- **Confess your sin**. Name the sin. Do not make it look better than it is. Naming sins **as** sins is the first step towards forsaking them.

- **Change direction**: change your mind. The Greek word for repentance is 'meta' or change, and 'noia' meaning mind.

- **Abandon all excuses**. The people invited to the wedding in Luke 14:18 made endless excuses as to why they could not obey the invitation and attend the wedding. Excuses are a sure sign of an unrepentant heart.

THE PLAN OF SALVATION

- **The cry of the repentant person is for mercy not justice.** The two men in Luke 18:9-14 had a totally different view of their worthiness before God. The first man appealed to justice which would reward him for being so good! The second man appealed for mercy and he alone found acceptance. If we get what we deserve we will never get salvation but hell.

- **The repentant person ceases to be critical** [Matthew. 7:1]. Romans 2:1 warns us that being critical of those who fail will expose us to dreadful temptation and shame along the same lines. If we criticise others, we are claiming to be above temptation on that line. This is very arrogant, and an indication that we have no sense of our need of grace. This unrepentant attitude can assail mature believers, who may begin to feel 'virtuous' as they live moral lives.

2. Faith

(For this section on faith read Luke 7:1-10 and Matthew 8:5-13.) This story reveals the true nature of faith. The Centurion had the greatest faith of any person that Jesus had met. Jesus certainly did not find any Israelite, whether Pharisee or disciple, with such a great faith. It is interesting to note that some of the greatest examples of people with faith were Gentiles.

The Centurion had never met or heard Jesus directly. He had only heard about Him [Luke 7:3]. He had admired the Jewish faith to the point where he had sacrificed much money to build the synagogue in Capernaum [7:5]. (Visitors to the ruins of the synagogue will notice Roman arches!) The elders of the synagogue were his friends [7:3]. They had probably instructed him on elements of the Jewish faith, such as the Law of Moses and the hope of a coming Messiah. The Centurion now heard of the miracles of Jesus and immediately believed. He sent the elders to ask Jesus for the healing of his slave.
The main elements of the Centurion's faith were as follows:

- He believed because of things he had **heard**, not things he had seen himself. Many Jews saw miracles, but did not believe the evidence of their own eyes [John 9:17-34]. 'Seeing' does not always 'believe' - *"faith comes by hearing, and hearing by the word of God."* [Romans 10:17].

- The Centurion believed in the **power of Jesus**. He believed that one word from Jesus was enough [Luke 7:7]. His belief in the authority of Jesus indicates that he believed him to be divine. There is no indication that he believed Jesus was merely a great prophet who was close to God. The Centurion believed that Jesus was the Son of God. Saving faith is to believe in the identity of Jesus, that He is Messiah and Lord, and risen from the dead [Romans 10:9].

- He believed in the **goodness of Jesus**. He believed that Jesus was open to his request, and that He would respond positively to that request. Faith has great confidence in the goodness of God - that He will respond with kindness and mercy [Romans 2:4].

- He **did not believe in himself** - he thought he was unworthy to receive a visit from Jesus. (This fact also confirms his sense of the deity of Christ.) He did not think that Jesus was rewarding his goodness, but had faith in the goodness of Jesus alone.

- His faith had a **specific object** - the healing of his slave - and this object was achieved.

Faith for a miracle and faith for salvation is rooted in the same Person. To be saved, we must believe that Jesus is the Son of God and God Himself. We must not believe in our own virtue or good works. We must believe and trust only in the mercy and kindness of God to save us.

3. Baptism in Water

The New Testament teaches that everyone who believes in Jesus should be baptised in water. Jesus told His disciples to go into all the world and make disciples of all the nations, baptising them in the name of the Father, the Son and the Holy Spirit [Matthew 28:19]. Jesus Himself, and all the believers in New Testament times, were baptised, and Jesus commands us to do the same as part of our obedience to Him.

Without spiritual understanding, baptism can become a merely religious ritual. The truth is that it is the outward sign of a mighty baptism with the Holy Spirit, which introduces the believer to the supernatural Kingdom of God. See Chapter 4 for a full treatment of this subject – Water Baptism and its Meaning.

4. Baptism in Spirit

There is a huge difference between the believers in the Gospels and the believers in the book of Acts. The foundation of salvation is that we believe in Jesus as Lord, Saviour and Messiah. This was the saving faith of the apostles in the Gospels. But the Kingdom of God came with power on the Day of Pentecost [Mark 9:1].

THE PLAN OF SALVATION

The Holy Spirit is the blood-bought inheritance of every saved person. He is not an optional extra, like some decoration on a Christmas tree! He is the essential dimension of the supernatural presence of God. No believer can make real progress until he receives the gift of the Holy Spirit.

The baptism with the Spirit brings:

- The indwelling of God's Spirit [1 Corinthians 3:16; Galatians 4:6]
- Heart purity [Acts 15:8-9]
- Boldness to witness [Acts 1:8 and 4:31]
- Deep unity among believers [Acts 2:44-46 and 4:32]
- Supernatural gifts of the Holy Spirit [Acts 2:4 and 6:8]
- The love of God [Romans 5:5]

Believers are brought into a new dimension of life and power and awareness of the presence of God. The baptism with the Holy Spirit is not a gradual process but a direct act of God, a sudden work of God.

3

THE BIBLE – THE WORD OF GOD

THE NEED OF THE HOUR: TO HEAR GOD SPEAK

The purpose of this chapter is to show the awful effect of neglecting the Bible and its consequences for the coming generation; and to show the amazing power of the Bible to transform our lives and Churches.

There has been a great decline in Bible preaching and Bible reading in some parts of the Christian Church today. Present attitudes and culture are the outcome of core beliefs in the population. These core beliefs underlie everything, from news reporting, to novel writing, to views of history and most importantly our view of God. It is useful to understand the change in thinking that has taken place over recent centuries. Here is a greatly simplified overview:

- **Scholasticism**: this is the foundation of philosophy pre-1600. The basic belief was that truth comes from God through revelation and that reason and faith are both important tools for understanding the world in which we live. The Bible was regarded as the great key to understanding the universe.

- **Rationalism** 1600–now: the foundation of modern thought. Truth comes through the power of reason alone. This is the foundation of modern science and has brought great advances to the human race. However, theologians increasingly applied reason to the Bible instead of faith. There was a denial of the supernatural and the miraculous. The result was liberal theology. Theologians began to discuss the merits of the Bible along with other literature.

THE BIBLE – THE WORD OF GOD

- **Relativism** 1960–now: truth comes through the exercise of will and choice, which results in a loss of absolutes - there is no right or wrong, no absolute divine revelation. Truth is arrived at through dialogue and discussion. No-one has 'the truth'. Each person creates their own world, and goes to their own heaven when they die. Opinion polls are more important than the Bible as a means of arriving at truth.

The 20th/21st century has suffered a loss of direction - there is no compass. Christians have become open to new ideas which are held to be of equal value to the Bible, e.g. words from angels, dreams and visions. Christians no longer ask, *"Is it in the Bible?"* As in Jeremiah's day, there is a tragic rise in false prophecies. Prophets are prophesying from their own imagination, not from the Lord. Prophets prophesy peace when there is no peace and *'heal the hurt of the people slightly'* [Jeremiah 6:14].

To major on the false is itself a tragic deception and derailment of many ministers. We must focus on God and on His Word, not on what is wrong around us. Nevertheless, while we seek to avoid unnecessary divisions, we do need to give a clear lead to God's people. Christians desperately need a compass, and that compass is the Bible.

WHY IS THE BIBLE SO IMPORTANT?

Smith Wigglesworth said: *"God's Word is supernatural in origin, eternal in duration, inexpressible in valour, infinite in scope, regenerative in power, infallible in authority, universal in application, inspired in totality. Read it through; write it down; pray it in; work it out; pass it on. The Word of God changes a man until he becomes an epistle of God."*

God has revealed Himself through the Bible [Luke 16:31]. If people will not hear the Scriptures then miracles will not help them. The Bible is God's Word spoken to God's servants, and is the key to all we know about God.

Voltaire expected that within fifty years of his lifetime there would not be one Bible in the world. His house is now a distribution center for Bibles in many languages...
                    Corrie Ten Boom

John Wesley said: *"I want to know one thing – the way to heaven; how to land safely on that happy shore. God Himself has condescended to teach the way; for this very end He came from heaven. He has written it down in a book. O give me that Book! At any price give me the Book of God!"*

Billy Graham said: *"The word of God hidden in the heart is a stubborn voice to suppress."*

1. The Bible is inspired by the Holy Spirit [2 Timothy 3:16; 2 Peter 1:20-21]

Many have opposed the Bible by asserting that it is the work of human beings. However, there are 24,000 manuscripts which confirm that the Bible has come down through the generations with no changes. Among ancient documents there is none that comes anywhere near the massive weight of evidence for the accuracy of the Bible. Homer's Iliad is the nearest rival, and for that there are only 643 manuscripts, with major differences.

Here are a few quotes on the authority of the Bible:

> **Thomas Arnold (English Historian):** *"I know of no one fact in the history of mankind which is proved by better and fuller evidence than the Resurrection of Jesus Christ."*
>
> **Sir Frederick Kenyon, Director of the British Museum:** *"The last foundation for any doubt that the Scriptures have come down to us as they were written now has been removed. Both the authenticity and the general integrity of the New Testament may now be regarded as firmly established."*
>
> **Dr. Simon Greenleaf of Harvard University** tried to refute the New Testament and the accounts of Jesus Christ. He became utterly convinced that they were true and accurate documents, and said: *"The Resurrection of Jesus Christ is one of the best established events of history according to the laws of legal evidence administered in the courts of justice."*
>
> **Werner von Braun, a top scientist working on the NASA space program,** said: *"I never really became a scientist till I came to know Jesus Christ as Saviour and God."*

2. The Bible is proved as supernatural by many prophecies

The Bible contains many prophecies that were spoken years before the events took place. Here are some examples of prophecies fulfilled:

- Psalm 22 describes the cross 1,000 years before the event, and hundreds of years before the Romans invented that cruel form of execution.

- Isaiah foresaw the virgin birth of Christ [Isaiah 7:13-14].

- Isaiah 53 describes the sufferings of Christ and their purpose, giving details about His execution as a common criminal, while being buried in a rich man's tomb. This chapter also explains that He died to take away our sin.

- Isaiah foresaw that Messiah would gather all nations together, both Jew and Gentile [Isaiah 42: 1-9].

- Daniel predicted that Messiah would be anointed 483 years after the command to rebuild the walls of Jerusalem [Daniel 9:24-27].

- Daniel also predicted that Messiah would die 3½ years later. The command was given in 457 BC, and this places the beginning of Christ's anointed ministry in 26 AD and His death in 29 AD, which, given the fact that our modern dating has been proved to be four years late, is perfectly accurate.

- Micah said that Messiah would be born in Bethlehem [Micah 5:2-5].

- Zechariah foresaw his betrayal for 30 pieces of silver [Zechariah 11:12-13].

These are only a fraction of the many prophecies regarding Messiah and they confirm the identity of Christ as God and Man.

3. The Bible is proved by archaeological evidence

There are countless examples of Bible details that have been unknown in history but have then been proved true through subsequent discoveries. Here are a few examples:

The Christian's Compass

- Babylon was completely covered by the sand, and all trace of it was lost. Liberal scholars suggested the Bible had invented Nebuchadnezzar and Babylon, but then in the 19th century explorers found the ruins of Babylon; and on every brick was stamped the name of Nebuchadnezzar.

- Luke 2:2 tells us that Quirinius was governor of Syria at the time of the birth of Christ. No evidence of this was found, so the Scriptures were taken to be in error. Then in the middle of the 19th century a stone was found with an inscription indicating that Quirinius had indeed been governor of Syria for a short three-month period exactly when the Bible said he had.

- For centuries the Hittite nation and culture were only attested to by the Bible and so sceptics regarded it as a myth. However, archaeological discoveries have now abounded regarding the historical accuracy of the Bible information.

- Sir William M. Ramsay (1851-1939) was born in the lap of luxury and was raised as a non-believer by his atheist parents. He graduated from Oxford University with a PhD and became a professor at Aberdeen University. Determined to undermine the historical accuracy of the Bible, he studied archaeology with the aim of disproving the biblical account, in particular the book of Acts. After 25 years of work, Ramsay was awestruck by the accuracy of the book of Acts. In his quest to refute the Bible, he discovered many facts which confirmed its accuracy. He had to concede that Luke's account was exact even in the smallest detail. Far from attacking the biblical account, Ramsay produced a book, *St. Paul, the Traveller and Roman Citizen*, which supported it. Eventually, William Ramsay shook the intellectual world by converting to Christianity. Ironically, this man who set out to refute the Bible, found himself accepting it as God's Word because of his explorations and discoveries. For his many books contributing to biblical knowledge, he was also knighted.

- Luke 3:1 records that Lysanias was tetrarch of Abilene in about 27 AD. For years scholars used this 'factual error' to prove Luke was wrong because it was common knowledge that Lysanias was not a tetrarch, but the ruler of Chalcis about 50 years earlier than when Luke described. But an archaeological inscription was found that said Lysanias was the tetrarch in Abila near Damascus at the time that Luke said. It turned out that there had been two people named Lysanias, and Luke had accurately recorded the facts.

4. The Bible has the power to create [Hebrews 11:3]

God's words are not merely ideas, as when people write what they think. God's words are both ideas and events. What God says, happens. When the leper said in Matthew 8: *"Lord, if You are willing, You can make me clean"*, he was recognising the Kingly authority of Jesus. Jesus replied: *"I am willing; be cleansed."* This is the word of the King, and what He says happens.

When Jesus said He was going to cross the lake, it was certain to take place. When He said, *"It is finished"*, the reign of sin and death ended at His command. The Bible must be read with faith in its sovereign power to change the lives of those who believe it; to bring healing, deliverance, forgiveness and full salvation.

5. The Bible is razor-sharp to give us clear understanding of ourselves and eternal things [Hebrews 4:12]

We cannot understand ourselves by psychology. Self-analysis is not fruitful in spiritual life. It is the word of God that alone gives light to darkened souls. We need supernatural discernment and wisdom in order to understand ourselves. This wisdom comes from the word of God.

6. The Bible is perfect and life-changing to the reader [Psalm 19:7]

The Bible has a perfection that baffles the mind of the sceptic. Rationalists will not accept the Bible as perfect since to do so would be to recognise its supernatural and miraculous quality. Numerous word studies have been made which show that there are patterns in the Bible text that are themselves an indication of an underlying perfection.
Jesus also said that not one jot (the smallest Hebrew letter) or tittle (a minute ornament over a Hebrew letter) would pass from the Law till all is fulfilled. This refers to the literal inspiration of the Bible through the writers. Peter says this in his second letter, where he affirms that: *"prophecy never came by the will of man, but holy men of God spoke as they were moved by the Holy Spirit"* [2 Peter 1:21].

This perfect quality of the Bible is not merely technical but also spiritual. Paul says in 2 Timothy 3:16 that, *"all Scripture is given by inspiration of God"*. Therefore its words have remarkable power in them.

Billy Graham had a close friend named Charles Templeton, who doubted the truthfulness and authority of the Bible. He tried to influence Billy Graham to follow his doubting path. In 1949, just before his great crusade in Los Angeles, Billy Graham wrestled in his own soul over the inspiration of the Bible. He went for a walk in a pine forest, and spread his Bible out before him, and at last embraced the Scripture in total submission as the authoritative and infallible Word of God.

Billy Graham noticed that whenever he quoted the Bible in his evangelism, the words had a distinct power to convict and bring illumination to the hearers. From that moment on he made it a deliberate policy to quote the Bible as often as possible while preaching.

7. The Bible produces faith in the reader [Romans 10:17]

The Bible teaches that faith comes as we perceive and apply God's word to ourselves. Faith is therefore a product of the word working on the heart and producing living faith as opposed to merely intellectual assent.

8. The Bible brings the wisdom needed to find salvation [2 Timothy 3:15]

There is no other book that explains the origins of mankind. Clearly speculation can never penetrate to things that happened at the dawn of time. The Bible, on the other hand, reveals these things - including the origin of evil, the purpose of Creation and the character of God. The Bible alone explains the cross and its meaning and power to save sinners.

THE SPIRITUAL ART OF READING THE BIBLE

1. We must read the Bible with the right attitude

The Bible must be read with the right attitude or it will not benefit the reader:

- ❖ **We are to receive the Word of God as seed**
  The Bible is a book of seeds. This seed principle is the key to the parable of the sower in Matthew 13:1-23. The purpose of the parable is to indicate the need to make room for the word of God. Worry, worldliness, unbelief, carelessness or a hard attitude will rob the word of God of power.

THE BIBLE – THE WORD OF GOD

The Bible shows that thoughts are seeds of actions. Jesus said that thinking adultery and murder were equal to committing the actions [Matthew 5:22, 28]. In the same way, if we entertain the thoughts of the Bible, they will be the seed-bed of our conduct. If we think on pure and honourable things then this will shape our lives [Philippians 4:8]. By reading, believing and obeying the Bible, we will become living epistles, and inherit its promises.

- **We are to read with humility**
  The key of knowledge is not the Bible alone, but the Bible read with the right attitude. In Luke 11:52 Jesus rebukes the lawyers for taking away the key of knowledge, and thereby neither entering themselves nor allowing others to enter. There is no doubt that the lawyers spent most of their lives debating and studying the Scriptures. It was not the knowledge of the Scriptures they lacked; it was a humble heart to read them properly.

- **We are to read with a heart that seeks God**
  Jesus reveals in John 5:39 that the Scriptures are a stepping-stone to come to Him. The Scriptures are not an end in themselves. He rebukes the Pharisees for searching the Scriptures for their own sake. As we meditate on the Bible, Christ reaches down and touches our lives.

- **We are to read with faith!**
  The Bible can be misinterpreted through unbelief: In Luke 24:25 Jesus reproves the disciples for not believing what the prophets had said about His resurrection. If they had believed, they would have understood. The same is true for us: if we do not believe the Bible, we will be tempted to believe that Jesus cannot do miracles today, or that our prayers will only be answered in difficult circumstances. Some Christians believe that since the time of the apostles God has stopped doing miracles. If we do not believe in a God of miracles, we will not experience miracles!

- **We are to check what preachers say with a true and honourable attitude**
  When Paul preached in Berea, the Jewish believers *"were more fair-minded* (Greek: honourable) *than those in Thessalonica, in that they received the word with all readiness, and searched the Scriptures daily to find out whether these things were so"* [Acts 17:11].

- **We are to read all of the Bible**
  The Bible can be misinterpreted by taking verses out of context, and by not considering the whole teaching of the Bible. Satan tempted Jesus by quoting the Scripture in Matthew 4:5-6, tempt-

ing Jesus to force God's hand to perform an amazing sign. But Jesus said, *"It is written again....."* [Matthew 4:7]. It is vital that Christians understand the whole counsel of God and not merely their favourite doctrines.

2. Keys to reading the Bible with our heart

(a) Wait on the Lord

It is vital to cultivate a quiet, peaceable spirit in which the Word of God drops like a pebble in a clear spring of water. We are to sit at the feet of Jesus like Mary and heed His Word as we meditate on the Bible [Luke 10:38-42].

(b) Stand in the Counsel of the Lord and Mark His Word
[Jeremiah 23]

We 'mark' His word by meditating on it. *"Reading without meditation is unfruitful; meditation without reading is hurtful; to meditate and to read without prayer upon both is without blessing."* [William Bridge, Puritan Writer].

Jeremiah exposed the false prophets and showed the right way to serve the Lord. Hearing what the Bible says is the foundational art of the true prophet. Isaiah 8:20 teaches: *"If they do not speak according to this word, it is because there is no light in them."*

(c) Receive the Spirit of Wisdom and Revelation
[Ephesians 1:17]

In Luke 24 Jesus approached two disciples on the Emmaus road. They did not recognise Him. Jesus corrected their blindness by expounding the Scriptures and explaining what they say about Him. In verse 32 the disciples state that Jesus *"opened the Scriptures"*. In verse 31 it says *"their eyes were opened and they knew Him"*. Later the same day Jesus appeared to the disciples and *"opened their understanding, that they might comprehend the Scriptures"* [Luke 24:45]. The Bible teaches here that we need help from Christ Himself if we are to understand the Bible.

(d) Ask, Take, and Eat!
[Revelation 10]

The Bible is the 'little book' that triggers prophecy. Revelation chapter 10 is an interlude in the teaching of Revelation and is a personal impartation of God to John to renew His prophetic ministry. It is an example to all ministers on how they can renew their ministry. The steps in the process are as follows:

- John is commanded to take the little book out of the angel's hand [10:8]. Bible reading is not an option; it is obedience to a command.

- John asks for the book [10:9]. Believers must ask for the Bible in prayer. Owning a copy is not enough.

- The angel commands John to take the book and eat it [10:9]. We must not merely read, we must take Bible truth into our spiritual hearts so that it will become part of our lives.

- The Bible is sweet to the taste, but bitter in its effects [10:10]. This is because it is incredibly beautiful and sweet to the soul, but has the power to convict, and to bring the believer into the groanings which are the fruit of the Spirit in us.

- The Bible in John unlocks even more prophetic utterance [10:11]. Where the Bible drops into believing hearts, the effect is to beget ministry, utterance and understanding of unseen things and of the future. The result is supernatural or prophetic understanding. This prophetic dimension is to be part of God's people at all times.

3. The Rediscovery of the Bible is a Prelude to Revival

2 Kings 22-23 gives us an example from the Old Testament.

The Temple had been locked up and neglected throughout the long 52 years of Manasseh's reign. Dust and decay had reduced the holy places to heaps of rubbish. Damp, mould and vermin had damaged the treasure of the nation to the brink of no return. Then King Josiah commanded the priests to cleanse the Temple. As they carefully sifted through the rubbish, there they found the ancient copy of the Law, probably the book of Deuteronomy. *"Then Hilkiah the High Priest said to Shaphan the scribe: 'I have found the Book of the Law in the house of the Lord.'"* [2 Kings 22:8]. When the Law was read out to the king, this led to great repentance on his part, and a partial revival in the nation - which did not, however, go deep enough.

There are treasures hidden in people's hearts, buried through years of sin, disobedience and prayerlessness. They neglect reading the Bible, but most serious of all, their inner faculty of knowing God is dead and buried. But God commands the cleansing of the temple of our heart.

He commands the treasures to be fully restored before they are lost forever.

How do we cleanse and refresh our inner life? Put away doubtful habits. Light up the heart with praise and wait quietly on God. As the inner eye becomes accustomed to the different light that shines from the presence of God, the believer sees his own heart in a fresh light for the first time. It is by the inner faculty of the heart that we know God. We are to 'sweep' our heart each day, expose our soul to the light of His presence, and look up to see the God who reveals Himself through His Son.

4. Discipline - the Mark of a Disciple

Disciples should be known by their commitment to knowing and obeying the Word of God. At its most practical level, this means that we read our Bibles at every opportunity. It is good to read several chapters a day. Someone who reads three chapters a day will read the whole Bible in one year.

As we read and meditate on individual verses, we can pray that God will speak to us. We can make a note of what God is speaking to us, and pray for wisdom how to obey. It is helpful to read a chapter and a book of the Bible over and over again, praying for understanding. We should read prayerfully, depending on God for understanding and the Holy Spirit for illumination.

The disciple knows that the Word of God is Jesus, not just a book. So knowing the Word is more than just Bible knowledge. The Pharisees knew the Bible but were not disciples of Jesus! The disciple uses the Bible to reach out and know Jesus, who is the Living Word of God.

5. Faith in the Inspiration of the Scriptures

This is a very basic point, but there is a danger, when believers are seeking God for fresh moves of His Spirit, that the Scriptures are no longer consulted and seen as the sole guide. Only where the Bible is honoured, and read with eagerness and hunger, is the Holy Spirit poured out. The parable of the sower indicates that the growth of the harvest is due to the conditions being right for the growth of the seed/word. The Word of God is the seed, and the water, the Holy Spirit, comes to germinate the seed/word in the hearts of believers.

There is a danger that believers become hungry for a move of God but neglect reading the Bible. When God comes with power then remarkable and unusual things begin to happen. Wesley tells of sinners lying on the ground prostrate before God, almost unconscious for hours. Jonathan Edwards tells of his wife going into a trance for hours.

THE BIBLE – THE WORD OF GOD

Thngs like this may occur, and also other manifestations that may puzzle the onlookers. While these things are exciting when they happen, there is the danger that we begin to believe that every such manifestation is from God. This is, of course, not the case, and we must try the spirits to see what is from God [1 John 4:1].

Believers must be firmly anchored in the Word of God, or there will be deceiving spirits at work in the midst of a move of God. If they are unchecked then the move of God will be weakened and may even be dissipated. In the worst cases there will be demonic activity that confuses and damages the confidence of believers. Sometimes a move of God will collapse if the Word is not preached and studied, along with the abandonment to the move of the Spirit.

The Book of Acts tells of the multiplication of the Church but also speaks of the growth of the Word. This implies that there is an essential life that is imparted as Scriptures are believed in and preached. The dramatic growth of the Church in Ephesus was described by Luke as: *"the word of the Lord grew mightily and prevailed"* [Acts 19:20].

Acts 6:7 tells of the multiplication of the Word leading to the multiplication of the numbers of disciples. (See also Acts 12:24.) The apostles devoted themselves to the preaching of the Word and prayer [Acts 6:2-4]. Paul gave to Timothy the most solemn charge in all of his writings:

> *"I charge you therefore before God and the Lord Jesus Christ, who will judge the living and the dead at His appearing and His kingdom: preach the word."* [2 Timothy 4:1-2]

If there is to be true lasting growth of the Church in depth and in numbers of truly converted men and women, then there must be a deep dedication to the preaching and teaching of the Word of God. Paul's letter to Timothy and the great charge quoted above is given in the context of other voices arising to tempt preachers astray from the clear path of the Spirit. This charge is more relevant today than ever.

This does not mean a return to intellectualism or exaltation of the mind! It means a soaking in the written word and in the presence of God so that the living prophetic application of the Word may shake and shape the culture in which we live, and destroy the strongholds of philosophies, religions and demonic powers that hold sinners in bondage. It also does not mean a return to a dry evangelicalism that exalts the Bible to the point of idolatry. God is revealed through the Bible, and so Bible study is not an end in itself but a path to fellowship with the living God, who lives and works in people today.

On the Day of Pentecost, Peter quoted from Joel and from the Psalms. There is great power to release the presence of God by the use of the Scriptures, both in private devotion and in public speaking. The Holy Spirit will be poured out upon the Word of God.

6. 'Soul Nourishment First' by George Muller

Finally, we will look at the example of George Muller, who found that his prayer life was dry until he began to meditate on the Scriptures before praying. Here is the text of a booklet he wrote:

Soul Nourishment First

"It has pleased the Lord to teach me a truth, the benefit of which I have not lost, for more than fourteen years. The point is this:

I saw more clearly than ever that the first great and primary business to which I ought to attend every day was to have my soul happy in the Lord. The first thing to be concerned about was not how much I might serve the Lord, or how I might glorify the Lord; but how I might get my soul into a happy state, and how my inner man might be nourished. For I might seek to set the truth before the unconverted, I might seek to benefit believers, I might seek to relieve the distressed, I might in other ways seek to behave myself as it becomes a child of God in this world; and yet, not being happy in the Lord, and not being nourished and strengthened in my inner man day by day, all this might not be attended to in a right spirit.

Before this time my practice had been, at least for ten years previously, as an habitual thing, to give myself to prayer, after having dressed myself in the morning. Now, I saw that the most important thing I had to do was to give myself to the reading of the Word of God, and to meditation on it, that thus my heart might be comforted, encouraged, warned, reproved, instructed; and that thus, by means of the Word of God, while meditating on it, my heart might be brought into experiential communion with the Lord.

I began therefore to meditate on the New Testament from the beginning, early in the morning. The first thing I did, after having asked in a few words the Lord's blessing upon his precious Word, was, to begin to meditate on the Word of God, searching as it were into every verse, to get blessing out of it; not for the sake of the public ministry of the Word, not for the sake of preaching on what I had meditated upon, but for the sake of obtaining food for my own soul.

THE BIBLE – THE WORD OF GOD

The result I have found to be almost invariably this, that after a very few minutes my soul has been led to confession, or to thanksgiving, or to intercession, or to supplication; so that, though I did not, as it were, give myself to prayer, but to meditation, yet it turned almost immediately more or less into prayer. When thus I have been for a while making confession or intercession, or supplication, or have given thanks, I go to the next words or verse, turning all, as I go on, into prayer for myself or others, as the Word may lead to it, but still continually keeping before me that food for my own soul is the object of my meditation. The result of this is, that there is always a good deal of confession, thanksgiving, supplication, or intercession mingled with my meditation, and then my inner man almost invariably is even sensibly nourished and strengthened, and that by breakfast time, with rare exceptions, I am in a peaceful if not happy state of heart. Thus also the Lord is pleased to communicate unto me that which, either very soon after or at a later time, I have found to become food for other believers, though it was not for the sake of the public ministry of the Word that I gave myself to meditation, but for the profit of my own inner man.

The difference, then, between my former practice and my present one is this: Formerly, when I rose, I began to pray as soon as possible, and generally spent all my time till breakfast in prayer, or almost all the time. At all events I almost invariably began with prayer, except when I felt my soul to be more than usually barren, in which case I read the Word of God for food, or for refreshment, or for a revival and renewal of my inner man, before I gave myself to prayer.

But what was the result? I often spent a quarter of an hour, or half an hour, or even an hour, on my knees, before being conscious to myself of having derived comfort, encouragement, humbling of soul, etc., and often, after having suffered much from wandering of mind for the first ten minutes, or a quarter of an hour, or even half an hour, I only then began really to pray. I scarcely ever suffer now in this way. For my heart, first being nourished by the truth, being brought into experiential fellowship with God, I then speak to my Father and to my Friend, (vile though I am, and unworthy of it), about the things that He has brought before me in His precious Word.

It often now astonishes me that I did not sooner see this point. In no book did I ever read about it. No public ministry ever brought the matter before me. No private intercourse with a brother stirred me up to this matter. And yet, now, since God has taught me this point, it is as plain to me as anything, that the first thing the child of God has to do morning by morning is, to obtain food for his inner man. As the outward man is not fit for work for any length of time except we take food, and as this is one of the first things we do in the morning, so it should be with the inner man. We should take food for that, as everyone must allow.

Now, what is the food for the inner man? Not prayer, but the Word of God; and here again, not the simple reading of the Word of God, so that it only passes through our minds, just as water runs through a pipe, but considering what we read, pondering over it, and applying it to our hearts. When we pray, we speak to God. Now, prayer, in order to be continued for any length of time in any other than a formal manner, requires, generally speaking, a measure of strength or godly desire, and the season, therefore, when this exercise of the soul can be most effectually performed is after the inner man has been nourished by meditation on the Word of God, where we find our Father speaking to us, to encourage us, to comfort us, to instruct us, to humble us, to reprove us. We may therefore profitably meditate, with God's blessing, though we are ever so weak spiritually; nay, the weaker we are, the more we need meditation for the strengthening of our inner man.

Thus there is far less to be feared from wandering of mind than if we give ourselves to prayer without having had time previously for meditation. I dwell so particularly on this point because of the immense spiritual profit and refreshment I am conscious of having derived from it myself, and I affectionately and solemnly beseech all my fellow believers to ponder this matter. By the blessing of God, I ascribe to this mode the help and strength which I have had from God to pass in peace through deeper trials, in various ways, than I had ever had before; and after having now above fourteen years tried this way, I can most fully, in the fear of God, commend it.

In addition to this I generally read, after family prayer, larger portions of the Word of God, when I still pursue my practice of reading regularly onward in the Holy Scriptures, sometimes in the New Testament, and sometimes in the Old, and for more than twenty-six years I have proved the blessedness of it. I take, also, either then or at other parts of the day, time more especially for prayer. How different, when the soul is refreshed and made happy early in the morning, from what it is when without spiritual preparation, the service, the trials, and the temptations of the day come upon one."

[George Muller, 9 May 1841]

4

WATER BAPTISM AND ITS MEANING

There are two conditions for baptism and one thing which must be understood. The conditions are:

- Repentance [Luke 3:8-14, Acts 2:38]
- Faith [Acts 8:36-7]

The thing which must be understood is that water baptism is a picture of baptism into death and resurrection, in and through the baptism with the Holy Spirit. The person being baptised may or may not have yet received the Holy Spirit, but it should be clearly in their minds that this is the goal of the believer - to receive the Holy Spirit.

When Cornelius heard the gospel he received the Spirit, and this convinced Peter that he should be baptised. In Acts 2:38 baptism is given as a preparation for receiving the Spirit. Clearly, God is not legalistic! He looks on the heart and gives the Spirit. Simon the sorcerer was baptised but clearly did not receive the Holy Spirit. He was not repentant to the point where he could receive life from God [Acts 8:9-24].

WHAT THE BIBLE TEACHES ABOUT WATER BAPTISM

1. *The Teaching of the New Testament*

The New Testament teaches that, when a person gets right with God through faith in Christ, they should be baptised in water as a sign of the step they have taken. This truth can be found in the teachings of:

(a) John the Baptist [Matthew 3:5-6 and Luke 3:3-18]

John the Baptist taught people to repent, including acts of restitution, in order to be baptised. Jesus submitted to this baptism at the hands of John. He had never sinned and so did not need to be baptised, but He did it as an act of identification with sinners, thus prefiguring His death on the cross. John even tried to refuse baptising Jesus, because he felt unworthy to do so. Jesus told John that, *"it is fitting for us to fulfill all righteousness"* [Matthew 3:15]. Jesus led His disciples in the way of obedience, and it is a simple enough lesson that where He led in baptism, believers should follow.

(b) Jesus Christ [John 4:1-2]

Jesus preached and practised the baptism of His followers. He Himself never baptised anyone in water [John 4:2] so that no-one would confuse the baptism in the Spirit that He gives; with the baptism in water ministered by human hands.

(c) The Apostles

From Acts 2:38, the apostles taught that, to be right with God, people should repent, believe in Jesus Christ and be baptised. The truths of repentance, faith and baptism are consistently taught throughout the book of Acts. See especially:

- Acts 8:12: *"But when they believed Philip as he preached the things concerning the kingdom of God and the name of Jesus Christ, both men and women were baptized."*

- Acts 8:36-37: *"Now as they went down the road, they came to some water. And the eunuch said, 'See, here is water. What hinders me from being baptized?' Then Philip said, 'If you believe with all your heart, you may.' And he answered and said, 'I believe that Jesus Christ is the Son of God.'"* See also Acts 10:47-48; 16:33; 19:5.

(d) The Church throughout History

The practice of baptism has been continued throughout all the centuries of Church history. There are different forms of baptism practised by different denominations, but generally all agree on the importance of baptism.

2. A Summary of the Bible's Teachings on Water Baptism

- It is an act of will, and was therefore ministered to children, young people and adults but not to infants who had no power of choice or understanding.

- It was commanded by Jesus to His followers [Matthew 28:19] and is an act of obedience to the will of God [Luke 7:29-30].

- It is conditional upon repentance [Acts 2:38].

- It is conditional upon personal faith in Christ as Saviour [Acts 8:37].

- It was by immersion, in rivers and lakes. John baptised in the Jordan, and the Ethiopian Eunuch was probably baptised in an oasis. The Bible speaks in Acts 8:38 of Philip and the Eunuch going *"down into the water"*.

- It was *"in the name of the Father and of the Son and of the Holy Spirit"* [Matthew 28:19]. However, there was no particular emphasis upon special words or rituals that had to be repeated. Acts 2:38 speaks of being *"baptized in the name of Jesus Christ"*. Acts 10:48 speaks of being *"baptized in the name of the Lord"*. Acts 19:5 speaks of being *"baptized in the name of the Lord Jesus"*.

WATER BAPTISM: A PICTURE OF DEATH AND RESURRECTION

Baptism is a picture of the believer's identification with the death and resurrection of Jesus Christ. The believer is to receive the benefits of the cross of Christ, which are:

- Forgiveness of sins [Luke 3:3 and Acts 2:38].

- Union with Christ and His death and all the power over sin that comes through His death and resurrection [Rom. 6:3-7].

- Baptism with the Holy Spirit - the infilling of the life and power of God [Acts 1:5, 8].

These blessings are not conferred by water baptism; they are conferred by faith and by the work of the Holy Spirit. Baptism is a **picture**, not a mystical work in itself. These blessings may be received before or after baptism.

Cornelius received all of them before being baptised with water [Acts 10:44-48]. The Ephesian believers received them immediately after baptism [Acts 19:5-6]. On the Day of Pentecost, Peter told the people that they would receive the Holy Spirit after fulfilling the conditions of repentance and baptism [Acts 2:38]. But there is no indication whether some received the Holy Spirit immediately, or whether some waited several days before receiving Him.

The lesson here is that each individual is different, and God is more concerned with the heart of the believer. He asks for our co-operation, and that means we must repent, believe and be baptised. God will fulfil His promises if we truly obey His Word from the heart. Only God can see the heart.

SOME IMPORTANT QUESTIONS ABOUT BAPTISM

Q. Can a person be saved by baptism in water?

A. No. Some have quoted 1 Peter 3:21 to suggest that *"baptism now saves us"*, but this is not referring to water baptism but to baptism into the death and resurrection of Jesus, of which water baptism is the picture.

Q. Must a person be baptised in order to be saved?

A. There is no verse to indicate that baptism is optional. But there are verses that emphasise that this is a vital step for every believer. Mark 16:16 and Matthew 28:19 clearly indicate that baptism is to be presented as part of the gospel. This does not mean that Christ will reject a person if they are not baptised for reasons beyond their control. The thief on the cross who accepted Christ minutes before dying had no opportunity to be baptised and yet he was given assurance of his salvation by Jesus's promise: *"...today, you will be with Me in paradise."* [Luke 23:43].

If a person rejects baptism, they will be in danger of being rejected by Christ: *"And when all the people heard Him, even the tax collectors justified God, having been baptized with the baptism of John. But the Pharisees and lawyers rejected the will of God for themselves, not having been baptized by him."* [Luke 7:29-30].

This verse teaches that if we are baptised we declare God to be just in His ways, but if we reject baptism we reject God's will for our lives.

WATER BAPTISM AND ITS MEANING

Q. How soon after conversion should a person be baptised?

A. Immediately – or as soon as possible. In Acts 16:33 the Philippian jailer was baptised along with members of his family in the middle of the night. It was the pattern in the Gospels and in the book of Acts that believers were baptised immediately upon their repentance and confession of faith.

Q. How sure should we be that everyone we baptise is truly converted?

A. The Bible emphasises the responsibility of the individual to repent and confess their faith to be saved. It does not indicate that the Church should conduct extended examination of candidates before baptising them. Probably Philip regretted having baptised Simon [Acts 8:13] because he clearly had not deeply repented [Acts 8:21]. Judas Iscariot was doubtless baptised either by John the Baptist or by Jesus's disciples.

Examination of people who wish to be baptised should be limited to the genuineness of their repentance and faith. Unless there is some compelling reason or revelation from God, the Church should accept the testimony of the person wishing to be baptised.

Q. What about infant baptism?

A. From around 300 AD some believers began the practice of sprinkling babies with water at birth to ensure that they would go to heaven when they died. From this idea, a second form of baptism developed, which has been practised since that time.

The act of baptising infants contradicts the plain teaching of the Bible. It was introduced as part of a loss of the gospel truth that a person is not saved until he or she repents and believes in Christ. From the 4th century onwards, many people were taught by the Church that they were Christians because they has been baptised as infants. This is a serious mistake, though not all who practise infant baptism believe that it saves.

Q. Is baptism found in the Old Testament?

A. The covenant seal for Israel was circumcision of baby boys on the 8th day after their birth, which prefigures water baptism in the New Testament. There are major differences in that (apart from the initial group of Abraham and his household) circumcision was to be performed on babies, not adults.

Circumcision is directly linked with baptism in Colossians 2:11-12. Both circumcision and baptism indicate that the people of God are set apart from all others to be His special nation.

Baptism into water is used symbolically in many Old Testament miracles:

- The whole earth rose from water in the first creation.
- God baptised the whole earth in the flood of Noah.
- Israel was baptised in the Red Sea unto Moses [1 Corinthians 10:1-2].
- Joshua led the nation of Israel into the Promised Land through the waters of Jordan. (Jesus was later baptised at this very spot.)
- Naaman was cleansed from leprosy through a form of baptism [2 Kings 5:14].

All these examples show that while baptism was not an Old Testament ritual, it was planned by God from the beginning.

Q. What about great men of God like Wesley and Finney who were baptised as infants? Were they saved?

A. Most people will have no difficulty in believing that these great men were saved. But the Bible warns us not to put the tradition of the elders above the Word of God [Mark 7:1-9]. The Church must be careful not to put its own practices above the Word of God. We are not to be guided by Church practice and doctrine, but by the plain teachings of the Scriptures.

5

THE PERSON AND WORK OF THE HOLY SPIRIT

Perhaps the most important truth concerning the Holy Spirit is that He is as active and present in the world today as in the days of the Acts of the Apostles. In fact Acts is one of the few New Testament books that does not end with the word 'Amen' - indicating that it is not yet a finished history! True the inspired account is complete, but it deliberately gives us the faith that God will be the same with all subsequent generations. Church history is full of miracles, prophecies and other manifestations of the outpouring of the Holy Spirit. The Bible is our infallible guide and is all-sufficient in all matters relating to spiritual life. However, we are not merely intellectual Christians and it is not an all-sufficient Bible that we worship, it is the All-Sufficient Christ, to whom the Bible leads us. He baptises with the Holy Spirit, heals, reveals and works wonderful things in and through His people. Christ ministers the Holy Spirit to His people and by this brings them into a dimension of life and power that is more than we could ever have dreamed of.

WHO IS THE HOLY SPIRIT?

1. He is Holy

This is a uniquely divine quality, and refers to His 'otherness' - the huge difference between the human and the divine. God is holy, pure, clean and in a different dimension.

In Isaiah 6:3, the seraphim cry out, *"Holy, holy, holy"* without ceasing. This cry is not a conscious decision; it is a response of their being to the presence of God. The astonishing thing about the seraphim is that they are not able to gaze upon God. It is entirely to be expected that a sinner should cover his face, but angels that have never sinned are not covering their faces from conviction of sin but from the overwhelming sense of awe at God's being. God in His holiness is above all that we can imagine Him to be. We become holy only through the work of the **Holy** Spirit. This means that we belong to God and bear His stamp and seal. Holiness means 'set apart for God'. This explains why the Holy Spirit is grieved every time we do or think something that is unworthy of a vessel in which God dwells.

2. He is Spirit- Uncreated and Non-material

God's being is in the dimension of spirit. God does not have a body like a human being, which means that He can indwell and be indwelt. Fallen humanity does not really know what 'spirit' is, as our eyes rest only on outward, external things. This means that faith is unnatural to fallen, carnal mankind. When the Spirit of God comes to us, we suddenly become aware of the supernatural realm. We become aware of God. The Holy Spirit brings this faith automatically, quickening our inner life, making us aware of God, and the reality of heaven and angels etc. 'Spirit' also refers to the essence or heart of a person. When we think of God's Spirit we should think of God's innermost, most intimate being - His heart. When God pours out His Spirit He pours out His heart. Christians rightly pray for God to pour out His Spirit, but they often do not realise the greatness of this request - that God should pour out and commit His innermost person to the lives of human beings. God rightly waits till our hearts are broken and deeply repentant before He will commit His precious inner Self in this way.

3. He is Invisible

Even some believers do not notice Him [Acts 19:2]! The Holy Spirit is content to be invisible as He loves the glory of Jesus. Though He is content to be invisible in order that Christ should be glorified, yet He is unknown by carnal mankind since there is no sensitivity to the Spirit of God in sinful people. Sinners can easily relate to the concept of God as Father and of God as Son. But they have no concept of what or who the Holy Spirit is. Most new Christians will think of Him as a power like electricity. But the Bible reveals that He is not a power but a person, with feelings and sensitivity.

Stephen said in Acts 7:51 that the Jewish leaders were *"stiff-necked and uncircumcised in heart and ears"*. This was a grave insult, especially to a Jew! Nevertheless, this is true of the whole human race. The human heart is hardened and our ears are covered with a thick layer of flesh, making us totally unaware of God. Many people are converted when they suddenly become aware of the presence of God through the Holy Spirit

4. He is Dove-like *[Matthew 3:16]*

The Holy Spirit is gentle and easily driven away; but yet never fearful or offended. Doves are clean, not scavengers. Seagulls and vultures, for instance, are among birds as pigs are among animals. They will eat anything in a greedy undiscerning manner. Doves, like lambs, eat clean food, and are gentle in nature. They symbolise the purity and gentleness of God's Spirit. When seeking the gift of the Holy Spirit, it serves us well to remember how He fell on the 'Lamb of God'. If we are rough and harsh by nature we will repel the dove, not attract Him. If we are broken and meek, then the dove will delight to fall upon us.

5. He is the Third Person of the Trinity, and is God

Many verses point to the mystery of the Trinity. In Matthew 3:16-17 Jesus is praying, the Holy Spirit descends and then the Father speaks from heaven. In John 15:26 Jesus describes that He will send the Helper, who proceeds from the Father. The Trinity is not a logical conclusion created by philosophical deduction through discussion! God is a person, and He is three in one. We can think of Him as a tripod, with three legs forming the whole. We can think of the Trinity as the vital organs of a body - heart, lungs and brain - each indispensable but part of one person.

The three persons of the Godhead indwell each other and love each other. The mystery of God is that He has invited humanity to join in the fellowship of the Trinity. This does not mean that humanity is invited to be God! But the Bride of Christ, the Church, partakes of the divine nature [2 Peter 1:4]. We are invited to partake of intimate fellowship with God [John 17:21].

6. He is the Servant, Carrying Out the Father's Will

The Holy Spirit carries out the Father's will. The Spirit hovered on the waters at the dawn of Creation [Genesis 1:2]. As God the Father speaks the Word (Christ), the Holy Spirit brings the spoken word into reality.

A waiter in a restaurant will watch the guests and keep in the background, meeting their needs as they arise, with as little fuss as possible. So the Holy Spirit watches over God's will to fulfil it in the hearts and lives of God's people. He has a servant heart, and it is **this** Spirit that fills the Church and also all of heaven. Christ came as a servant, and washed the disciples' feet. How wonderful that the Holy Spirit can shape our lives and conform us to the atmosphere of heaven!

7. The Holy Spirit and the Cross

The Holy Spirit is linked with the cross – since He cannot live in a carnal, sinful heart. He is gentle and submissive. He would never be able to function in an uncrucified heart. The human heart cannot receive the Spirit unless that heart is first prepared by the work of the cross. The cross works in brokenness and cleansing to prepare a vessel for God that is clean and pure and submissive to His will. The cross makes the human heart like the heart of Jesus. The Holy Spirit fills us when we embrace the death of self and sin, and we experience the wonder of the resurrection life as His Spirit washes through us.

WHAT DOES THE HOLY SPIRIT DO?

1. He Changes Our Nature [John 3:1-21]

Our problem is our nature; God's solution is a new nature; God's method is the cross.

Jesus said that we must be *"born again"* or literally *"born from above"* [John 3:3]. He said that the nature of sinful flesh gives birth to a person of sinful flesh [John 3:6]. Our problem as humans is that we cannot change our nature by external things, since our nature goes down to the spiritual DNA of the heart. It is no more possible to change a sinner into a Christian by teaching him, than it is possible to turn a pig into a child by sending it to school! You might dress up the pig in clothes and do all in your power to make the pig respectable, but in the end the pig will instinctively be what it is by nature. So it is with the human heart.

Since mankind's problem begins at birth, there is nothing we can do about it apart from the power of the gospel. There is no human power to change our own heart. We are born sinners and we must live and die sinners. Our spiritual DNA has set us on a train track that leads to death and hell. But God has intervened, and has allowed the destructive power of sin to fall on His Son when He died at Calvary. By the power of the cross, Christ has reached into the depths of our hearts and changed our nature, if only we will repent of our old nature and our old ways.

It is for this reason that Christ died - to change the DNA of our hearts by a miracle. The key is to realise that the problem is not just what we have done, but what we ARE in our life and nature. We have offended God by what we do, by what we say, and by what we are. When we open our hearts to the power of the Holy Spirit, a miracle takes place and our hearts are changed. This miracle takes place in the unseen places of our inner person, and the effects of this change are deep and surprising. Most people are amazed at the depth and the power of new birth.

THE PERSON AND WORK OF THE HOLY SPIRIT

2. He Washes Us [1 Corinthians 6:11]

The work of the Holy Spirit can be likened to washing. Things which are dirty may require different methods to clean them. Soap will remove many marks, but some stains will require strong detergent or even bleach. But the stains of sin on the human heart and soul are ingrained and do not yield to anything but the power of the fire in the Holy Spirit. There are hurts and wounds in the human heart that go deep into the subconscious. God longs to minister such deep healing to our aching hearts. The baptism with the Holy Spirit is also a baptism of fire [Matthew 3:11], indicating His purging work.

The Holy Spirit baptism purges the depths of our hearts, but it is also penetrating, like a whitening dye. The Spirit removes stains, and imparts the life and love of God. Our lives are then empowered to live for Christ. The Holy Spirit imparts spiritual LIFE, including faith and expectancy, and wonderful confidence in God.

3. He Applies the Cross [1 Corinthians 12:13]

The word 'baptism' is always associated with death and resurrection in the New Testament, as in Romans 6 which describes the work of the Holy Spirit in the heart. Water baptism prefigures the work of the Holy Spirit. It indicates a dying to self by faith. This is not a negative death; it is an entrance into life, bringing the death of everything that is negative. The cross is like an operation to remove cancer. The patient may fear the surgeon's knife, but he also blesses it and is grateful for it. By it the poison and sickness is removed from his life. So too the baptism with the Spirit is an experience of the cross; there is loss and there is gain. This is because God will not mix His Spirit with sinful flesh.

In the Old Testament there are examples of sinful people such as Samson who received an anointing of power - which is never described in the Old Testament as the baptism with the Spirit. From this we can understand that the Old Testament saints experienced something similar to the baptism with the Spirit, but with the important difference that there was no power of the cross in their experience. Also, we can understand from it that in the New Testament there is the danger that people may experience an anointing of the Spirit and miss the true baptism with the Spirit. There is, of course, a true and a false. Some speak of the Holy Spirit without ever mentioning the power of the cross. This can easily lead the sheep to wrong pastures.

4. He Teaches and Guides [John 14:26, 16:13]

The Holy Spirit teaches and guides believers. He does this in many different ways, but the main way is through the 'witness of the Spirit' or the inner 'anointing' by which we 'know' things. John writes that by this inner anointing we *"know all things"* [1 John 2:20]. He does not mean that we know Church history or that we no longer need to hear preaching and teaching! John is referring to things that not only **are known** by the inner anointing, they **can only be known** by this means.

By the inner witness we know we are children of God [Romans 8:16]. By this inner witness, believers can sense a deceiving spirit [1 John 2:18-20]. Of course we use our minds to detect wrong doctrines, but we know wrong spirits by the anointing. Not everyone who has a strange doctrine is of a wrong spirit, and not everyone who has correct doctrine has a right spirit!

The witness can lead believers to make choices in their lives. Acts 16:6-7 describes how the Spirit enabled Paul and Silas to discern the next place for them to preach the gospel. The Holy Spirit communicated God's will to them, perhaps through the inner faculty of knowing or perhaps through some other means.

A British preacher named Dave Wetherley was praying in his house in South London, when he felt a sudden prompting to go to one of the famous London bridges. When he got there, Dave noticed a soldier standing near the middle of the bridge, so he approached the man and shared the gospel with him. The soldier was amazed and confessed that he had come to that bridge to commit suicide, but had instead found new life in Christ!

A similar story is told by Jonathan Paul, the founder of the Pentecostal Church in Germany. He spent his retirement in a village in the mountains on the Czech border. One night he was woken by the Spirit and felt a strong urge to go to the house of a neighbour who lived close by. He resisted the idea at first, but finally got up and knocked on the door of the man's house. The neighbour stood there, with a shocked expression on his face, holding in his hand the rope with which he was about to hang himself. Jonathan Paul led the man to Christ.

The Holy Spirit guides by prophecies, dreams, visions, words of knowledge, circumstances - in fact by many different methods. He sometimes speaks with an audible voice. Many people have suddenly heard the audible voice of God with such clarity and authority that they have looked around to see if there was another person with them. There are many examples in the testimonies of Christians and also in the Scriptures. God guides His people, and the Holy Spirit communicates His will. Many have testified that they entered into a new dimension of guidance through the baptism with the Holy Spirit. Joel says that young men shall see visions, old men dream dreams and that all of God's servants shall prophesy. These things reflect the true dimension of the supernatural into which God brings us through the Holy Spirit.

5. He Loves and Glorifies Jesus [John 16:14]

The Holy Spirit loves Jesus, and He inspires the reading and the preaching of the word of God. At colleges and universities, the lectures are designed to give students information they did not previously know. But when Christ is preached, the Holy Spirit reveals Jesus to those who never knew Him, and also afresh to those who do know Him. This work of revelation imparts a sense of God and of the power of the cross in a way that no lecture could ever do. Believers need the Holy Spirit to preach the gospel, since there is no other effective way that the gospel can be communicated [1 Thessalonians 1:5].

The deep love of the Spirit for the Father and the Son means that one of the great effects of the baptism with the Spirit is a love for God. There is a melting power in the Holy Spirit, and a fire of unswerving devotion to Jesus Christ. He will never compromise but will always bring the soul back to this point of focus.

6. He Convicts of Sin [John 16:8]

In the presence of God's holiness, sinners are troubled and begin to sense the dangerous state they are living in. The result is that many turn spontaneously to Christ and fall on their knees in deep repentance. Believers can also experience deep conviction of sin if they fall into a life of backsliding, prayerlessness or unbelief.

7. He Empowers Believers [John 14:12]

The Holy Spirit can empower believers to do supernatural works of power, ranging from the gift of tongues, to raising the dead. This realm of God's supernatural moving is exciting, but Jesus warned His followers not to get carried away with this breathtaking ministry of power:[Luke 10:17-20]. Jesus warned that it is not a sign of being right with God when He uses us in ministry [Matthew 7:22-23]. There are many examples of godly people who have been full of pride and have fallen, despite being mightily used by God.

However, these examples should not take away our belief that God can work in powerful healing and deliverance. When troubled, suffering or sometimes even dying people are healed and delivered, God is glorified. We must simply and naturally believe that God will use us to minister all of His love and power to needy souls. This power of the Holy Spirit is manifested through the use of the gifts of the Spirit (see later in this chapter).

HOW DO I RECEIVE THE HOLY SPIRIT?

1. Introduction

❖ ***We must receive the Holy Spirit!***

Perhaps the most important part of this study is to realise that we can and indeed must receive the Holy Spirit. The word 'must' should not be intimidating. Some people will ask: *"Can I be saved without the baptism with the Holy Spirit?"* There is clear evidence throughout the New Testament that this is possible, even quite common. From the thief on the cross, to the believers in Samaria [Acts 8:4-8] and in Ephesus [Acts 19:1-6], even to the apostles themselves, there is abundant evidence that salvation is a gift bestowed upon those who repent and believe. But to then think of living without the life-empowering gift of the Holy Spirit is like buying a car but refusing to put petrol in the tank!

The Church is formed through the baptism in the Spirit. We ourselves become members by this means [1 Corinthians 12:13]. The apostles received life in a new dimension through the baptism in the Spirit. If we have truly repented then there can be no good reason to reject it. Rather, there is every reason to seek this wonderful gift with all our hearts.

❖ ***We can know we have received the Holy Spirit***

Can we know by experience that we have received the Holy Spirit? Yes, we can! Tozer said that if we were to accept that the Holy Spirit was in us with no noticeable change, then we would never know if He left us! The coming of the Holy Spirit makes such a difference in our lives that we know He has come. Opinions may differ as to how we know. Many emphasise the gift of tongues. Others have said that the real mark of the baptism with the Spirit is trouble! But the main point is that we enter a dimension of the **supernatural life of God in us**. This means that gifts of the Spirit will be real, but also prayer and faith will take on another dimension.

> Some have suggested that we may experience an initial sign and thereafter nothing more! Rather, the opposite is true - the real sign of life is growth and development. A seed that never grew would be a great disappointment. A child that never grew would bring distress to its parents. When the Holy Spirit comes we can expect a fountain of abundant life, and not just once but as a pattern of the new life. The key is: do not be satisfied with a taste! Press in till you have the fullness within you. **At all costs – receive the Holy Spirit!**

How then do we receive the Holy Spirit? Here are seven elements that will help us understand the mind of God on this vital matter.

2. Repent [Acts 2:38]

We cannot change our nature, but we can change our attitude and our direction, laying aside all sins, doubtful habits, repairing broken relationships through forgiveness, and restitution. There are many aspects of true repentance, including:

- **Confession:** often we use euphemisms for sin such as 'mistake', 'error', 'I wasn't myself' etc. But when we truly confess our sins we do not make them seem better than they are; we name them in all their shameful horror.

- **Forsaking:** confession is good but is not full repentance. Some people, especially those from a Catholic tradition, find relief in 'confession'. However, there is no repentance in merely confessing. It is the first step, but the second is to forsake – to utterly turn our back on former habits and sins. We need faith for this, and Hebrews 11:27 tells us that it was by faith that Moses *"forsook Egypt"*. Moses had the inner power from God to give up all the wealth, privileges and honours that were his in the royal court of Pharaoh. He turned his back on it all, embraced the life of a simple shepherd and was content to live out the rest of his days in the wilderness, trusting God.

- **Restitution:** there are some sins, like stealing or fraud, that not only must be forsaken but if possible require restorative action to put the wrongs right. If a person has been evading tax, then God will not give them the baptism with the Holy Spirit unless there is a change of heart and a commitment to pay the tax owed.

3. Obey [Acts 5:32]

If the Holy Spirit reminds us of something we need to put right, we should promptly obey. It might be a relationship that is not right, and requires us to write a letter or make a phone call. It might be an object that does not belong to us - either it was stolen or borrowed, but it must be returned. It might be not paying debts as promised, despite having the ability to pay. It might be declaring income to the tax authorities.

Sometimes, when the Holy Spirit has moved in this way, the police have been overwhelmed with stolen goods returned and firearms and knives handed in. While many of us may not have been involved in stealing or violence, yet all of us need to obey the Holy Spirit quickly. When the Holy Spirit touches us this is a great blessing, though it may seem negative at first and involve conflict of conscience and will.

4. Love Jesus *[John 14:15-16]*

Love is a **response**, and if we respond to Jesus, then that love will drown out every competing love and become the dominant note of our lives. The Holy Spirit loves Jesus; it is not possible to receive the Holy Spirit and not have love for Jesus. It is possible to have faith and use the name of Jesus for miracles, but it is not possible to be filled with the Spirit who loves Jesus, and not love Him!

Love is an **act of will** - choosing Jesus above everything else, above every other competing relationship, whether it be husband, wife, children, mother father etc.

5. Thirst *[John 7:37]*

This is the inner drive that carries us to God. If you do not have a thirst for God, then pray for one. This is not the superficial kind of thirst that makes a person sip a little water. It is the deep disquiet of heart that is more like the thirst of someone who is wandering in the desert, dying for water. Jesus said in John 4:14 that whoever receives the gift of the Holy Spirit will never thirst again. By this He means that the awful emptiness of life will disappear for ever, though there will be a constant healthy desire for God.

The Bible bids us pray for the Holy Spirit [Luke 11:13]. But prayer is not merely speaking religiously to God! The key to prayer is an inner longing that is directed up in faith to God. Some people pray for revival but do not long for it. A mother may not think she is very good at prayer, but will groan all day with longing for her son to be saved. She may not realise that she has been praying all day, but the inner thirst is heard by God. Jesus said that He will give the Holy Spirit to those who thirst.

6. Believe *[John 7:38]*

This is not a mere mental position, but an attitude of heart, and inner commitment and entrustment of our lives into His hands. Many believe God exists and that He loves them, but are not willing to **let God take control** of their lives.

A famous high-wire performer in the USA was able to walk across the Grand Canyon and other famous places. Once he asked the crowd if they believed he could walk on the wire with a wheelbarrow. "Yes!" roared the crowd!

"Do you believe I can do it with a man in the wheelbarrow?" "Yes!" roared the crowd! "Who will be the first to volunteer?" There was embarrassed silence from the crowd....

If people were asked whether they believed the current US President exists, everyone would immediately answer, *"Yes - of course!"* But if they were then asked, *"Do you trust him?"*, their answers would vary widely, based on their assessment of his character. Belief in Christ is a statement not merely that we think He exists, but that we have entrusted our entire life to Him. It is a statement of total commitment.

7. Drink/Receive *[John 7:37]*

This is the action of letting go our fears and receiving the life-changing living waters. This action of drinking in the Holy Spirit is based on trust. But we should not give this kind of trust to everyone who asks it of us. After all, we are not entrusting our souls to other people; we should know that we are yielding to Jesus, not to people. God has promised us that if we ask for bread, fish or an egg, He will not give us a stone, nor a serpent or a scorpion [Luke 11:11-12]. So too, as we come to the living presence of Jesus, our confidence will grow and we will learn to yield our lives to Him and drink of His Spirit.

8. Ask *[Luke 11:13]*

This is not like asking for a cup of coffee, but more like asking for someone's hand in marriage. It is a deeper step in an eternal partnership. When a young man asks a girl to marry him, he will prepare the moment as well as possible. If he truly loves the girl he will wait for the answer with bated breath and beating heart! The Bible describes God as a young man in love [Song of Solomon]. The most common picture of the Church is as the Bride of Christ, making herself ready for her wedding day [Revelation 19:7-9]. God is inviting us to share eternity with him.

God has promised to hear our prayer if we ask with all our heart [Jeremiah 29:12-13]. Ask with faith, believing in God's unswerving faithfulness to His promise.

The sermon that sparked the Welsh revival of 1904 was by Evan Roberts, and it was incredibly simple. God gave him four things that he should share with his home Church:

- *That they should confess all known sin and put right any wrong done to anyone.*
- *They should put away every doubtful habit.*
- *They should obey the Holy Spirit quickly.*
- *They should confess their faith in Christ publicly.*

This sparked such a hunger for God that the revival began.

EIGHT BIBLICAL TYPES OF BAPTISM IN THE HOLY SPIRIT

1. The Creation of the World

This is the first of this series of eight miracles through water that teach us things about the baptism with the Holy Spirit. The first creation was under water, and it rose out of the water on the third day. Here already is the biblical picture of death and resurrection. The lesson here is that the baptism with the Spirit is a work of creation, of re-creating the human heart, making a new person, and of producing in us a quality and dimension that simply did not exist before.

This creation is not the act of moulding something, like a piece of clay; it is the act of calling something into existence that simply was not there before. In the baptism with the Spirit, the Holy Spirit creates in us a clean heart [Psalm 51:10]. The Holy Spirit creates a new person in Christ who is motivated by a new nature. The nature of sinful mankind is to rebel. But the nature of someone who is baptised with the Spirit is to obey. This promise is explicit in Ezekiel 36:26-27. Here God promised the gift of a new heart through the gift of the Spirit. Through this gift, God would cause His people to walk in His ways.

2. Noah's Flood

THE PERSON AND WORK OF THE HOLY SPIRIT

The purpose of Noah's flood was to deal with the awful state of sin that had spread to the whole human race. There are three main aspects of the sinful states that God was seeking to deal with by this miracle:

- There was a **demonic interference** that was producing human monsters [Genesis 6:4]. The baptism with the Spirit wipes out the devil's hold on our lives. Souls troubled by demons find relief, not merely through the sending away of evil spirits, but through welcoming the power of God to fill and replace the inner rooms of the heart. The great danger is to think we can have empty hearts. This is very dangerous, since Jesus warned that this cannot continue long. In Luke 11:24-26, Jesus said that if someone is delivered from an unclean spirit, he will be like a swept, clean house. But if that evil spirit returns and finds the house clean but not occupied by a new master, then it will bring seven more evil spirits with it, thus making the final condition of that soul worse than at the beginning.

- Sin had reached a level where it was the **only obsession** of the human race [Genesis 6:5]. Sin is addictive and obsessive. Lust for money, sex and pleasure through substance abuse (alcohol, drugs, tobacco) or mental stimulation (videos, magazines, internet games etc.) is a dangerous drift, and there is a need for the power of God to cut deep into the human heart and set us free from inner sins. The baptism with the Holy Spirit delivers us from these obsessive sins.

- **God Himself regretted that He had created mankind** [Genesis 6:6]. This is the great question-mark over our lives. Many want hell not to exist, but the Bible reveals that God has put a question-mark over the right of human beings to continue in a life of sin. God will end this right by a punishment that is both awful and eternal. The baptism with the Spirit is God's wonderful, complete answer to change our eternal state of heart and put heaven within us, to prepare us for heaven after we die. The Kingdom of God has come now in power through the baptism with the Holy Spirit. The kingdom comes in two stages - first inwardly through the Spirit and then outwardly when Christ returns.

The flood, then, was God's answer to the awful state of the human race. He baptised the whole world under water, returning it to the original condition of the first creation. This act was repeated through the death and resurrection of Christ. When Christ died, though the earth was not covered with water, it was covered with darkness [Genesis 1:2 and Luke 23:44]. God made a new world. When we receive the baptism with the Holy Spirit, God drowns the work of Satan and sin in our souls, and remakes us.

3. The Crossing of the Red Sea

One aspect of the crossing of the Red Sea has to do with the destruction of Pharaoh and his armies. What does Pharaoh signify spiritually? The answer is, he signifies the fallen nature of Adam, which Romans 6:6 refers to as the 'Old Man'. The Old Man, who is in league with Satan, is the enemy within and there is no miracle that can bless or heal him. He must die!

There are several characteristics of Pharaoh that identify him as the Old Man:

- He is seated on the throne, and will not share it. There is a throne in every human heart, in every home, in every church and in every nation. These power centres are misused unless God is invited to sit on these thrones. All thrones belong to Him [Colossians 1:16], and all must bow to Him, but the Old Man sits as king and will not bow to Jesus.

- He is cruel and heartless, persecuting the Israelites and forcing them to hard labour [Exodus 5:11]. The Old Man is selfish and hard in his handling of those under his power. Husbands, wives, children, office or factory workers can all suffer from the heartless rule of this nature in those around them.

- He has a hard heart to God and to other people [Exodus 7:13]. Hardness indicates an insensitive state of life, not sensing the presence of God or the needs of other human beings.

- He is manipulative and seeking to control God. In Exodus 8:8 he asks for prayer for relief from the plagues, but changes his mind quickly when relief comes. Similarly, the Old Man will ask for prayer for help but will not yield his will to God unless it is to his benefit!

- He is untouched by sufferings, and resists all pressure to change his attitude, even though God sends plagues to humble him and make the human heart teachable [Exodus 9:14].

- He repents with false repentance [Exodus 9:27]. He confesses he has sinned, but this is all part of the manipulation he uses to stay on his throne. Confession of sin is good if it is accompanied by a deep desire to change. But if not, it is just a sinful manipulation of God and his ministers to get them to feel sorry for the poor suffering sinner. Sin must be forsaken, not merely confessed.

o The Old Man is a supreme bargainer, and Pharaoh attempts to bargain his way out of the situation by trading with Moses. He suggests that Moses lead the people out - but not far [Exodus 8:28]! He later suggests that they may go but they must leave their flocks and their herds [Exodus 10:24]. The Old Man bargains with God over salvation, seeking to maintain a worldly lifestyle alongside a 'Christian' life. God will not bargain - it is all or nothing!

There is only one answer for the Old Man, and that is death! Our release from sin takes place in two stages:

(a) The Passover lamb is slain. When God passed over in judgment, Egypt's firstborn, including Pharaoh's heir, died [Exodus 11:5]. The lamb died as a substitute for the firstborn of every family that ate it – their firstborn was saved. Jesus is our Passover lamb [1 Corinthians 5:7]. He died as our substitute; He suffered separation from God's presence to save us from eternal death and damnation.

(b) God's people passed through the waters of the sea [Exodus 14:21-30]. It was a baptism; God's people were baptised. This is a picture of Jesus and the believer. Jesus went through the baptism of death and resurrection [see Luke 12:50]. And every believer is baptised with Him. When Christ died, all died [2 Corinthians 5:14]; when He died, so did the Old Man that was enslaved to sin [Romans 6:6]. And when Christ rose again, so did the believer. Their New Man was born [see Ephesians 4:24]; they were raised again with Christ to a new life of freedom from bondage to sin [Romans 6:4]. By the Holy Spirit, we are baptised with Christ; by baptism with the Spirit we are set free from the body of sin, from our old nature. This is the wonderful truth: through faith, Christ's death and resurrection are now ours.

4. The Priests' Laver *[Exodus 30:17- 21; 38:8; John 13:2-10]*

The laver or basin that the priests washed themselves in represents the cleansing action of the Holy Spirit that prepares us for the closeness of a relationship with God in prayer and intercession. This Old Testament picture teaches us that those who are washed can then approach God, to minister to Him. The laver is seen in type again in John 13 in the hands of Jesus as He washes His disciples' feet. Only when we are washed do we have the necessary heart state to pursue the high calling of prayer. The laver of the Holy Spirit, ministered through Jesus, produces in us a deep longing for prayer and for the ministry of intercession.

5. The Crossing of the Jordan [Joshua 3:13]

The key phrase in this event is *"cut off"*. The waters of Jordan were cut off and this represents the power of the cross to cut us off from the heredity of sin - from all the generational sins and curses that a human soul may have inherited from his or her parents.

All souls are troubled with the general heredity of sin from Adam. There are further problems that many people have inherited from the sins of their ancestors. For instance, if a person's grandfather was a Freemason or a spiritist, that person may find they have strange psychic powers, along with depressions and oppressions. The cross cuts us off cleanly from our heredity and we are free!

6. The Anointing of Elisha at Jordan [2 Kings 2:1-14]

The anointing of Elisha at Jordan is a type of the mantle (or cloak) of power that came upon the disciples on the Day of Pentecost. Jesus used the phrase *"clothed* (translated 'endued') *with power from on high"* in Luke 24:49. There are many lessons in this event:

- There are divine discouragements! Three times Elijah told Elisha not to follow him (verses 2; 4 and 6), but each time Elisha gave his stirring answer: *"As the Lord lives and as your soul lives, I will not leave you!"* These discouragements parallel the temptations that the Lord passed through and which His disciples also had to pass through in some measure: *"But you are those who have continued with Me in My trials."* [Luke 22:28]. The pursuit of a deeper life with Christ is in the face of strong winds of discouragement and trials. If we are not determined, we will give in. God does not plan to make it easy for us, knowing that He can only build His kingdom on proven character, including qualities such as perseverance and self-control [2 Peter 1:5-7]. Ruth demonstrated this unswerving commitment when offered the possibility of leaving her mother-in-law Naomi [Ruth 1:16-18].

- The crossing of Jordan is a picture of union with Christ through His death and resurrection. It is this wonderful redemptive act that not only takes sin away but enables us to partake of all of His wonderful life.

- Elisha prayed a difficult prayer [2 Kings 2:9-10]! Elijah said that such a prayer could only be answered if Elisha saw him as he ascended. This refers to the truth that we must keep our eyes on Jesus at all times [Hebrews 12:2]. Jesus is the fountain of faith. He is the beginner and perfecter of faith, and as we keep our eyes on Him, so faith is formed and grows. There are easy prayers: *"Give me money"*, *"Help me pass this exam"*, etc. And there are hard prayers: *"Make me like Jesus!"*, *"Give me true spiritual authority!"*, *"Give me a double portion of the Spirit of Jesus"*!

- The 'double portion' refers to several things. It refers to the firstborn's right to have twice as much as the other sons because he had the responsibility of caring for all the family members who were in need, such as orphans and widows. To have the double portion meant to have the double burden!

  It also means that Elisha did not want merely a taste of Elijah's blessings, but he wanted to go further than Elijah had done - building on the work and ministry that had gone before. Jesus said the same thing would be true of His disciples when He sent the Holy Spirit [John 14:12].

- The whole event signifies that believers must follow Jesus and see Him high and lifted up on the throne of the universe. It is the glorified risen Christ who ministers the Holy Spirit [Acts 2:33].

7. The Baptism of Naaman in Jordan *[2 Kings 5:1-27]*

The baptism of Naaman in Jordan represents the washing of the Holy Spirit to deliver us from the power of sin, symbolised here by leprosy. Naaman was a famous general in Syria and yet his life was ruined by the secret beginnings of this disease. It must have been a terrible blow, since as the disease progressed it would have led to him being isolated and cut off from friend and family alike.

In Naaman's household is an Israelite servant girl who was captured on one of Naaman's military campaigns against Israel. This girl is not bitter or afraid, but boldly witnesses to the power of the living God to deliver Naaman from his disease [verse 3]. Naaman, sadly, does not go first to the prophet Elisha but to the King of Israel. The king has the outward symbols of power, but has no spiritual power. The prophet has no outward symbols of power but is close to God. The same can be true today. We do not always find the Churches to have the answers we are seeking. Sometimes the bishops, with their robes and crowns, are actually devoid of all spiritual reality, although many bishops are godly, spiritual men.

Naaman goes to Elisha at last and is instructed to baptise himself seven times in the Jordan. This reminds us of the seven sayings of Christ from the cross, and reinforces the sense of baptism into death and resurrection. Naaman is at first angry at such a simple solution, but is at last persuaded. The result is that his skin is restored like that of a little child. This is the wonder of the baptism in the Spirit - that it refreshes and cleanses our inner life and makes us new again.

Elisha is offered money as a reward for this wonderful healing, but he refuses. This is a vital point for all ministers to note: we should never accept money as a reward for blessings that God alone has bestowed, even though it is through our ministry. We receive support from believers to continue our ministry, but the blessings of the ministry come without charge. The story contains a fearful warning, as Gehazi secretly takes the reward that Elisha has refused. The result is that the plague of leprosy that afflicted Naaman now comes on Gehazi.

8. Jonah in the Belly of the Whale (or Great Fish)

The story of Jonah depicts the impartation of the power to love our enemies and to take the gospel to the whole world. This is what Jesus imparted to His disciples by the baptism with the Holy Spirit. The Holy Spirit gives us the power and urge to evangelise the world.

Jonah is commanded to preach the gospel in Nineveh, the capital of Assyria. It was the Assyrians that had afflicted Israel and were ultimately to lead the northern kingdom into captivity. Jonah had had a hand in strengthening Israel against the attacks of Assyria [2 Kings 14:25]. Jonah's reaction can only be described as racist. He so loathes the Assyrians, that he wants God to judge them and destroy them. He disobeys God and flees from the presence of the Lord.

In the ship, he sleeps during the storm! This may well have been the deep sleep of a depressed soul. When at last the sailors awake him, he is immediately aware that he is the cause of the storm and the danger that the ship is in. Instead of repenting, he chooses rather to die! The sailors throw him into the sea, but to his amazement and horror he is swallowed by the whale.

The three days and nights that he spends in the belly of the whale (or huge fish) must have been like a living hell. He would have been unable to move. The air would have been so foul that he would have found it hard to breathe. He would have vomited and probably passed from consciousness to unconsciousness with the heat, the lack of air, and his distress of soul. Jonah here is a picture of Christ bearing our punishment on the cross. Christ bore our sins. The key here is that the sense of time is relative to our sufferings. A minute watching our favourite movie passes unnoticed. Ten seconds with our hand in a flame would seem like ten hours! Christ on the cross for six hours, separated from the Father by being made sin, would have seemed like an eternity. It was on the cross that Christ destroyed our unloving, prejudiced sinful soul and recreated us in Him [Ephesians 2:10].

Jonah cries to God from the depths of his living hell. So, too, sinners must cry with all their heart to God in order to experience the inner transforming power of the resurrection. Jonah was raised from the dead! We do not have to go through the same suffering, but we must cry out to God and give our souls to God in death and resurrection. Jonah is raised, and now finds that he has a love for the Ninevites. Jonah preaches to that great city, with such clear fervour that the whole city is shaken and repents, from the king downwards.

The story also has a warning that even after such deep dealings of God; a Christian will always have temptations to revert to his former sins. Jonah is grieved that the power of God has changed Nineveh. He reverts to his former prejudices and even mourns the loss of his shade more than the souls of the people of Nineveh.

From Jonah's story we can see that in the baptism with the Spirit, God imparts to us His love for the lost. If we walk in that love, we will be a missionary people, moved with a great passion for the lost, and involved in God's worldwide plan to reap the nations with a great harvest of believers who will spend eternity with God.

THE GIFTS OF THE SPIRIT

Spiritual gifts are supernatural abilities uniquely imparted to believers who are baptised with the Holy Spirit [1 Corinthians 12:13] to aid them in: - Their personal life of faith
- The edification of God's people
- The ministry of reaching the lost

A gift is bestowed on every believer [Ephesians 4:7-8]. A gift may be common to all (e.g. the gift of tongues) or may determine the whole ministry of the individual (e.g. apostles, prophets, evangelists etc.). We will consider a full list of the gifts from all the Scriptures.

1. The Gift of the Word of Wisdom *[1 Corinthians 12:8]*

This is the supernatural ability to understand the hidden causes of problems, and to bring a clear word that answers the problem.

A pastor was advising a couple and found that they were opposites in character. Their differences were leading to an irreconcilable breakdown of their marriage. One was tidy and the other messy. The pastor, prompted by the Holy Spirit, advised them to have one week when both would be messy, and then one week when both would be tidy. This word of wisdom led to the mutual appreciation of each other and the healing of their relationship!

---

2. The Gift of the Word of Knowledge *[1 Corinthians 12:8]*

This is best illustrated by the word of knowledge that Jesus demonstrated when he told the woman of Samaria that she had been divorced five times [John 4:18]. God simply reveals hidden factors that cause the person concerned to believe the gospel, and to come to real repentance and faith. There are many times when we could do with this gift, and there is a need for faith to receive the operation of this gift often as we pray.

A Church in the UK was having great difficulty and a time of heaviness. A group of pastors gathered to pray and to seek God for a breakthrough. During the time of prayer it was revealed to one of the pastors that the hall that the Church met in had formerly been used as a Freemasons' Lodge. This revelation was later confirmed. The pastors prayed against the spirit of this secret society and the atmosphere in the Church changed.

~~~~~~~~~~~~~~~~~~~

Once, the famous London preacher Charles Spurgeon stopped during his preaching and, pointing at a young man, declared: "Young man, those gloves you are wearing have not been paid for. You have stolen them from your employer." The young man confessed this to be true and made restitution.

On another occasion, he pointed at a man and said: "You have a bottle of gin in your pocket!" This startled the man and led to his conversion.

---

3. The Gift of Faith *[1 Corinthians 12:9]*

This is the gift of extraordinary faith for a specific situation, perhaps in the face of great danger or difficulty. The use of this gift is quite varied. Jesus used this gift to calm the storm on the sea and to give a sign to Israel by cursing the fig tree!

During a boys' summer camp in the UK the weather was so bad that the organisers had to make a decision whether or not to cancel it. The campsite was covered with mud, and heavy rain was making the conditions worse by the hour. At the early morning prayer meeting, a young man prayed with tears that God would send a wind and grant strong sunshine to dry the camp out. As the prayer meeting was ending at 7.30 am, the rain stopped and the sun shone all day, accompanied by a strong wind. The extent of the miracle was only fully appreciated as cars began arriving in the evening from surrounding towns for a meeting. All the drivers reported heavy continuous rain in all directions. Only in that locality were there dry conditions!

4. The Gift of Healing [1 Corinthians 12:9]

There are numerous examples of healing in the Bible and in the writings of believers from Bible times to the present day - although sceptics will rarely accept even well-documented examples.

5. The Gift of Working Miracles *[1 Corinthians 12:10]*

It is not important to differentiate too precisely between all the gifts. Some people have the gift of working miracles that are like signs, which require great faith and may involve a healing. God does all these wonderful signs for His glory.

John Welch was a preacher in the 16th century in Scotland who once refused to allow a man to be buried for two days. Welch prayed fervently and, to the astonishment of the doctors, the man rose from the dead!

6. The Gift of Prophecy *[1 Corinthians 12:10]*

The gift or prophecy has two different forms - foretelling and forthtelling. Foretelling is the revelation of future events, such as when Jesus prophesied that Jerusalem would be completely destroyed [Matthew 24:2].

George Fox prophesied the great fire of London the year before it happened. Jan Hus prophesied the coming of Luther 100 years before the Reformation. Such prophecies have occurred regularly over the whole Church age. Have there been mistakes made? Of course, but these do not discredit the whole ministry of prophecy. Preachers have made many mistakes but this does not discredit the whole preaching ministry.

There is a great need for humility in the exercise of the gifts. It is better if, instead of saying, *"God has told me"*, a person prophesying says, *"This is what I believe God is saying to me/us."* And no-one should be completely dismissed for getting things wrong and perhaps prophesying mistakenly. Anyone who makes mistakes should be treated with grace and forgiveness.

7. The Gift of Discerning Spirits [1 Corinthians 12:10]

This is the ability to discern when an evil spirit is at work. There are true prophets and there are false prophets [2 Peter 2:1]. John instructs believers not to believe every spirit [1 John 4:1]. John is here describing the ability given to every believer to discern what is from God and what is from the devil. However, sometimes there is a need to discern the particular demonic bondage that is binding a soul.

8. The Gift of Tongues [1 Corinthians 12:10]

This is the supernatural gift of speaking in either known or unknown languages. This gift has been severely attacked - often with methods of exegesis that no Bible scholar would normally accept. There is no Biblical evidence that the gift of tongues was a temporary manifestation, any more than preaching and teaching. Some have suggested that the *"perfect has come"* [1 Corinthians 13:10] now that the Biblical canon (writings) is complete. Such an explanation of this text is highly unusual. The establishment of the canon was itself only completed at an indeterminate date, and was not marked by any particular event.

The gift of tongues can be abused, as can the gift of preaching! But Paul says that this gift is of great value in personal edification. Jackie Pullinger and David Wilkerson have written extensively of their successful work with drug addicts, leading them to faith in Christ and relief from addiction. They use persistent prayer in tongues to help the addicts through 'cold turkey' (slang for the symptoms that accompany withdrawal from drug addiction). If such an addiction can be broken with the gift of tongues, should not all God's people seek the use of this gift for their personal edification and the breaking of the addiction of sins of body and mind?

Testimonies of this gift may be quite subjective, but they do include the apostle Paul himself who claimed that he had great benefit from this gift and used it copiously [1 Corinthians 14:18].

9. The Gift of Interpreting Tongues [1 Corinthians 12:10]

This gift is similar to the gift of prophecy but is initiated by a person giving a message in tongues. The value of this gift is that it turns the minds of all present to the Lord in a specific way, in order to seek a clear word from the Lord. The use of this gift can lead to a period of quiet listening to the Lord and to the voice of the dove in the heart.

10. The Gift of Apostleship [1 Corinthians 12:28]

There are different levels of apostleship, and there are more than twelve apostles in the New Testament. The first twelve were to be personal witnesses of the resurrection. Judas fell, and it seems likely that Paul, not Matthias, was God's choice to replace him. Certainly, Paul believed that he had had a unique apostolic revelation of the resurrection in the same way as the original apostles [1 Corinthians 15:8]. Paul does, however, refer to the twelve apostles [1 Corinthians 15:5], indicating that he respected the early Church's choice of Matthias. But this cannot be interpreted as indicating absolute divine sanction, since it was Jesus and not the Church who chose His apostles. The manner of choosing Matthias is lacking in divine inspiration, since Jesus did not instruct them to do this. Also, there is no indication that this choice of Matthias had any effect on his life and ministry.

The original twelve were unique in that they witnessed the resurrection in a remarkable and clear way. Also some of them wrote documents that were soon recognised as divinely inspired and were quickly added to the canon of inspired Scripture. Peter refers to Paul's writings as 'scripture' in 2 Peter 3:16.

The Bible clearly indicates that there were other apostles, including Barnabas [Acts 14:14] and Titus [2 Corinthians 8:23]. We can readily agree that there are no apostles adding to the Scriptures today, but then, not all the original twelve wrote parts of the Bible. It is also apparent that apostleship did not automatically mean equal status, with gifting similar to that of the apostles Paul or Peter.

It seems that the word 'apostle' refers to someone chosen by God to fulfil a special work for God, related to the foundations of the Churches. Many men have had such clear calling and gifting, including Wesley, Luther, Finney etc. The Bible clearly teaches that there are men of such stature in every generation. It may also be true that there are more apostles than we realise, simply because the word has become synonymous with the ministry of 'giants' such as Wesley and Finney. It may be that many pioneers have been apostles. Certainly the Greek word means 'missionary', though it would clearly be wrong to equate everything we understand by the modern word 'missionary' with apostolic gifting.

11. The Gift of Teaching *[1 Corinthians 12:28]*

Of all the gifts, this is the easiest one to think of in natural terms. After all, the universities are full of theological professors and teachers. Do they have the gift of teaching? No, they have a natural gift, not the gift referred to in the Bible. Sadly, the ministry of teaching in the Churches is often purely natural - built on intellectual perception of truth and lacking in divine revelation. Human effort alone can yield results that satisfy human pride, but it will bring no revelation or spiritual refreshing to God's people.

It is sometimes thought that evangelists and preachers are interesting, but that teachers are dry, intellectual and boring. The truth is that all the gifts and ministries are to be inspired and empowered by the Holy Spirit. All of them are given to build up God's people in faith, and so bring deliverance, healing and the life-giving presence of God.

12. The Gift of Assistance (Helps) *[1 Corinthians 12:28]*

Gifts like this are so easily overlooked; but God has set many in the Church who faithfully reveal the glory of Christ by their constant availability and servanthood. They do this cheerfully and with faith and love in the Holy Spirit. The Church is poorer without these gifted individuals. They can be seen cleaning floors, cooking meals, setting out meeting rooms, etc. They are an army without which the Church would cease to function.

13. The Gift of Governing or Administration *[1 Cor12:28]*

The gift of governing includes administration. So many preachers have to do this work, but not all are called to it. The mark of such gifting is that it is carried out without heaviness, and certainly without the faceless spirit of the world. This work of governing is made easy by the oil of love. It is fascinating to see Jesus as the administrator of His disciples and His kingdom. He clearly knew that Judas was not handling the money well, and yet He did not become worried or fearful but allowed things to take their course. There is an administrative ease in the Gospels and the book of Acts that makes the reader amazed at the enabling of the divine presence to make things happen.

14. The Gift of Evangelists *[Ephesians 4:11]*

The gift and ministry of the evangelist is simply that of freely sharing the gospel without embarrassment and with complete ease. The world has seen many great evangelists, but there are just as many individuals who share their love and faith in the workplace in the most gifted and wonderful manner.

15. The Gift of Pastors [Ephesians 4:11]

Peter was called first to be an evangelist [Matt. 4:19] and then later his calling was redirected to include that of being a pastor [John 21:15-17]. God is able to widen or even change the calling He lays upon a life. Pastors are those who are caring for the flock, and as such this gift encompasses all the main ministries of the Church. There is a dimension of pastoring in apostles, prophets, evangelists and teachers. Nevertheless there is the distinct and unique ability to care tirelessly for God's people - visiting the sick, the lonely, the widows, etc.

16. The Gift of Liberality [Romans 12:8]

This is the gift of supplying money and hospitality to believers and unbelievers alike. It is a God-given generosity that motivates individuals to share with abandonment and faith, knowing that God will supply. This is not the ministry only of rich people. Those who follow this call and give freely, sharing what they have, will find that the divine principles will be fulfilled: *"Give, and it will be given to you"* [Luke 6:38]. Many big givers in the Church started by giving from their poverty, but found that God provided them with more and more to give.

17. Conclusion

We can readily see that the above list of gifts is a description of the functions of the body – the Church. It is important to realise that the Holy Spirit can give gifts as He pleases, and that each gift is a remarkable ability that cannot be explained by natural gifting. Also, the above list is not exhaustive, and there are other Spirit-given gifts and abilities that are not expressly included. For example, a person may have a gift of handling souls that may be described as a 'counselling gift'. God has given supernatural ability to His people to accomplish His will in the earth. By the gifts of the Spirit, Jesus Christ is continuing His ministry through His people.

The greatest gift is, of course, Jesus Himself. This fact should make us aware that we may receive a gift through the Holy Spirit, but by it we ourselves become a gift to the Church. The Bible says: *"He Himself gave some apostles..."* [Ephesians 4:11]. The **person** is to be a gift to God's Church. Present yourself a living sacrifice, being ready to speak what He gives you to speak and do what He gives you to do; knowing that, with the call, there comes the divine ability to fulfil His commands.

THE PRICE AND POWER OF DISCIPLESHIP

THE GREAT COMMISSION TO MAKE DISCIPLES

"*Go therefore and make disciples of all nations, baptizing them in the name of the Father and of the Son and of the Holy Spirit, teaching them to observe all things that I have commanded you; and lo, I am with you always, even to the end of the age.*" [Matthew 28:19-20.]

These are the words of the Great Commission, and they are still the command of Jesus to His people today. The key word is 'disciples'. It is relatively easy to get converts or decisions at a crusade. But it is not so often that the converts who fill in decision cards are found following the Lord and learning the ways of the disciple.

Making one disciple is probably worth much more in the long run than getting 100 decisions. This is because it is not how we start the race that matters, but how we finish. Also, one disciple will make another disciple, whereas those who make decisions for Christ without understanding the implications are not likely to disciple others.

It is the same principle as someone being offered a choice between receiving $5,000 as his fixed wage, or being paid one cent on the first day he works, which then doubles for every subsequent day he works. The mathematics alone proves that after 18 days he will be earning over $5,000 for that day, and at the end of one month he will be earning more than $21 million per day! In the same way, Jesus' example shows us that to disciple 12 men over 3 years is by far the best investment of our ministry.

The focus of our ministry must include discipleship. Some discipleship movements hold the belief that if the early Church had really discipled believers, then the whole of mankind would have been won to Christ within a generation, and He would have been able to return to earth! This view is rather mechanical, to say the least, - nevertheless, the principle is true that disciple-making is much more effective than evangelism alone.

THE EXAMPLE OF JESUS

1. Jesus was a Disciple of the Father

At its simplest level, a disciple in New Testament times was someone who was taught by a Rabbi, a teacher. In the synagogue, all boys would go to the school called The House of Books from the age of 6-12 and learn the Torah - the Law - which is the five books of Moses. This was to them the way, the truth and the life.

The boys who succeeded at this level would move on to The House of Learning from the age of 12-15. At this stage they would learn the 39 books of the Old Testament by heart and learn to discuss questions with their Rabbi.

If a Rabbi noticed a young man who was willing and able, he would invite that young man to 'follow' him, and the scholar would then become a follower of the Rabbi, learning his ways - learning to become like him in speech, understanding and even habits of life. The young man would follow his teacher until he reached 30 years of age. At this point the disciple would become a Rabbi himself.

Jesus Himself learned from His Father - He learned the hard disciplines of submission and listening and obeying. John describes all these qualities of Jesus as a disciple of the Father. He only did what He saw the Father do [John 5:19]. He was personally taught by the Father [John 8:14-17]. Jesus was a disciple on a totally different level from any person who had ever lived before. The cost of this discipleship was death to self.

Key lesson: we must die to self and be disciples of the Father.

2. Jesus was a Rabbi - a Disciple-maker

Jesus chose men who had not succeeded in the first stage of the House of Books and had not progressed beyond it. They were uneducated and untrained men [Acts 4:13]. Jesus personally tutored them for 3 years. He shared His daily life with these twelve men. They were by no means perfect men; the worst of all being Judas, who was a thief and constantly disobedient to the teaching he heard. But Jesus persisted, and longed that Judas would somehow come through all his personal struggles and become a true disciple. This was not belief in Judas! It was belief in the power of God to take the worst of men and transform him, if he will only co-operate with God.

Jesus suffered the disciples' ways for 3 years as they only slowly realised their need to change, from an outward relationship of Rabbi/disciple, to an inward one through the Holy Spirit. The Holy Spirit was to become their teacher and the focus of the disciples' ability to know and follow Jesus. Jesus is still making disciples! He is still the teacher and He is still calling people to follow Him and learn of Him.

Key lesson: we must give time to people to work with them, be available to them, to answer their questions and teach them the ways of God. Making disciples is not simply a classroom exercise; it is the investment of ourselves.

Key lesson: we must believe that God can take the worst of people and make them disciples.

Key lesson: we must not be discouraged by people who fail and fall away like Judas, but we must believe that some will be like Peter, who won many others to Christ.

CHARACTERISTICS OF TRUE DISCIPLES

1. A True Disciple is One who Carries the Cross [Luke 9:23-26 and 14:26-33]

Of all the qualifications of a disciple, this is the most important and the foundation of them all. Jesus taught us about denying ourselves and taking up our cross.

- **Self-denial** [Luke 9:23] - without great renunciations there will be no great Christians!

> **Lilias Trotter** *lived and died in Algeria as a missionary to the Muslims. John Ruskin (a famous English painter) said that she was the best painter he had met, with the brightest prospects. She renounced this career to work in obscurity.*

THE POWER AND PRICE OF DISCIPLESHIP

> ***J.O. Frasier*** *was an outstanding pianist and musician but gave it all up to walk in the mountains of Lisuland and bring the gospel to the mountain tribes.*
>
> ***John Sung*** *earned numerous degrees in America, but dropped all but one of his certificates into the ocean as he sailed back to China. He had appeared in Time Magazine as an outstandingly brilliant man of his generation. He was offered professorships from many prominent universities in America and Germany but he had decided to renounce a bright future as a university lecturer and preach the gospel. John Sung preached for only 20 years but turned China upside down with his powerful ministry.*
>
> ***C.T. Studd*** *was the son of a millionaire but he gave all his money away and became a missionary first to China and then to Africa.*

Disciples must let go not only of their sins, but also of good things, in order to give themselves entirely to following Jesus Christ. Jesus called Peter to leave fishing, and the Bible says he left all. Self-denial means we must leave habits of self-indulgence and self-pleasing and embrace hardship where necessary. We do not have to create lives of hardship! But we must forsake all that competes with our devotion to Jesus.

- **Taking up our cross** - this means to embrace death to self and to the world. Jesus was dead to the world - to flattery, to reward, to pleasure-seeking. For this reason his focus was clear. Only someone who has taken up his own cross can teach the principles of the cross! John Sung could have had a prestigious university teaching career, but gave it all up to preach the gospel.

- **Hating those we love most** [Luke 14:26] - this teaching seems unnecessarily hard! Why should we hate our fathers, mothers, wives etc? The answer is that we are not to develop feelings of hatred for anyone! But whenever there is a conflict of interest between our relationship with a loved one and with Jesus, we must always choose Jesus. This is cross-bearing at its simplest. We love Jesus first, we put Him first and everything else must be second to that master passion of our lives.

In order to pioneer a work in central Africa, **C.T. Studd** *did not see his wife and children for years. He was joined by many young men inspired by his commitment. Many died of malaria within a few months. One young man who had joined him on the mission field, burst out in frustration one day, when the food supply was quite low, and said to Studd: "Well we have got to live haven't we!?" Studd calmly replied: "Not necessarily."*

Parable 1 – building a tower *[Luke: 14:28-30]*
If we do not have this master passion, we will not be able to stay the course, finish the race and complete the building. Better rather to be among the spectators than to kit up, start the race and just give up halfway for no good reason! The Christian who does not have the heart of the disciple will look like a person who never put a roof on his house. It aspires to be a great house, but it actually looks like an incomplete shell.

Parable 2 – war with an enemy *[Luke 14:31-33]*
If we do not have this master passion we will not be able to defeat our enemy, the devil. Victory is not based on numbers but on passion. Little Vietnam defeated the USA and China because their passion for victory was greater. If we do not have this passion we had better make peace with our enemy! But how can we ever do this? He will only accept our surrender to him, and that is what the half-hearted disciple is doing. He is surrendering to the powers of darkness. Discipleship is the path of victory.

- **The cross and relationships** - *the* cross has two dimensions. The vertical line of the cross points upwards, teaching us that we need to obey the Lord. The horizontal line teaches us to focus on caring for others. Jesus emphasises these two teachings:
    (1) To passionately and wholly love God
    (2) To love others as we love ourselves.
These are the sum of all the commandments. This biblical structure must be carefully laid in each Christian's life. The cross in discipleship means that we love and worship God, and that we love and care for all around us, from our closest family and friends to our neighbours and colleagues.

- **Dying to self and sin** - of all the aspects of carrying the cross, this is the most important. Paul said that believers are already dead and crucified with Christ [Galatians 2:20 and Colossians 3:3]! Paul makes it clear that, by baptism with the Holy Spirit, we are baptised into the death of Christ, and we are already dead. This happened by faith to the apostles on the Day of Pentecost and was the great release of their lives from self and sin to discipleship.

- **Paul said "I die daily"** *[1 Corinthians 15:31]* - this means that although we have already died, we must renew our discipleship by daily denying ourselves and surrendering to the cross and the power of the Holy Spirit. Paul exhorted the believers to count themselves dead to sin, and to yield their members to righteousness. Though we have died with Christ as a spiritual fact, yet we must bring our lives into line with this fact by total surrender to the Holy Spirit.

- **Surrender leads to commitment** - we are empowered by the Holy Spirit to be commited, which is the heart of cross-bearing. Commitment by the power of our will is too weak to fulfil the demands of discipleship. We need the supernatural power of God to fire our hearts to true discipleship.

2. A True Disciple Knows Victory over Sin

"Then Jesus said to those Jews who believed Him: 'If you abide in My word, you are my disciples indeed. And you shall know the truth, and the truth shall make you free.' " [John 8:31-32]

There is a difference between being a mere 'believer' and being a disciple. Many people believe that Jesus exists, that He is the Son of God etc. but they are not committed to this truth. They have not done anything about it, and their lifestyle is not affected by what they believe. A disciple is so committed to the truth that it dominates his or her world view.

- *A disciple loves his or her Bible and should be totally commited to knowing and obeying the word of God.*

- *A disciple is personally devoted to Jesus and will find ever greater freedom from sin as they follow the Lord. This is the true mark of discipleship – that we are free from religion and sin, from law and from lust. We are followers of Christ, and our holiness is not based on keeping a few rules, but on personal devotion to Jesus. A true disciple has discovered the miracle that true holiness is a by-product of loving Jesus.*

- *A disciple's heart is 'good ground' - the disciple knows the word abiding in his or her heart. The word of God is not lost by the wayside, nor stolen by the devil as a result of negligence. It is not choked by the thorns and thistles of worldliness, but thrives in the good ground of a heart that is focused on Jesus.*

3. A True Disciple Knows the Power of Prayer

"If you abide in Me, and My words abide in you, you will ask what you desire, and it shall be done for you. By this my Father is glorified, that you bear much fruit; so you will be My disciples." [John 15:7-8]

Here Jesus explains the power of abiding in Him. This is the secret of fruit-bearing. This teaches us that discipleship is not mechanical but a living, growing plant that is nurtured by the presence of Jesus. Jesus teaches us that we cannot create fruit by our own efforts. Neither can God create the fruit of the Spirit, which is LOVE. If God merely created love then it would not be love! It would be a sad imitation of love. In the same way, parents cannot force their children to love them. Neither can they bribe them by buying presents! Love must be nurtured in the right atmosphere, and this atmosphere is JESUS. We must abide in the presence of Jesus and nourish our souls by His word, and so we will grow in grace.

The effect of abiding and storing His word in our hearts will be to produce a closeness to God in prayer which will be seen by answered prayers. Answered prayer is a mark of true discipleship.

4. A True Disciple Loves Others

"By this all will know that you are My disciples, if you have love for one another." [John 13:35]

The greatest mark of true discipleship is LOVE. Jesus teaches in John 13 that the foundation of all ministry is humility motivated by love. He gave us the example of true ministry by taking the garments of a slave and washing the disciples' feet. This indicates that the true heart of ministry is washing, and that it is exercised by humility, and is powerful in proportion to the love that is poured out. As water washes and refreshes tired and dusty feet, so love washes and refreshes the souls of God's people.

True discipleship is not competitive. It is not a race against other disciples! It is a race in which we are to keep a loving heart, ministering to and encouraging others in their walk with God.

A disciple is someone who witnesses for Christ as a way of life. As Christians we are to bear fruit, according to John 15:8. This includes the fruit of souls brought into Christ's kingdom, as well as the fruit of the Spirit. This is part of our love for our neighbour. Reaching out to the lost is as essential a part of loving our friends, relatives and neighbours as giving them medicine when we know that we have the only medicine that will heal them.

A disciple loves his brothers and sisters by a deep commitment to his local Church.

> *Oh to dwell with saints above!*
> *Yes, that will be glory,*
> *But to live with saints below...*
> *Now that's a different story!*

Many believers will find difficulties in attending Church. Churches require commitment and discipline. They require submission to the plans of the leading team, and believers may have to accept a humbler position than they think they deserve. But a disciple welcomes this discipline, because he is seeking to live out a life of commitment through total surrender. Because of this, he loves the Church and lays his life down for it. He finds the various aspects of Church life naturally fit in with loving his brothers and sisters. These include:

- Giving through tithes and offerings
- Fellowship, hospitality, readiness to help others
- Worshipping regularly with God's people
- Partaking of communion

5. A True Disciple has Learned Three Golden Rules

(a) The Absolute Demands of Discipleship

The demands of Jesus Christ on our devotion are absolute. A husband will never share his wife, a slave cannot be owned by two masters, and so Jesus will never share us with anyone else. We must *"forsake all"* to be disciples [Luke 14:33].

This was Paul's experience of – he suffered the loss of all things and counted them as dung in order that he might win Christ [Philippians 3:8]. This is not devotion to a cause or to an ideal, but to a person. It is the absolute devotion of love that Jesus requires, and nothing less will do. Jesus said that we cannot serve two masters, or we will love the one and hate the other. We may say that we do love Jesus and yet find times when we have turned our backs on following Him and His ways. The truth is that when we have a divided heart, we actually do still love Jesus but only part of the time. This means that Jesus does not regard us as disciples, unless we love Him with an undivided heart all of the time.

(b) The Impossibility of Discipleship

" 'You are not also one of His disciples, are you?' He (Peter) denied it and said, 'I am not!' " [John 18:25]
This was the moment of supreme revelation to Peter, that he was not a disciple. He could not meet the absolute demands of discipleship in his own strength. Peter had boasted that he would lay down his life for Jesus, which is the very heart and centre of discipleship. All the disciples agreed with this expression of devotion, but they were not able to keep to it, and they all forsook Him and fled when their lives were in danger [Mark 14:50]. This proves that discipleship is based on devotion that is empowered by the Holy Spirit. The self-willed fanatic longs to die for his cause. But the Spirit-filled disciple longs to be true to a person. Peter discovered that he did not have that level of devotion, and he could not fulfil his dream to be a disciple. We must see the emptiness of human commitment or we will never become true disciples.

(c) The Supernatural Power of Discipleship

Jesus gave a personal prophetic promise to Peter that is true of all who would be disciples: "...you cannot follow Me now, but you shall follow Me afterward." [John 13:36]. Jesus gave this promise to Peter just before Peter said that he was willing to die for Jesus. Jesus warned him clearly that before the cock would crow twice, Peter would deny him three times [Mark 14:30]. Such a word is devastating to the one who hears it. But for Peter, and for all disciples, it is vital to realise that Jesus knows that the discipleship He requires cannot be produced by human zeal alone.

What then is the power of discipleship and when did Peter truly become a disciple? The answer is, in and through the Holy Spirit. It is through the Holy Spirit that Peter became a true disciple, and although the word 'disciple' is not prominent in the book of Acts, there is no doubt that the believers described there were disciples of Jesus through the leading of the Holy Spirit.

6. A True Disciple is a Love Slave of the Lord
"Paul, a bondslave of Jesus Christ." [Romans 1:1 KJV]

(a) A Disciple is the Property of his Master

Paul does not refer to himself as a disciple anywhere in his writings. His preferred word is *"bondslave"*, indicating that he saw himself as belonging entirely to Jesus Christ. This concept of slavery underlies his whole view of discipleship. A slave has no rights; he has no free time, no right to choose what clothes he wears, or when and where he will go on holiday. The slave has no rights at all, and no wages. The reason is that he is owned by his master.

(b) A Disciple is the Responsibility of his Master

While a slave has no rights, he also has no burden to carry for his own life. His only burden is the master's will. But all his food, shelter and means of transport are provided for by his master. So, he is not anxious about any day or the future, knowing that his master has everything under control.

A famous hymn expresses this love-slavery of the disciple:

Make me a captive Lord, and then I shall be free,
Force me to render up my sword, and I shall conqueror be,
I sink in life's alarms, when by myself I stand:
Imprison me within thine arms, and strong shall be my hand.

My heart is weak and poor until it master find,
It has no spring of action sure: it varies with the wind;
It cannot freely move till thou hast wrought its chain,
Enslave it with thy matchless love, and deathless it shall reign.

My power is faint and low, till I have learned to serve
It lacks the needed fire to glow; it lacks the breeze to nerve.
It cannot drive the world, until itself be driven,
Its flag can only be unfurled when thou shalt breathe from heaven.

My will is not my own, till thou hast made it thine,
If it could reach a monarch's throne, it must its crown resign.
It only stands unbent, amid the clashing strife.
When on thy bosom it has lent, and found in thee its life.

[George Matheson 1890]

7. A True Disciple Follows Christ – Even Through Failure

A true disciple picks himself up when he falls and carries on following Christ through pain, failure and suffering. The stages of Peter's discipleship have major lessons for us as disciples today:

❖ **Peter knew the call of God** - " *'Follow Me and I will make you become fishers of men.' They immediately they left their nets and followed Him."* [Mark 1:17-18]

This moment of Peter's call is the starting point of the 'Way', as the Christian gospel was first known [Acts 9:2]. A person hears the call and is faced with a huge choice. Following this call will cost a person everything that they own. Peter and his fellow disciples left all immediately - there is no indication of any preparation. They were suddenly faced with a spiritual reality that presented itself and then would pass on with or without them. They answered with an act of renunciation.

- ❖ **Peter received the anointing and ordination for ministry** - *"He went up on the mountain and called to Him those He Himself wanted. And they came to Him. Then He appointed twelve, that they might be with Him and that He might send them out to preach, and to have power to heal sicknesses and to cast out demons."* [Mark 3:13-15]

A few months after being with Jesus, He gave the twelve spiritual power and ordination. The first thing they were ordained to do was to be with Jesus. This is still the central ordination of any follower of Jesus. We must spend time with Him, and then we will know the full outworking of the power of God resting on our lives.

- ❖ **Peter received special insights into the teaching of Jesus** - *"And when they were alone, He explained all things to His disciples."* [Mark 4:34]

Jesus gave special understanding to His disciples. He took time to explain things to them. They were not intellectually strong men, but they were given the grace to understand things that were hidden from others. Disciples will receive deeper understanding of mysteries quite beyond their intellectual power and education.

- ❖ **Peter's faith was tested in the storm** [Mark 4:35-41] - Peter and all the twelve were allowed to pass through a storm in which their lives were in great danger. They cried out in great fear of losing their lives. But this was a test, which although Peter failed, he nevertheless kept following Jesus. Disciples are not super-human, but they have an unusual perseverance.

- ❖ **Peter received revelation about the divine identity of Jesus** - *"Simon Peter ... said: 'You are the Christ, the Son of the living God.' "* [Matthew 16:16].

This was the moment of great revelation to the disciples, the moment that Jesus had carefully prepared. Peter was impetuous and he blurted out the great confession before he realised the full importance of what he was saying. This was saving faith, and Peter was the first man to fully realise the identity of Christ, as Messiah and God.

THE POWER AND PRICE OF DISCIPLESHIP

- **Peter received a rebuke from the Lord** - *"But He turned and said to Peter: 'Get behind Me Satan! You are an offense to Me, for you are not mindful of the things of God, but the things of men.' "* [Matthew 16:23]

  Moments after his great revelation in verse 16, Peter is lifted up with pride and begins to talk to Jesus as an equal. The Bible says in Matthew 16:22 that Peter rebuked Jesus. Jesus then turns to Peter and gives him a rebuke that would have devastated most people. Doubtless Peter was deeply broken by this admonishment; but this is part of the disciple's strength - that he is not discouraged by Jesus' rebuke. Like Peter, the disciple must pick himself up and follow on with Jesus.

- **Peter received mountain-top revelation of the glory of God** [Matthew 17:1-13] - Peter saw the glory of God in the face of Jesus at His transfiguration. It was moments like this that prepared him for the trials and persecutions that would come later. The person who has seen the glory of God will never be the same.

- **Peter was commended for his persevering heart** - he was given the promise of ruling one day with Jesus [Luke 22:28-30]. It was the great quality of perseverance that made Peter the most outstanding disciple of the Gospels, to be matched later by the same quality in the discipleship of Paul.

- **Peter failed Jesus by not watching with Him in prayer** [Mark 14:32-42] - despite all the revelations and promises, Peter failed the Lord in prayer when Jesus needed him the most. This crushing failure is one of many, but Peter never wavered or accepted these failures as the last word on his discipleship, but picked himself up and continued right on following the Lord.

- **Peter denied the Lord with cursing and swearing** [Mark 14:71-72] - of all the moments of bitter failure, this was surely the most awful. Peter failed and collapsed in a terrible display of moral cowardice. Jesus had foreseen this and had prayed for Peter [Luke 22:31-34]. Disciples must experience inner brokenness, which is a major preparation for power and service that will follow.

- **Peter received a personal visitation to restore his broken heart** [Mark 16:7; Luke 24:34; 1 Corinthians 15:5] - Peter was restored by personal touches from the Lord. With great tenderness, Jesus mentioned Peter by name through the angels, and then appeared personally to him, doubtless reassuring him of His unchanging love. Jesus must also have renewed the call of God on Peter's life. Peter would have seen himself as disqualified, but Jesus sees deep

- **Peter was God's chosen vessel to bring the gospel to Israel and to the Gentiles in the full power of the Holy Spirit** [Acts 2 and 10] - Peter was called and chosen to preach on the Day of Pentecost, using the keys of the kingdom to unlock heaven itself - first for the Jews, then for the Samaritans and finally for the Gentiles. Peter was weak and failed often, but none of these things deterred the Lord or Peter! How Peter must have marvelled at the great grace that made him a true disciple of Jesus Christ.

Peter's life is a great encouragement to all who falter in their discipleship. Jesus Christ is the anchor and the boasting of all who have the honour of calling themselves a disciple of the Lord Jesus Christ!

8. Conclusion

Finally, a quote by the American evangelist Bill Bright:

"You can be a great scientist, a famous statesman, or even a great theologian, and still fall short of God's plan for your life. If you do not understand and experience basic truths about discipleship taught by the apostle Paul and Jesus Christ, you are not his disciple, and you won't be able to disciple others."

"The apostle Paul wrote to his spiritual son, his disciple Timothy, in 2 Timothy 2:1, 2: 'Oh, Timothy, my son, be strong with the strength Christ Jesus gives you. For you must teach others those things you and many others have heard me speak about. Teach these great truths to trustworthy men who will, in turn, pass them on to others.' " [Living Bible]

"A disciple is one who loves God, our Lord Jesus Christ, with all his heart, soul, and mind, and tries to become more and more like him through a life of faith and obedience."

7

THE MINISTRY OF PRAYER AND INTERCESSION

WHAT IS PRAYER?

All religions pray. Buddhists have prayer flags and prayer wheels; Catholics light candles at shrines. Many Churches have liturgies or written forms of prayer that are repeated, often including the Lord's Prayer. However, in themselves these things are not prayer.

- Prayer is talking to God.

- Prayer is reaching out to discover the living God and to meet with Him.

- Prayer is opening a door for God into our lives and circumstances.

- Prayer is the true exercise of the human soul, in co-operating with God so that His plans and purposes can be fulfilled in the earth.

- Prayer is like the tracks for a train. The train is powerful, but can only move if there are tracks. So God has ordained that unless human beings request Him to do certain things, He will not do them.

- Prayer is the highest activity of the human soul, and involves the exercise of that faculty of our spirits that can commune with God.

- ➢ Prayer is a longing, a thirsting for God. Some say prayers for revival but do not thirst for it.

- ➢ Prayer is not the spare tyre on the car of our lives, it is the steering wheel [Corrie Ten Boon]!

- ➢ Prayer is not for the strong who need no help; it is for the powerless who need a miracle. We have to be weak enough to pray.

There are different ways of studying the biblical teaching on prayer:

> The teaching of Jesus on prayer
> The example of Jesus in prayer
> Examples of prayer in the Old Testament
> Examples of prayer in the New Testament
> The teaching of Paul on prayer
> Examples of prayer in history

THE TEACHING OF JESUS ON PRAYER

There are four key passages in which Jesus taught His disciples how to pray.

In Matthew 6 and 7, Jesus taught that prayer is not only an activity, it is a place.

1. The Poison of Insincerity! *[Matthew 6:5]*

Jesus warned the disciples about the great danger of hypocrisy or insincerity in prayer. This is when someone prays from the place of unreality, without care, burden or hunger for God. People who pray like this are motivated by duty, not by passion. It is a searching truth that the Pharisees were not insincere in their fulfilment of duty, but they lacked any sense of spiritual reality and so pretended to have love and spiritual depth. The same can be true of Christians at any moment of their life or in any position they may occupy. This may afflict pastors, elders, worship leaders etc. How awful if a person with a dry heart has the role of trying to lead passionate worship!

Insincerity in prayer poisons the atmosphere of prayer meetings, and blocks the true activity of the Holy Spirit. If you have no burden, do not pretend by imitating those who have one! Instead, confess your need. If we are ashamed to pray publicly, God has no agenda to humiliate us publicly! Jesus told us to go and pray in secret, and God will hear our prayer. In secret it is difficult to be insincere! The Pharisees loved to impress their onlookers by their piety.

The great missionary to the Eskimos, Wilfrid Grenfell, was a sceptic before he was converted. He reluctantly went to hear the great evangelist D.L. Moody, but almost turned away when he had to endure a long empty prayer, by an elder, before Moody was to speak. Suddenly Moody jumped to his feet and declared: "While our brother is finishing his prayer, let us sing hymn number...!"

Grenfell was so struck by the down-to-earth reality of Moody's Christianity that he stayed to hear him preach, and was soundly converted.

2. We Have Free Access through Grace - *"Pray to your Father" [Matthew 6:6]*

Jesus is so simple in the way He describes the wonder of prayer. Although the words 'justification by grace' are absent from the Gospels, yet the Justifier of human beings is always present. Yes, the cross was still in the future, but in the Old Testament God anticipated the justification of sinners, and Christ justified sinners in the way He treated them and still treats them. He speaks to sinners in a way that invites them simply to come. The great fact is that we are not justified by faith in a **doctrine** of justification; we are saved by faith in the justifying welcome of a **person**! God in Christ welcomes us into the holiest of all [Hebrews 10:19]. Christ teaches this same thing here in Matthew 6:6 - that we are simply to come to God in prayer, and He will receive us.

This is a truth that can baffle a believer when he is a new convert, and can return to puzzle the oldest saint. The human soul is prone to believe that we must earn acceptance with God, and that we must earn answers to prayer. So people who feel that they have failed God in some way, or have sinned, will simply stop praying because they feel unworthy. Some mature Christians will pray with a sense of pride at their spiritual stature! They will recount the hours they spend in prayer as a badge of superiority, as if they had earned some answers to prayer, and it was through their efforts that souls are being saved and people healed. The truth is that we can never earn acceptance with God, and that we are unworthy ever to approach him. But God is full of grace and mercy and invites us to approach Him. It is by this grace and by this grace alone that we are made BOLD to approach the holy throne of God. It is the grace of God that we have answers to prayer. God will simply grant our request, whether we are able to spend hours praying or minutes!

3. The Presence of God and the Human Spirit – the Inner Room

When Jesus teaches about the *'inner room'* He does not mean our bedroom! While it is true that we are wise to choose a quiet spot to pray, many people will not actually find a room with a door to close. In the homes of the wealthy this is common, in the homes of the poor it is rare, and it is to these people that Jesus was speaking.

When Jesus says 'go to your Father in the secret place', He is referring to the God-given ability to enter the direct presence of God. This is not just a mental attitude or the exercise of our imagination. This is a real experience of the living presence of God. The Holy Spirit is the inner place, and we ourselves have within us something that is best described as a room. The Tabernacle itself is a description of a human being, with the outer body, then the soul, then the inner sanctuary of the heart or spirit of the individual.

Jesus himself *'tabernacled'* among us (the Greek for 'dwelt' in John 1:14). Jesus had the inner room that no-one saw or entered while He was on earth. When we enter the secret place, we surrender our inner life to the Holy Spirit; then, as we are filled with the living Presence of God, we begin to pray in the Spirit. It is this act of surrender by faith that is the foundation of Jesus' teaching on the life of prayer.

4. The Order of Prayer

The 'Lord's Prayer' is contained in this chapter [Matthew 6:9-13]. Some have noted that it is not strictly the Lord's Prayer, in that He never prayed for His debts or sins to be forgiven! It can only be understood as the Lord's in the sense that it is the prayer He gave His disciples; so it may be called the 'Disciples' Prayer'.

Whatever title we give it, it was not intended to be repeated by rote, since this contradicts the teaching of the verses that precede it [Matthew 6:7]. It gives us the order or pattern of prayer. We may and surely will pray spontaneously and freely, but we must learn the order of things in the will of God if we are to learn to pray in a manner that pleases God. There are, then, six prayers within this one prayer - the first three for God and the second three for mankind. We do well to learn these principles and to seek to apply them as we pray.

THE MINISTRY OF PRAYER & INTERCESSION

- Prayer 1: Praying for the Glory of God - *"Hallowed be your name"*

Praying for the glory of God means that all prayer begins with **worship**. The great centre and motive for all things is that God be glorified. If God is not glorified by something I am praying for, then I have no business praying for it! All believers do well to take time to contemplate the greatness of God and to speak forth this greatness in praise. We may contemplate God in silence, but we are always to lift up our voices and speak out what we see and know when we are before God. It is not always easy to find words, and so God has given the gift of tongues, but we are to pray both with the Spirit and with the understanding also [1 Corinthians 14:15]. Take time to worship, sing to God, and exalt Him with all of your heart.

- Prayer 2: Praying for the Rule of God - *"Your kingdom come"*

This prayer for the rule of God is marked by **submission**. We must consciously deny ourselves and submit our plans, minds and lives to God. Only as we do this can we really pray for the Kingdom of God to be manifest in and through us.

- Prayer 3: Praying for the Will of God - *"Your will be done"*

This is bringing the offering of **obedience** to God. It would be madness to pray for the will of God unless we were unconditionally prepared to obey Him. This is prayer that seeks for God's will to be done in answer to our prayers, but also as His Spirit touches us, through the absolute surrender of our own will to obey everything that He tells us.

- Prayer 4: Praying for Physical Needs - *"Give us this day our daily bread"*

This is prayer for our most basic physical needs. At first sight it may seem as if *"this day"* and *"daily"* is needless repetition. But really it is God's perfect wisdom that He gives only the supply for the immediate future. We might prefer that God give us today enough bread or money to last a year or even a lifetime! But God teaches us to pray for enough bread to last each day.

- Prayer 5: Praying for Spiritual Needs – Forgiveness

Of all our human needs, this is the greatest - to be forgiven and to forgive. Sin that is not brought in repentance before God will cloud our hearts and minds, and make our lives full of a miserable dread of the future. Guilt is a destroying power, and if we will only confess our sins and humble ourselves before God then our sin will be forgiven. Note the link in the chain - if we do not pass forgiveness on, then God will not only *not* forgive us, but will call back all our former sins and make us account for them too. This is the clear teaching of Matthew 18:21-35.

The king's servant owed him an impossibly big debt. It was 10,000 talents, and each talent was 3,000 shekels, which was 12,000 days' or 33 years' wages! This can be calculated as US$ 330,000 if we assume a wage of $10,000 per year. Ten thousand talents then would be $3,300,000,000 - nearly 3½ billion dollars. The servant promised he would pay the debt given time! But the king had compassion and forgave him freely. Then the servant went out and met a fellow servant who owed him 100 denarii, which was 100 days' wages; this, on the same scale, would mean $3,000. The servant threw him into prison, but when the king heard of it, he had the servant arrested and thrown into prison till he should pay the $3½ billion that had been cancelled just hours before.

The point of the story is clear. Our debt to God is so big that we can never pay it. Christ paid the price for our sins to be cancelled, and so we in our turn must freely cancel all the debts and sins that have been committed against us. This attitude of thankfulness to God and mercy towards our fellow human beings must be maintained if our prayer life is not to be paralysed.

- Prayer 6: Praying for Spiritual Needs – Deliverance

It is easy to forget that we are engaged in battle, and that prayer is the cutting edge of that warfare. For this reason, praying believers must be on their guard to notice things that happen to oppress their souls. Perhaps we will be criticised or scorned. Perhaps we may get involved in a heated argument with another believer about something we feel very passionately about. Even a wave of fear or depression may come upon us without any clear reason. Whatever the cause of the attack of Satan on our soul, we must pray for deliverance, and resist the devil with determination and faith. Some people labour far too long under clouds of condemnation. We will be attacked. We will be subject to temptations and problems. But we must not yield ground to the enemy, but must pray - crying to God to deliver us from the evil one. God will deliver us. The help we need is promised and available: *"Resist the devil and he will flee from you."* [James 4:7].

5. The Enemies of Prayer

In Matthew 6, Jesus mentions some of the enemies of prayer. Many other adversaries are taught about in different Bible passages.

(a) *An Unforgiving Heart* [Matthew 6:14-15]

This has been sufficiently explored above, but it is vital to realise the connection between forgiveness and an open heaven. If we shut our hearts in refusing to forgive others, our prayers will not be answered.

(b) *Worry* [Matthew 6:25-34]

Worry has a twin brother called Fear, and together they form the opposite of faith in the heart. The person who worries is gripped by unbelief; in fact that person is gripped by the opposite of faith - they believe that bad things are going to happen to them! The person of faith believes that, even if bad things happen to them, then those things are allowed by God, so that they may learn warfare and come out conquering!

Worry distracts the mind, it is a sin, and will destroy the spiritual life of the person who yields to it. Jesus warned us not to be anxious about food or clothing, and gave the great antidote to worry: *"your heavenly Father knows"* [Matthew 6:32]! When we realise that Father knows, our hearts are safe and protected from this chill wind and from the frozen heart of unbelief. Jesus taught us that if we put our priorities in the right order then God will make sure that all our needs will be taken care of. *"But seek first the kingdom of God and His righteousness, and all these things shall be added to you."* [Matthew 6:33].

(c) *Worldliness* [Matthew 6:19-24]

Worldliness will hinder our praying. Why? Because it will steal the heart away from God. Jesus said that if we serve two masters, we will end up loving one and hating the other. The divided heart will attend meetings and respond with tears to the challenge of the word, with great words of dedication. But the next day it will make worldly decisions that destroy all the work of the day before. The divided heart is not free to enjoy God and not free to enjoy the world. It moves from love to hate, sometimes loving God and sometimes hating Him, sometimes loving carnal pleasures and sometimes hating them. Jesus said it is impossible to serve two masters, and He will not receive such service, and will not answer prayers until the matter is resolved.

(d) Not Listening

"One who turns away his ear from hearing the law, even his prayer is an abomination." [Proverbs 28:9]. If we will not listen to God, then God will not listen to us! This is a warning against reading the Bible without due attention. We must take care to hear what the Bible is saying, which is not a matter of *just* reading the Bible, but *how* we read the Bible. God says we are to listen to His voice as we read, and if we do, then God will listen to us when we pray.

(e) Lack of Compassion

"Whoever shuts his ears to the cry of the poor will also cry himself and not be heard." [Proverbs 21:13]. This verse indicates a chain of events which takes place when a person closes their heart to those in need. God warns here that if we do not listen to others then we ourselves will find that we cannot get through to God. God tells us that we must pass on to others what we ourselves receive. This includes love, money, forgiveness, listening and answering. It is a great thing to realise that God will treat us as we treat others:

"With the merciful You will show Yourself merciful; with a blameless man You will show Yourself blameless; with the pure You will show Yourself pure; and with the devious You will show Yourself shrewd." [Psalm 18:25-26]

(f) Sin

"If I regard iniquity in my heart, the Lord will not hear (me)." [Psalm 66:18]

"Behold, the Lord's hand is not shortened, that it cannot save; nor His ear heavy, that it cannot hear. But your iniquities have separated you from your God; and your sins have hidden His face from you, so that He will not hear." [Isaiah 59: 1-2]

Quite simply, God will not suffer religious hypocrisy. God loves righteousness, and those who pray must subject themselves to God's word and righteousness.

6. The Power of Unity in Prayer

"... if your brother sins against you, go and tell him his fault between you and him alone. If he hears you, you have gained your brother. But if he will not hear you, take with you one or two more, that by the mouth of two or three witnesses every word may be established. And if he refuses to hear them, tell it to the church. But if he refuses even to hear *the church, let him be to you like a heathen and a tax-collector. Assuredly I say to you, whatever you bind on earth will be bound in heaven, and whatever you loose on earth will be loosed in heaven. Again I say to you that if two of you agree on earth as concerning anything that they ask, it will be done for them by My Father in heaven. For where two or three are gathered together in My name, I am there in the midst of them."* [Matthew 18:18-20]

These words indicate that where there is agreement and harmony between believers then there will be great spiritual power. The great power of unity was shown when God came down to see the progress of humanity in building the tower of Babel. He declared that, because of their great unity through one language, mankind was on the verge of enormous discoveries and breakthroughs. God even said that *"nothing that they propose to do will be withheld from them"* [Genesis 11:6]. This is true in the merely human sense of linguistic unity. It has proved to be true in that the medium of English has united the world's scholars, and has enabled the human race to make great strides forward in technology. But if it is true in a natural sense, it is much truer in a spiritual sense.

In our first year as missionaries in Cameroun, Vicki went down with a bad attack of malaria. This left her quite weak, causing an outbreak of boils, and then she contracted hepatitis from drinking contaminated water. Unable to eat or drink properly and totally weak, she was told to rest completely for several weeks and to expect a long recovery time.

Back in England, our home Church was praying for us, unaware of what we were going through. The Lord revealed to them that the devil was trying to wear us down in our health. They immediately cried out to God for our full restoration and healing.

The next morning, Vicki woke up and noticed how dirty the bedroom windows had become; so she set to and started washing them. She suddenly realised that her lethargy had gone, her yellow skin and eyes were a normal healthy pink – she was totally healed!

The great key for the Church is not to allow the devil to divide and conquer. If brother can be divided against brother, then the prayer life of the Church will be paralysed. If only the Church can walk in unity and love, then the Lord will take its prayer life to such a level that the

Church prayer meeting will be wonderfully united with the throne room on high, where all the great decisions are made.

In this context, we must resolve to restore any wrong relationships. Perhaps we have blamed others, but is there anything we have done wrong that we should confess? If we restore and heal broken relationships, we will come into a new dimension of power in prayer.

7. The Need for Persistence in Prayer

In Luke 11:1-13 Jesus taught the disciples about prayer. They had observed Him praying and must have been deeply stirred as they realised the depth and the spiritual reality He lived in, which was His natural element. When they made the great request, *"Lord, teach us to pray"*, He partly repeated the teaching He gave in Matthew 6 - the Lord's Prayer.

Then Jesus told them the famous parable of the man who disturbed his neighbour because he had received visitors in the middle of the night and had no bread to give them. The neighbour was at first reluctant to get up and give him bread, but because of the man's shameless persistence, he did rise and give him what he was asking for.

What is the lesson of this parable? Jesus contrasts the attitude of the reluctant neighbour in the parable with the eager heart of the Father in heaven, who longs to give us what we need. However, Jesus clearly is teaching here that we must keep on praying even though it may *seem* as if God is reluctant. We are to believe in God's generous heart, so Jesus says, *'Go on asking, seeking, knocking and God will give the Holy Spirit.'*

There are several details of this parable which are important:

- *"Ask and it will be given to you."* By this Jesus teaches that the Holy Spirit is a gift to be received as we persevere deeper in prayer.

- *"Seek, and you will find."* This teaches us that the Holy Spirit is a discovery, like an undiscovered continent to be explored as we pray.

- *"Knock, and it will be opened to you."* By this Jesus teaches that the coming of the Holy Spirit in answer to prayer will be like a door opening into another realm of life.

- Bread, fish, and eggs indicate that the Holy Spirit is wholesome nourishment, imparted when we pray.

- Scorpions, snakes and stones are the deceiving power of Satan, but God will make sure that they will be kept out of our souls by His watchful goodness; He will not allow us to be deceived or disappointed as we seek His face.

- The man who was praying did not seek something for himself, but provisions for the friends who came in the night. By this Jesus teaches that many of the blessings we can receive through prayer will come to unselfish souls who are not seeking only to be blessed, but to bless and feed others on their journey in the night of sin and darkness.

8. Prayer in the Name of Jesus *[John 15-17]*

In many passages of the New Testament, Jesus teaches that we are to pray in His name. This was clearly the practice of the Church in Acts. They boldly preached the name of Jesus and proclaimed Him as Messiah, Son of God, crucified, risen and ascended to the throne of the universe. Only through this name can God be approached. Jesus is the way to God, and there is no other.

This of course does not mean that there is any magical quality in using the phrase *"in Jesus' name"*. The key to praying in Jesus' name is to **have faith in the person and work of Jesus** - in the person who is represented by that name, and in all the qualities that the Bible reveals in the person of Christ. If we approach God through faith in Christ, Jesus teaches us that we can be assured of the answer to our prayers.

THE EXAMPLE OF JESUS IN PRAYER
1. His Childhood Prayer Life

We know only a little of the prayer life of Jesus. Nothing is said of His prayer life before His Bar Mitzvah at the age of 12, when as a Jewish boy he became a man and joined His father's business. This was the age at which Jesus wanted to stay permanently in the Temple, which was the house of prayer. Instead He had to go and learn carpentry with His stepfather, Joseph.

We may imagine Jesus as a child communing with His Father, but nothing is said of it, except a few verses in the Psalms, which indicate that from a baby He had the attitude of hope in Father. *"But you are He who took Me out of the womb; You made Me trust while on My mother's breasts. I was cast upon You from birth. From my mother's womb You have been My God."* [Psalm 22:9–10]. Such verses as these (see also Hebrews 10:5-7) indicate that Christ's inner life had roots that made Him a person constantly dwelling in the presence of His Father.

2. His Ministry Begins

The first time we see Jesus praying is in the waters of Jordan, and the Holy Spirit is descending upon Him. The Bible says: *"while He prayed, the heaven was opened. And the Holy Spirit descended..."* [Luke 3:21-22]. This already should teach us the wonder of praying in the power of the Holy Spirit. By our praying, we too can open heaven if our hearts are right with God. The heart of all ministry is to pray and see the Holy Spirit descend on those we minister to, revealing God and doing the works of God.

This pattern was to continue as Jesus preached and worked miracles. He was in touch with Father and so great works were seen through Him. Often the anointing is seen as an impersonal power, but in reality the power of Jesus' ministry was in the simple fact that He had a clear, unbroken relationship with the Father, hearing His voice, and knowing that His prayers were heard. Jesus did not have to withdraw for hours every time He needed to do a miracle. He prayed in the midst of the crowds; nothing was ever allowed to disturb His communion with the Father.

3. Praying and Fasting for 40 Days in the Wilderness

This is the first great prayer phase of His life. Jesus has been equipped for ministry, but before preaching and healing, He has an intense period of prayer with fasting. These 40 days remind us of Israel's 40 years in the wilderness, and Jesus quotes Moses three times in countering Satan's temptations. These three Bible quotations came directly from the experience of God's people in the wilderness. This context explains why they had to go through the wilderness in order to learn the three severe lessons:

- That mankind must live by the word of God.
- That we must worship God alone.
- That we must not put God to a foolish test.

These three lessons were burned into the soul of Jesus the Son of Man as He suffered the loneliness and pain of His vigil in the wilderness. He doubtless suffered the loss of all pleasure relating to His desires for food, conversation, a comfortable room etc. This teaches us that there is a measure of the cross in the lessons of prayer, and that we must die to the world if we are to go deeper with God. Moses also went up the mountain with God for 40 days and nights, where he neither ate nor drank, and passed into a deeper experience with God.

4. The Habit of Early Morning Prayer [Mark 1:35]

While it is wrong to glorify the morning hours as more spiritual than the evening or afternoon, yet it is true that Jesus spent His early mornings with God. The habit was clearly that of seeking a quiet and undisturbed environment, where He could settle His soul in quiet waiting on God and on His word. If Jesus, as a mature man, felt the need for this, how much more should we who are learners in the divine mysteries! Many men of God have practised early morning prayer, but if we are not able to pray in the early morning, nevertheless we must make room in our daily schedule for prayer. Luther said that if he had a busy day with little spare time, he had to devote more time in prayer, not less, in order to know God's blessings!

5. Prayer Before Big Decisions

Luke 6:12-13 tells us that Jesus *"went out to the mountain to pray, and continued all night in prayer to God* (literally 'in the prayer of God'). *And when it was day, He called His disciples to Himself; and from them He chose twelve whom He also named apostles."* There are many lessons contained in these few verses:

- **Jesus spent the night in the prayer of God!** How can this be possible? The definition of prayer is often 'people talking to God', but this is a very narrow definition. Clearly, when Jesus prayed it was God talking to God! The Bible teaches that Jesus, who is God the Son, is constantly in prayer to His Father for people's salvation and for the blessing of His saved ones. How then can we understand this phrase? It is best understood as God's longings for fallen mankind. God has longings, and these are expressed in deep groanings in the Holy Spirit. We also are to have deep longings and direct them towards God. Many say prayers for revival, but true prayer is when a soul is gripped with a deep longing for God to move. This is the deep, convulsing passion that moved Jesus to pray.

- **Spending all night in prayer is not easy**, but Jesus did it often and doubtless without checking the time! In other words, He was not doing it out of some superstitious idea that prayer through the night was better than prayer through the day. He was gripped with the whole matter and could not sleep till it was resolved.

- **The choosing of the twelve apostles came after this night of prayer**. Waiting in the presence of His Father was the prelude to this momentous decision. Such a choice must have weighed heavily on His soul and caused Him much agony of heart as He wrestled with what the faults of leaders can do to the flock they lead. Leaders are of course imperfect, and God the Son prays for leaders, that they may be true shepherds for His flock. This is one of the greatest longings of God's heart, and a deep prayer in the Spirit of God.

- **Jesus prayed till the sunrise**. This is the marvel of His prayer life, that He prayed through the night of sin and opposition to God, and overcame it. On the cross there was darkness until the third hour, and then when He cried, *"It is finished"*, the sun reappeared. What a new dawn on the human race! We must pray through and hold fast till the breaking of day. Jacob prayed and wrestled all night with God until the sun rose. Jesus rose from the dead at the rising of the sun. *"Weeping may endure for a night, but joy comes in the morning."* [Psalm 30:5].

6. *Praying in the Glory – The Mountain of Transfiguration*
[Luke 9:29]

While Jesus prayed on the mountain, He was transformed before Peter, James and John. He entered into glory; glory descended; glory shone from within Him. This experience was in one way unique to Jesus in that the glory radiated from Him. We can receive the glory of God, but it does not emanate from us!

When Moses went up the mountain he also prayed to see the glory of God [Exodus 33:18], and was so filled with glory himself that his face shone [Exodus 34:29]. We are to experience glory, which means that we are to know the overwhelming greatness of God. God is not merely great; He is beyond human power to bear. Human beings cannot bear to look upon God, and the closer we come, the more overwhelmed we are. Some people tremble, others fall on their faces unable to continue standing before Him.

7. *Praying in an Agony – the Garden of Gethsemane*

In Luke 22:44 we read that the sweat of Jesus was like great drops of blood. This indicates the awful depth of burden He felt in prayer for the lost. This is not a burden we can carry. It was Christ who carried our sins, and Christ alone; but there is no doubt that He shares the burden for the lost with us when we pray, so that we intercede with groanings which cannot be uttered [Romans 8:26]. This burden of love is the intercessor's burden. Christ is interceding now in heaven for us [Hebrews 7:25] and we are to enter into this fellowship of prayer for men and women.

8. The Seven Prayers of Calvary

The words of Jesus on the cross are prayer words that were spoken to God and mankind, and as such they determine the future of the whole human race. It is well to remember that words have more power than most people ever realise. The words of God are not only ideas, they are events! When Jesus said *"It is finished"*, He was not observing something happen, He was making it happen! *It* (i.e. the rule of Satan, death and sin) was finished because He said so. His is the word of a King. Jesus spoke from the cross and the Father answered from heaven; and the result is the amazing victory of the cross.

The words from the cross established our salvation, as follows:

- **Our justification/forgiveness**: *"Father, forgive them, for they do not know what they do."* [Luke 23:34]. Forgiveness is the first and greatest need of the human heart, both in relationship with God and with others. It brings peace and healing. Christ had the right to curse the human race for what they had done to Him. But He felt no resentment, and did not have to overcome negative feelings in order to forgive us. Forgiveness was the spontaneous reaction of His heart. It burst from His lips as the great reaction to the injustice that was being inflicted on Him.

- **Our adoption into the family of God**: *"Woman behold your son! ... Behold your mother!"* [John 19:26-27]. Jesus was leaving His mother without His loving care in old age. He was also leaving her with a huge gap in her own heart – her capacity to love her son. Here He joins together the disciple John and Mary in an act of adoption that was as real as a marriage ceremony. What Christ did on the cross caused those who receive Him to be adopted into the family of God, to love and care for each other. All around us there are lonely ones - old sisters who need the loving care of a son, and young men who need the love of a mother. Christ from the cross commands us to make this spiritual adoption real and practical in the way we receive each other.

- **Our assurance of eternal life**: *"Assuredly, ... today you will be with Me in Paradise."* [Luke 23:43]. The thief crucified beside Jesus cried out for a drop of mercy from the great King. He had recognised His royal majesty, sinlessness and Lordship. So he pleaded to be remembered. Christ gave Him the unshakable decree from a royal throne. He gave Him immediate assurance of eternal life. Those who trust in Him will receive the same assurance of a place in heaven beyond this life.

- **Our deliverance from the God-forsaken state of sin and hell**: *"My God, My God, why have You forsaken Me?"* [Matthew 27:46]. This cry came from the midst of the deep darkness that covered the earth. It was no eclipse that covered the earth, since it lasted 3 hours (eclipses last only 12–15 minutes) and covered the whole earth (eclipses cover only a narrow strip). This was an act of God, returning the earth to the original darkness from which He created it. Here He recreates the human race. Christ was made sin; He was identified with sinners at the deepest level. He died our death, that we might be raised to life with Him.

- **Our restored fellowship with God** – the deep thirst of God for every person: *"I thirst!"* [John 19:28]. Christ went to the cross with this thirst for the friendship and love of men and women, just as a father longs for sons and daughters to be his friends. Jesus longed for communion - heart friendship and mutual understanding without effort or strain. He longs for this today and delights when his beloved followers spend time with Him. This is the great fruit of His passion, that we, who made Him the Man of Sorrows, can now fill His heart with joy.

- **Our complete salvation** – the all-sufficient sacrifice of Jesus: *"It is finished!"* [John 19:30]. The cross is completely sufficient for all our spiritual needs. It has completed our salvation so that there is nothing to be added to it. It is perfect and complete, and needs only to be received by faith.

- **Our reconciliation**: *"Father, into Your hands I commit my spirit."* [Luke 23:46]. Jesus was separated from the Father for the few hours of the cross as He was made sin. When Jesus cried *"My God"* to His Father, it was in a way that He had never spoken before. Jesus had only ever addressed God as *"Father"*. *"My God"* is the way a forsaken sinner cries out from the depths of despair. Christ felt all the forsaken states as He was made sin, but here, as the work is completed, He calls God *"Father"*. This is now a cry, not only on His own behalf, but on behalf of sinners, now perfectly reconciled as sons of God, co-heirs with Jesus, given the same clear standing before God as the Son of God Himself.

Christ established these foundations of our salvation in an agony as He became the sacrifice for sin. Our prayer life knows nothing of this agony. But we can base all our praying on His sufferings, His all-sufficient sacrifice.

Christ's prayer ministry did not end with His entry into heavenly glory. He continues His heavenly ministry of intercession from the throne above [Hebrews 7:25], and it is through this ministry that the Church is watched over and supplied with the Holy Spirit, poured out in answer to His prayers.

AN EXAMPLE OF PRAYER IN THE OLD TESTAMENT

There are of course innumerable examples of prayer in the Old Testament, and a study of them would have to include the prayer life of Abraham, Moses, Daniel, Elijah and many others. Here is one from the life of Jehoshaphat.

The Deliverance of Judah from the Moabites [2 Chronicles 20]

- Judah is attacked by an overwhelming army [v2].

- Jehoshaphat is afraid, but sets his heart to seek the Lord, and proclaims a fast. The prayer that follows comes from a man who has set his heart - this refers to the whole area of the human will, and the direction of its intention. The human will is not sovereign, but it must be directed towards God.

- Jehoshaphat's prayer begins with praise [v6].

- Jehoshaphat reminds God of His promises [v7-9].

- Jehoshaphat pleads for God's intervention [v10-12].

- God answers with a declaration through His prophet, *"the battle is not yours but God's"* [v15].

- God commands the people to *"stand still and see the salvation of the Lord"* [v17].

- The army of Judah is led forward not by armed soldiers but by a choir of singers praising the Lord [v21]!

- When they began to sing, the Lord causes their enemies to fight and destroy each other [v22–25]!

What great lessons can we learn from this event?

(1) We must not be disheartened, no matter how great the problems facing us.

(2) We must begin our prayers with praise

(3) We must remind God of His promises. The promises of God are unshakeable and are given to us so that we can lay hold of God in time of need.

(4) Believe God! Jehoshaphat put the singers in the front of the army because he believed what God had said. In the end we must believe God, and it is faith that pleases Him.

AN EXAMPLE OF PRAYER IN THE NEW TESTAMENT

The New Testament has many examples of prayer apart from the great example of Jesus Himself. Often people praying in the New Testament were simply asking Jesus to do something. It was not often religious, and probably not often thought of as prayer. The prayers of the New Testament are often quite raw and unrefined, which is probably one of the reasons they were so powerful.

The Prayer of the Thief on the Cross [Luke 23:39-43]

What great lessons can we learn from the prayer of the thief on the cross? This man was crucified beside Jesus. His experience must have been overwhelming, not only in the sense of the horror of his pain, but also as he witnessed the awesome events that transpired beside him.

- The man begins by mocking Jesus - Matthew tells us that both of the robbers mocked Jesus at first [Matthew 27:44].

- He is gripped with the fear of God [Luke 23:40]. He was probably struck by hearing the words of forgiveness that Jesus uttered, and also by observing the meekness of Christ as He was led like a lamb to the slaughter. His eyes are opened and he changes his mind and rebukes the other robber for mocking Jesus.

- He confesses his sin by accepting that it is a just punishment for him to be crucified [Luke 23:41].

- He confesses that Jesus is righteous [Luke 23:41].

- He confesses Jesus as Lord and King [Luke 23:42].

- He prays for mercy - that Jesus will remember him and think of him when He is in His kingdom [Luke 23:42].

- He receives an immediate, total assurance that his prayer is heard and that he will be saved from hell and be with Jesus in Paradise before the end of the day (a Jewish day ends at sunset). This answer probably gave him peace of heart despite the physical agony.

- Jesus welcomes him into Paradise. His legs are broken before sunset, causing instant death [John 19:32]. A crucified man would support his weight with his legs and thus be able to continue breathing. If the legs were broken, the weight of the body made breathing impossible. As he stopped breathing and closed his eyes on earth, he would have opened them on eternity and seen the Lord welcoming him into Paradise.

This prayer is magnificent since it is a model of simplicity. It is a cry from the heart in the midst of extreme pain and imminent death. Eternity was pressing in on the man. While the other thief reacted to the same circumstances with mockery and anger, this man reacted with the fear of God, repentance, brokenness and prayer. God answered his prayer immediately.

God will answer us when we pray and cry out to Him. He will hear whoever calls on the name of the Lord!

THE TEACHING OF PAUL ON PRAYER

Paul's teaching in Ephesians 6:10-20, makes several vital contributions to our understanding of the ministry of prayer and intercession:

Prayer is warfare! The powers of darkness are opposing those who pray. We may not understand why we feel so lethargic when we go to pray, or so discouraged and in a fog, but the reason is because there are evil spirits and principalities all around us who oppose us when we pray [v12]. Paul likens prayer to a wrestling match!

We need God's armour. The will of God is that we stand. There is great victory when we keep our position in Christ.

- We need the belt, of the truth that we are seated in heavenly places [v14].

- Our heart needs the protection of the breastplate which is righteousness [v14].

- Our feet must be shod with the readiness to preach the gospel. This involves a readiness to be bold in witnessing of our faith in Christ [v15].

- We need the shield of faith to extinguish the fiery darts of thoughts and accusations that Satan whispers into our minds [v16].

- We need the assurance of salvation as a helmet to protect and keep our minds strong in the battle [v17].

- We need the sword of the Spirit – our knowledge and application of the Bible to our life and circumstances [v17]. This is our weapon of offence - to use the Scriptures with the wisdom of the Holy Spirit and attack the strongholds of Satan.

- The warrior who stands will be able to pray. The purpose of all this armour is to stand and pray with *"all prayer"* [v18]. This means all the fullness of prayer, from praise and worship to intercession and quiet waiting. There is a world of prayer to be discovered.

The key to Paul's teaching is to see the unity of our whole personality in the matter of prayer! We cannot see prayer as an activity of the Spirit alone. Our whole life must be conformed to the things of God and the victory in prayer. As we wear God's armour we will be able to continue steadfast in a victorious prayer life.

EXAMPLES OF PRAYER IN HISTORY

The examples of praying people in history are so vast that it would fill a library to study them all. Here are a few extraordinary examples. We should not be disheartened by these people's depth of devotion. God raises up 'apostles of prayer' who have a special calling both to pray and to be an example to the whole Church of the truth that God answers prayer.

1. John Welch

One of the most remarkable men in Scotland's history was John Welch, son-in-law of John Knox, the great Scottish reformer. John Welch put it on record before he died, that he counted the day ill-spent if he did not put in seven or eight hours of secret prayer. When John Welch died, an old Scotsman who had known him from his boyhood said of him: "*John Welch was a type of Christ.*" Of course, that was an inaccurate use of language, but what the old Scotsman meant was, that Jesus Christ had stamped the impression of His character on John Welch. When had Jesus Christ done it? It was in those seven or eight hours of daily communion with Himself. John Welch became famous in his day for prophetic utterance.

2. Praying Hyde

John Hyde (1865-1912) was born in Illinois. His father was a Presbyterian minister who faithfully proclaimed the gospel message and called for the Lord to thrust out labourers into His harvest. He prayed this prayer not only in the pulpit but also in his home. This made an indelible impression on the life of young John, as he grew up in such an atmosphere.

THE MINISTRY OF PRAYER & INTERCESSION

John graduated with such high honours that he was elected to a position on the college faculty. However, he had heard the divine call to the regions beyond, and was not disobedient to the heavenly vision. So he resigned his position and entered the Presbyterian seminary. He graduated in Chicago, in the spring of 1892, and sailed for India the following October.

On board the ship that took him to India, he received a letter asking him if he had yet received the baptism with the Holy Spirit. He was angry at first, that someone should ask him, a missionary, if he had received the Holy Spirit. However, he quickly realised his need and prayed for and received the baptism with the Spirit. He quickly entered into a new dimension in prayer.

His ministry of prayer in India during the next 20 years was such that the natives referred to him as *"the man who never sleeps"*. Some people called him 'the apostle of prayer'. But more familiarly he was known as 'the praying Hyde'. Deep in India's Punjab, he engaged with his Master and, face to face with the eternal, he learned amazing lessons in prayer. Often he spent 30 days and nights in prayer, and many times was on his knees in deep intercession for 36 hours at a time.

His work among the villages was very successful, as for many years he won four to ten people a day to the Lord. Hyde was instrumental in establishing the annual Sialkote Conferences, from which thousands of missionaries and native workers returned to their stations empowered afresh for the work of reaching India with the gospel. Hyde's life of sacrifice, humility, love and deep spirituality, as well as his example in the ministry of intercession, inspired many others in their own lives and ministries. When he died in February 1912, his last words were, *"Shout the victory of Jesus Christ!"*

3. The 1859 Revival in New York

A young Dutch businessman named Jeremiah Lanphier was appointed as a city missioner by a Church in downtown New York. The Church was depleted because of its members moving to the suburbs. Lanphier had been converted in 1842 in Broadway Tabernacle, Charles Finney's church. He felt led by God to start a weekly prayer meeting at noon for businessmen. Anyone could attend - for a few minutes or for an hour. Prayers were to be brief. He printed some handbills announcing the prayer meetings.

At 12 noon on 23 September 1857 the door was opened to the room on the third floor. Lanphier waited. Five minutes went by and no-one appeared. Ten minutes, and still no one came. The missioner paced the room in the midst of personal conflict. Fifteen minutes went by. After 35 minutes a step was heard on the stairs, and the first welcome person arrived! Another and another came until there were 6 people at the prayer meeting. On the following Wednesday 20 people attended and on the third Wednesday there were 40 to pray. In the first week of October it was decided to meet daily, rather than weekly. In the second week of October a great financial crisis took place. It is impossible not to link these events together and recognise the sovereign hand of God, preparing the stage for what was about to follow.

Within 6 months, 10,000 businessmen were gathering daily in New York for prayer, and within 2 years a million converts had been added to the US Churches. New York at noon became one vast prayer meeting, with all rooms in all Churches packed with people praying. Here was no fanaticism, no hysteria, just an incredible movement of people to pray. When Churches could not contain the numbers of people praying, the theatres began to open their doors to those who wanted to pray. *Anyone* was free to pray.

In February the press began to notice the deluge of blessing. Other prayer meetings were established, and the hour became generally known as the 'Hour of Prayer'. These meetings were non-denominational. This was the greatest revival New York had experienced, and the whole nation was curious. Here is a quote from a New York Christian journal at the time:

> *"Without any alarming event, without any extraordinary preaching or any special effort or other means that might be supposed peculiarly adapted to interest the minds of the people, there has within a short time past been, in several towns and villages ... a revival so extraordinary as to attract the attention of all classes of the community . . . The work is still going on, they expect the whole town will be converted - for this they pray. The work does not appear to be confined to the churches; hundreds are converted at prayer meetings, in private homes, in the workshops and at their work in the fields. Men of fortune and fashion, lawyers, physicians and tradesmen and indeed all classes, ages and sexes, are the subject of it."*

LET US PRAY THAT GOD WILL DO EVEN GREATER THINGS IN OUR GENERATION!

LET US RESOLVE TO SET HABITS OF PRAYER IN OUR LIVES, PRAISING GOD AND INTERCEDING FOR OTHERS.

Practical helps to follow God's order in prayer

1. Spend some time praising God using songs and Scriptures.

2. Spend time meditating on God's word, and turn what you read into praise and intercession.

3. Remind yourself of His faithfulness to His own character and promises and of His unfailing goodness.

4. Intercede for your loved ones.

5. Intercede for your nation, for the government and for the world situation, that the gospel will be preached [1 Timothy 2:1-4].

6. Pray for your own needs, that God will transform you and make you a powerful intercessor.

7. Pray for your pastor, leader, elders, deacons etc.

8. Pray for the prayer ministry in your Church.

9. Pray for the preaching ministry in your Church [Ephesians 6:19].

10. Pray without ceasing; pray when you feel like it and when you don't feel like it; pray always [1 Thessalonians 5:17]!

8

DIVINE HEALING AND DELIVERANCE

DIVINE HEALING

The Bible reveals that God created the world without sickness, pain and death. God looked on the world He had made and, *"it was very good"* [Genesis 1:31]. When God creates a new creation at the end of time, it will be a world without a curse [Revelation 22:3], without death, sorrow, crying or pain [Revelation 21:4].

Pain, sickness and sorrow came into the world as a result of original sin [Genesis 3:16-19]. The Bible indicates that God wills for us to be in good health [3 John 2]. The Bible also teaches that God can make people sick as a direct act of judgment, as in Acts 13:10-11 and 2 Chronicles 26:16-23.

1. Healing: a Blessing for God's People in Old Testament Times

In Exodus 15:26 God promised His people Israel that if they obeyed Him, He would not allow the sicknesses of the Egyptians to afflict them, as *"I am the Lord that heals you"* (Jehovah Rapha). God sent His word to Israel *"and healed them"* [Psalm 107:20], though this verse refers directly to their spiritual state rather than to sickness. Psalm 103:3 tells of God's faithful care of His people, forgiving their sins and healing all their diseases. God's desire for Israel was that their days should be as heaven on earth [Deuteronomy 11:21]. The nation of Israel was to show God's kingdom. Sadly, through disobedience, Israel passed through long years of exile and difficulty.

2. Jesus and the Kingdom of God

When Jesus was anointed at Jordan, He began to preach the gospel of the kingdom. Through His rule, Israel began to experience the marvellous conditions of heaven. Sickness, death, and demon possession were all swept aside through His ministry. God's will for Israel was fulfilled in Christ. However, it was not immediately clear what price had to be paid for the Kingdom of God to come with power.

3. Healing: a Blessing through Christ and His Cross

Isaiah 53:5 tells us that all healing is possible because Christ bore our sins and our sicknesses when He died on the cross. Isaiah 53:4 tells us that Messiah carried our infirmities and sorrows. Matthew 8:17 tells us that this was fulfilled when Jesus began His healing ministry. The Bible teaches that all the redeeming power of God is through the death and resurrection of Christ. Many blessings of the cross were available in the Old Testament in anticipation of the sacrifice of Jesus. 1 Peter 2:24 confirms that it is through the cross that we are healed. God loves the human race and feels for us in our suffering and longs to heal. 1 John 3:8 teaches that Christ was manifested to destroy the works of the devil. This includes sin and the effects of sin, including healing of the body and deliverance from evil spirits.

Sickness has many causes. Some sicknesses are caused by demon possession, such as the woman bent double in Luke 13:11. The Bible teaches here that her condition was caused by an evil spirit, and that when she was delivered she was immediately healed. However, most of the cases of healing in the Bible are not in this category. In most cases there is no reference to demon possession or to the need for deliverance. Clearly, discernment is needed.

In Luke 9:37-43, a demon-possessed boy was delivered, and some have assumed that the boy had epilepsy; but this is an assumption, and not plainly stated in the text. Some mental illnesses have physical causes, and ministers need to be careful not to jump to conclusions. Fever and high blood pressure can cause hallucinations and physical effects that may lead to a mistaken conclusion that spiritual powers of darkness are causing the problem. Whatever the cause of the problem is, there is healing in the name of Jesus.

I was once asked to minister deliverance to a lady in the north of England who had had an 'out of the body' experience. She had felt tingling sensations in her body, and had various hallucinations. In great distress, she had contacted her pastor, who called me for help. After a few moments' conversation, the Lord put it in my heart to tell her to go quickly to see the doctor. He checked her blood pressure and found it to be sky high. If she had not gone in quickly, she would have had a stroke and possibly died!

Matthew 9:35 teaches that Jesus healed every disease and sickness, which indicates that there is nothing too hard for God. The New Testament abounds with examples of healing:

- Blindness: Matthew 9:27; 20:30-34 and Mark 10:46-52
- Leprosy: Matthew 8:3
- Dumbness: Matthew 9:32 and Mark 7:35
- Fever: Mark 1:30-31
- Paralysis: Mark 2:1-12
- The crippled: Acts 3:2, Matthew 21:14
- Deafness: Mark 7:32
- Resurrection from the dead: John 11:43-44

God can heal any and every disease. Barren women can have children [Genesis 30:22]. God can even raise a dead body that has begun to decompose [John 11:39]. Maimed people can have their limbs restored [Luke 14:13, 21; Matthew 15:30, 31].

Jesus' healing ministry has many wonderful characteristics:

♦ Luke 4:18 indicates that the anointing that is upon Jesus covers all the ills that afflict human beings, including: a broken heart through disappointment; deliverance from addiction and curses; healing for the blind; and freedom from hurts and abuse. The anointing heals from grief and sorrow and all the traumas that afflict the human race through bereavement, divorce and physical and mental abuse. *"Surely he has borne our griefs and carried our sorrows"* [Isaiah 53:4].

♦ Healing was nearly always immediate and complete [Luke 5:13].

DIVINE HEALING AND DELIVERANCE

- ♦ On rare occasions healing was not instantaneous, such as the blind man who needed a second touch from Jesus [Mark 8:23-25] and the lepers who were healed *"as they went"* [Luke 17:14]. However, these 'exceptions' still indicate that healing was virtually immediate. There are no examples in the Bible of people being asked to claim they were well, while still having the symptoms. The act of believing brought instant relief.

In the late 1970s a young Frenchman named Marcel became a drug addict. His life descended into the misery of severe addiction. On one particular day, he was indulging in his habit together with some friends. In despair, he suddenly swallowed a large dose of LSD in order to take his own life. His friends fled in dismay as they witnessed what he did. As he fell unconscious he cried out to God, and suddenly there, before his eyes, was a cross of flame which he knew was the cross of Jesus. Marcel did not die, but he was severely brain damaged, as brain scans clearly showed.

Unable to function normally, he wandered around various cities and ended up in Amsterdam, where he met Christians. They cared for him in a Church-based drug rehabilitation centre. Many of the Christians there had been former addicts. Through his dulled mind, he could hardly comprehend the message they told him, but during times of worship, his reasoning faculties sharpened and became clear. Then afterwards the pall of dullness would return.

After some time in the centre, he was alone in his room one day, and stirred by something deep within, he formed a purpose to surrender to Christ. Suddenly Satan appeared to him, and threatened him: "If you give yourself to Christ I will kill you!" But Marcel was desperate and cried out: "Then kill me, because I must surrender to Him!" As Marcel prayed this desperate prayer, the power of God descended and changed his life completely. And most wonderful of all, his brain became clear and sharp. When he returned to France, the doctors who examined him with fresh brain scans were amazed, and wrote in his medical records: "This man has been healed by a miracle from God."

4. Conditions for Healing

(a) Confession and Forgiveness

Healing is often linked with confession and forgiveness [Psalm 103:3; James 5:15; Mark 2:1-12]. In Mark 2 Jesus ministered to the paralysed man's spiritual need, indicating that obtaining forgiveness was the first step in his physical healing. The inference from this event is that human beings are spiritually paralysed until we receive forgiveness. In another case Jesus told the man at the pool of Bethesda not to return to sin, or a worse sickness would befall him. The word 'dis-ease' indicates a lack of peace, through guilt, worry or fear. These conditions must be dealt with if the person is to be whole and remain whole.

(b) Desire

Jesus expected those He healed to have a desire to be healed [John 5:6; Mark 10:51]. It may seem surprising that some people might not want healing. The Guinness Book of Records tells of a woman who was sent to bed by her doctor because she had a bad cold. Some 40 years later she was still in bed, though the cold had disappeared long before. Clearly she loved the life of an invalid!

(c) Faith

Jesus asked many sick people if they believed He could heal them - as in Matthew 9:28. James 5:15 tells us that it is the prayer of faith that makes the sick person well. Faith is not a power - it is a channel that allows God's power to work. Scripture says that in His home town, Jesus *"could do no mighty work because of their unbelief"* [Mark 6:5-6]. This unbelief was caused by familiarity with Jesus, to the point that the people who had known Him since He was a child did not believe He could do such mighty things.

It is vital to remember that faith is a gift from God, and that it is not a virtue or a good work that we must do. Some people have taught that healing is ours to take by faith and that therefore it is our own fault if we are not healed. Some have preached that, if we are sick, or our children die, we have allowed Satan to rob us. This error places impossible burdens of guilt and condemnation on souls. Some well-meaning Christians have thrown away their glasses as a step of faith, expecting that their eyes will be healed, only to have to rummage in the rubbish bin to find them the next day! More seriously, however, some diabetics have stopped taking insulin, and have suffered terrible consequences. Faith comes by the word of God (the Greek 'rhema' word) made personal in application by the Holy Spirit.

(d) Obedience

This is especially true of those who are God's people. God said that He would bless His people if they obeyed Him [Exodus 15:26; Deuteronomy 28:4-6] but would make them sick if they went against Him [Deuteronomy 28:22-35]. God's Word teaches that God's ears are deaf to the unrighteous, and this includes His people if they disobey.

(e) Grace for Unworthy Sinners

God expects people to get right with Him in order to be blessed, but it is also true that He is full of grace and mercy and heals unworthy sinners so that they may come to Him and be reconciled with Him. In John 9, Jesus healed a man who had been blind from birth; he was healed without even knowing the name of Jesus! This man was so moved, that he became a true follower of Jesus.

(f) Laying On of Hands

The laying on of hands is often a way in which healing is ministered [Mark 16:18]. This is probably as a means of increasing the faith of the person seeking the healing. In many cases it was not necessary, and in Luke 7:1-10, Jesus did not even need to be physically present.

(g) Anointing with Oil

The anointing with oil is similar to the laying of hands, in that while it is encouraged [James 5:14; Mark 16:13], it is not a legalistic condition of healing. It would be wrong to be superstitious about anointing with oil. It is through faith in Christ that we are healed, not by His Holy garments [Mark 5:27-34]. The practice of selling prayer cloths and holy oil is to be condemned, as these are against the whole spirit of the New Testament, which states that *"freely* (without paying) *you have received, freely give"* [Matthew 10:8]. Hezekiah destroyed the ancient bronze serpent that Moses had used to heal the Israelites. He destroyed it because the people had begun to worship it, but it was only a piece of brass, with no healing power in itself [2 Kings 18:4].

5. God Does Not Always Heal

There are many mysteries that are difficult to explain. It is clear that healing is not ultimately within human power; it is a gift from God, and He alone knows why He allows some people to suffer. Even great men of faith have experienced much physical suffering. Smith Wigglesworth suffered from kidney stones and sciatica. His daughter Alice was half deaf and his son died very young. John Wimber saw many remarkable healings but was seriously ill himself for most of his life, with heart problems, strokes and cancer. His biography makes clear that he showed great faith even in the midst of extreme pain and suffering.

Although the origin of all pain and sickness may be Adam's sin, yet the Bible teaches that sickness is not always the result of sin in the life of the sufferer. There may be many causes of sickness:

- ❖ Job's sickness was *"without cause"* [Job 2:3]. The book of Job teaches that God sometimes has a higher purpose in allowing His children to be ill - a purpose that will purify their character, and also lead to a greater triumph over the powers of darkness.

- ❖ Epaphroditus was sick through his great exertions for the sake of the gospel [Philippians 2:26-30].

- ❖ The blind man healed in John 9 was not sick because of his personal sin nor any sin which his parents had committed. John 9:1-5 indicates that, through all that has gone wrong, God will be glorified as His love and power are made manifest.

- ❖ Romans 8:28 indicates that all things work together for good if our hearts are right with God. This is a great mystery but goes to the heart of the Christian's perception of life and of things that happen to them.

- ❖ Old age! Isaac lost his eyesight in old age [Genesis 27:1]. While old age may be a heavy burden, Christians are able to bear it with patience and inner trust in God.

- ❖ It is also true that some people are not healed because of unbelief [Mark 6:5-6].

- ❖ Healing may be lost if there is a return to sinful ways [John 5:14].

6. Two Kinds of Faith

There are two kinds of faith:

(1) Faith to be healed. This kind of faith may bring great power to our bodies, but people may feel condemned and full of despair if they are not healed. They lack the most important kind of faith, which is:

(2) Faith to trust God through times of suffering and sorrow. Faith of this kind accompanies martyrs to their execution. This is the faith of the Christians who were thrown to the lions in the Roman amphitheatre. This is the faith of Meshach, Shadrach and Abednego, who confessed that they knew their God was able to deliver them miraculously, but if He didn't that would not deter them from following Him to death [Daniel 3:17-18]. This example of faith is one of the most triumphant in the whole Bible.

7. The Gift of Healing

The gift of healing is a special gift of the Spirit that is not given to every minister of the gospel [1 Corinthians 12:30]. All believers can prophesy but not all are prophets; all are to evangelise but not all are evangelists; all believers can pray for healing, but not all have the gift of healing. This is a vital point to understand, otherwise it will lead to striving, disappointment, condemnation and a sense of frustration. If God has not given us the gift of healing, we should not try to make healing the centre of our ministry. If God has given us the gift of healing, then it will work without striving; it will be easy to minister to people in need. It is clear that some people have other gifts - like John the Baptist, whose ministry brought powerful conviction of sin. But no doubt healings and deliverance took place as a secondary result of John the Baptist's ministry. Peace of heart heals many diseases! Also, people may lose their healing and deliverance if they do not repent of sin.

All ministers do not have the gift of healing, but the Bible indicates that part of preaching the gospel of the kingdom is to announce that through faith we can experience the power of God now. This should be preached and ministered by all believers [Luke 10:9]. It is right to point people to Jesus as the one who can make them whole through faith in His name.

The Bible also does not encourage us to boast of our power or our gifts. These gifts operate by the grace of God, and God alone is to receive the glory for miracles that He does. Peter was very careful to point out that the lame man in Acts 3 was healed by the power of God through the name of Jesus [Acts 3:12, 16]. Jesus taught that His followers were to keep their eyes on making sure of their salvation rather than glorying in their spiritual power to heal and deliver [Luke 10:20].

In the early 1980s a lady named Sally, in a Church in North London, became ill and the doctor diagnosed fibroids. These growths were as large as oranges and could be felt by external examination; the doctor advised surgery. But there was a complication - Sally was pregnant. The doctor gave regular check-ups and planned to perform surgery after the delivery.

Meanwhile, Sally continued to attend her Church regularly. Although the pregnancy combined with fibroids was life-threatening, a word of prophecy in one meeting assured her that she would not die of this condition. An evangelist with a gift of healing, named Ian Andrews, visited the Church and Sally was prayed for. During the meeting, God's power touched her and the growths disappeared. At her next appointment, she told the doctor: "My fibroids have disappeared. God has healed me!" But the doctor was a sceptic and told her to be rational. He even refused to examine her to see if the fibroids were still there, because it was not medically possible to think they could be gone.

A month later, during a check-up, the doctor said: "I can't explain it, but I can no longer feel the fibroids, they have disappeared!" "Well, I did try to tell you!", laughed Sally.

DELIVERANCE: WHO IS SATAN?

The Bible reveals very little about Satan, and so we must piece together the few things that we know.

1. The Anointed Cherub in Paradise

Satan was created as one of the great angels that abide in the presence of God. Some people have speculated that there were once five mighty angels around God's throne, and not just the four mentioned in Revelation 4. This is, of course, simply speculation. The Bible does reveal more in Ezekiel 28, where the prophet describes the Prince of Tyre as embodying the evil heart of Satan. Ezekiel describes first the Prince of Tyre and then Satan who inspired and motivated him.

It is interesting to notice at this point that the short-cut to political power over the nations is to bow to Satan! Satan even offered this short-cut to Jesus [Luke 4:6]. Probably evil politicians such as Hitler and Stalin held some very dark secrets in their hearts, of transactions they had made with the power of darkness. But all politicians and leading businessmen must be watchful not to lie, bribe, deceive, or harm others in order to attain high office or positions of power. Success by deceit is at a price that is simply not worth paying.

Further information on Satan is provided by Isaiah 14 where, in a similar way, Isaiah begins by describing the ruler of Babylon and then proceeds to describe the spirit that inspired him.

Ezekiel describes Satan as dwelling in Eden, the garden of God, in the midst of precious fiery stones. He is described as the *"anointed cherub"* [Ezekiel 28:14]. Whatever these verses mean, they indicate the high calling he had before he sinned. Isaiah describes Satan as having the name Lucifer, or 'Day Star'. This is one of the most prominent stars in the sky. Lucifer is perhaps the planet Venus, which is the brightest heavenly body in the night sky and the first to appear in the morning. Jesus holds a similar title, but one indicating that he is like the sun shining in its strength: *"the bright and morning star"* [Revelation 22:16]. When Jesus rises, no other star is visible. While all the other angels are full of joy at the greatness of Jesus, Satan became envious of Jesus. His hatred and envy of Jesus, the Son of God, are the main motives of his being.

2. What Do We Know about Satan from the Bible?

- **He is full of wisdom** [Ezekiel 28:11 and Genesis 3:1]

    No-one should try and argue with Satan, since he is so clever that he will tie us in knots. It was not with clever answers that Jesus responded to him, but by quoting the word of God. Eve made the mistake of entering into discussion with the arch-deceiver. We must be very careful not to believe what he says nor fear his threats.

    A pastor in Manchester, UK was threatened by a demon-possessed man, who said that he would die on a certain date. The pastor was, of course, mildly troubled by this threat. But as the threatened day drew near, he examined his heart and, knowing he was right with God, he decided to ignore the threat completely. The day came and went and that pastor has lived on, serving God for many years since that date.

- **He was perfect in beauty** [Ezekiel 28:12]

    This means that we should not only expect him to appear in an ugly form. Evil is ugly but Satan is the master of deceptive outward beauty. The word 'serpent' in Hebrew is 'nahash', meaning 'shining one'. 2 Corinthians 10:14 describes Satan as appearing as an angel of light. This means that Satan probably appeared to Eve as an incredibly beautiful angel. When you read books that describe visits from angels, take great care! Check what the angels have said by the word of God. If there is no basis for their revelation in the Bible, then you know certainly that these are not angels from God but deceiving spirits. Satan will not present himself to us in a negative light since most people are repulsed by evil. (A small number of people are attracted by evil, including people like Hitler, and other mass murderers.) The key here is not to take things at face value but to listen to the witness of the Spirit and check things out with the word of God.

- **Satan was lifted up with pride because of his beauty** [Ez 28:17]

    Self-congratulation is the first step towards self-worship. Narcissus, in Greek mythology, was a handsome young man who, while walking over a bridge, noticed his own reflection in the river below. He fell in love with himself and was unable to leave the bridge, and starved to death gazing at his own reflection. Self-love and self-loathing are closely linked. Satan leads people down the path of self-love and self-harming. He is full of himself and is therefore an intensely miserable being.

- **Satan rebelled against God** [Isaiah 14:13-14]

  He tried to exalt himself and set his throne above God. Pride was the original sin and is the most satanic of sins.

- **God cast Satan down** [Isaiah 14:15; Ezekiel 28:17-18]

  Satan fell to the lowest pit. Jesus was a witness of this event and mentioned it in Luke 10:18.

- **Satan plagues the human race**

  From his fallen position, Satan strikes the nations continually [Isaiah 14:4-6]. Satan oppresses the human race by innumerable means - stirring people up in their carnal lusts, tempting them to vile acts, placing misery and depression on human minds.

3. Satan's Power is Limited

In the Garden of Eden, God condemned Satan to walk on his belly [Genesis 3:14]. It is not clear what this means, and we must assume that Satan's speed of movement was significantly curtailed by this curse. Satan is neither omnipresent nor omniscient, since these are qualities of God alone. The Bible confirms this in Job 1:7, where Satan is described as roaming up and down in the earth.

Revelation 2:13 reveals that Satan has a throne on earth, and that in the first century it was located in Pergamos. There was a temple there in Pergamos, dedicated to Augustus, which had a serpent on its doors. The ancient altar of Pergamos was taken by archaeologists to Berlin at the end of the 19th century. This immediately preceded the evil developments in the German government which led to the First and Second World Wars, the holocaust and the death of millions. While it may be going too far to assert that the altar of Pergamos was the cause of these things, it is nevertheless easy to believe that Satan's throne at that time was in Berlin.

(a) The Father of Lies [John 8:44]

Jesus called the devil *"the father of lies"* and *"a murderer from the beginning"*. This means that Lucifer rebelled against God's will for him almost from the moment he realised what that will was. He rose up against the truth, and lied against it, declaring that God is not good [Genesis 3:5] and inferring that God is keeping something back from the human race. The devil rose up and murdered Adam and Eve by his lies. He poisoned the human race. His murderous anger against God culminated at Calvary, where he stirred up the human race to demand the crucifixion of God the Son. He no doubt delighted in the sufferings of God, but was doubtless also shocked to realise that his malice had not deterred God from loving sinners even to death. 1 Corinthians 2:8 teaches that if the powers of darkness and the political rulers had realised what was happening on the cross, they would not have crucified the Lord of Glory.

(b) Troubling of the Human Race

The human race has been disturbed by Satan and all the fallen angels since the Fall. In the pre-flood era there were evil spirits at work that interacted sexually with mankind [Genesis 6:4]. This activity stopped after the judgment of the Flood and it may be assumed that many evil spirits were bound at that time, some in the bottomless pit, and others in the river Euphrates [Jude 6-7; Revelation 9:14, 16:13-14]. These evil powers provoked the human race to sex acts that were extreme and abnormal – called *"strange flesh"* in Jude 7.

(c) The Countdown to the Return of Christ

The Bible reveals that in the last days these spirits will again be unleashed on the human race as part of the countdown to Christ's return, the end of the world and the Day of Judgment [Revelation 9:1-11]. Some have speculated that this has already happened, with the wave of drugs and drug-inspired music that spread like a wave over the earth in the 1960s and 70s.

(d) The Final Defeat of Satan

The imprisonment of Satan in the bottomless pit, followed by his eternal punishment in the lake of fire, are both clearly prophesied in Revelation 20:1-2 and 10. The devil knows that he has only a short time left before his final banishment in eternal weakness [Revelation 12:12; Isaiah 14:9-11].

DIVINE HEALING AND DELIVERANCE

HOW DO PEOPLE BECOME TROUBLED BY EVIL SPIRITS?

What are the dangerous activities that lead people into demonic bondage? It is important to realise that while Satan is called *"the god of this world"* [2 Corinthians 4:4], yet his power is not absolute. He works in the sons of disobedience, i.e. fallen humanity, but his control is severely limited [Ephesians 2:1-3]. The human race is afflicted with the spirit of disobedience; humanity is not devil-controlled nor demon-possessed. To escape Satan's power, it is enough that men and women believe the gospel. The same is true of all bondage. Satan cannot ultimately hinder any soul from running to Jesus and experiencing salvation and deliverance [Mark 5:6-15].

Nevertheless, it is possible to identify ways by which people become bound and come under more specific control from the devil and demons. The boundary between demon possession and demon oppression is not easy to determine. Human beings cannot see demons, and it is fruitless to try and pretend knowledge that we do not have.

Many have debated whether Christians can be demon-possessed. This is clearly a grave assault on the power and authority of Christ, who is Almighty God and lives in the hearts of believers. Opinions may differ, but it is better to realise that Satan does attack and deceive whoever is willing to follow his lies and temptations. It is right to assert that Jesus and the devil will never indwell the same heart, yet it is nevertheless agreed by most believers that he can deceive and oppress believers and even ministers of the gospel. While the distinction between possession and oppression is a very important one to those who are jealous for the glory of God, yet for the soul who is afflicted, the key is to find the path of deliverance, and the principles are the same in either case.

Some of the following cases described are only possible for unbelievers, but others are possible as oppression in the life of believers.

1. *Witchcraft*

This sin was outlawed by the Law of Moses [Exodus 22:18; Deuteronomy 18:10]. This was to protect Israel from the flood of demons that invade nations through the ministry of witches and mediums. Included in this is *all* attempts to contact the dead (necromancy [Deuteronomy 18:11]), clairvoyants, spiritists, tarot card readers, crystal ball gazers, astrologers, white magicians and black magicians.

The sin of witchcraft, and all the other sins listed above, are an outright defiance against God, and an invitation to Satan to invade the life and personality of the person who practises them. In some cultures, magic charms are attached to children to protect them from sickness and evil. These charms, on the contrary, attract evil spirits and can cause sickness and oppression of all kinds, including nightmares and visions. Many cultures are based on witchcraft, and in such cultures large numbers have witnessed supernatural apparitions that have terrified them. The use of witchcraft opens a wide door to the devil and slams the door shut in God's face.

2. *Idolatry*

The worship of idols is found in every nation. In its worst form, people worship dogs (e.g. the Egyptian god Horus), elephants (e.g. the Hindu god Ginesch) and every other animal form. Many gods have snakes entwined around them – Pharaoh's statue typically had a serpent above it, and the same is true of Hindu temples. Many idols depict strange creatures that are not found on earth - creatures with staring eyes, large teeth, many arms, fire-breathing dragons and so on. This is the worship of the devil and of demons. To worship them is to fall down and invite their power and spirit to dominate the life of the worshipper. Idolatry opens the door wide to demons. The above description does not include the grosser forms of idol worship, and many heathen temples have a large number of temple prostitutes.

3. *Western Idolatry or Covetousness*

"Covetousness is idolatry" [Colossians 3:5]. There is little worship of idols as such in western society. Nevertheless, there is widespread idolatry of a different kind. **Money** is worshipped and accumulated as a god that has power to protect and provide for all needs in this life. Jesus called money 'mammon'. Mammon was a Babylonian god which was associated with wealth, avarice and greed. Western society is built on the myth that money will make a person happy; but the evidence is to the contrary. The wealthiest societies have increasing numbers of suicides, not least among teenagers.

This idolatry spills over into the love of possessions. People become obsessed with their cars, their homes, their holidays, their possessions in general. Ultimately, advertising is directed at awakening the idolatry of self-image. Someone once said that advertising's aim is: *"to make people buy things they don't need, using money they don't have, to impress people they don't know"*.

It is strange how important **image** is to the human heart. This also brings with it the worship of appearance and the human body. In Greek culture, to have physical beauty and strength was to be god-like. This was worshipped and displayed in statues of perfect male and female naked bodies. Modern western society is full of similar worship. Diets, clothes, fashions, are all preoccupied with the perfect human form. Young women diet more and more, with a mixture of self-love and self-hatred. There are evil spirits that will bind the mind to these extremes. Obsession with exercise and sport can also be idolatrous.

4. Substance Abuse, including Drugs and Alcohol

Deliberate substance abuse for pleasure opens a person's will to being invaded by external forces that excite and manipulate the human imagination. Drug addicts often hear voices and see visions or faces that threaten and frighten. Many who use drugs have had near-death experiences, others have had out-of-the-body sensations or visions of the devil. Many musicians have used drugs to enhance their sense of the supernatural in order to find inspiration for new songs. The Beatles wrote several of their songs under the influence of drugs.

All substance abuse is a doorway to another world, but it is a trap - easy to get into and almost impossible humanly to get out of. Government rehabilitation centres for alcohol and drug abuse have commonly failed to provide lasting relief. Many governments have acknowledged the gospel as the most lasting form of cure from drug abuse. Jackie Pullinger worked in Hong Kong for years and wrote a book about her successful work with drug addicts: 'Chasing the Dragon'. The Hong Kong government recognised the importance of her work and provided land and buildings free of charge to help the development of drug rehabilitation. The Queen of England conferred on her the Order of the British Empire in recognition of the importance of her work. Jackie led the drug addicts to Christ and to receive the Holy Spirit. When they experienced withdrawal symptoms (cold turkey), she counselled them to speak in tongues. This method was effective and often led to the supernatural alleviation of all cold turkey symptoms.

5. Prostitution, Pornography and Sexual Fantasies

The devil excites the imagination and seeks to open doors into forbidden territories. The Bible reveals that in sexual union there is a mixing of the personalities into one flesh: *"Or do you not know that he who is joined to a harlot is one body with her? For 'the two', He says, 'shall become one flesh'. ... Flee sexual immorality. Every sin that a man does is outside the body, but he who commits sexual immorality sins against his own body."* [1 Corinthians 6:16, 18].

The point is that sexual sin, including adultery and fornication, requires the submission of the whole body to another person. Sexual sin is dangerous physically, since terrible diseases can be contracted by this means. But the spiritual impact of sexual sin cannot be perceived or measured externally. There are spiritual forces at work to deceive, bind and ultimately possess the human personality. The doorway to these bondages may be fantasies, or pornography, but in the end the answer is the gospel.

6. Curses

The subject of curses is very wide, ranging from specific curses put upon people by witches, to words spoken in bitter or angry spite. Sometimes an attitude can bring a cursed state on a child.

One pastor was called to a young woman who had gone blind at the age of 21. When he visited her in hospital, he noticed that she was lying in the bed in an extreme foetal position. As he talked with her, she told how she had had a terrible self-hatred since childhood. When she was about 5 years old, she overheard her mother say to the neighbour, while pointing at her: "We didn't want this one." Her whole life from that moment had been shaped and scarred by those words. He was able to minister the love of God to her which resulted in her complete healing.

Some people have felt rejection from childhood and have later discovered that their parents had wanted to abort them, producing a feeling of rejection right from the womb. Others have found that some relative cursed the family as a form of revenge for some wrong committed. Curses are a form of open door to the devil. Words spoken hastily in bitterness and anger can be a channel for the devil to scar the character of a child. These curses can produce a pattern of failure and of mental and physical disease. But all of them can be broken through prayer in Jesus' name.

7. Sects, Heresies and Doctrines of Devils

Sects like Jehovah's Witnesses and the Mormons are inspired by deceiving spirits, which make their victims almost impervious to normal persuasion or argument. Such spirits will attack the deity of Christ, and minimise His importance. They will cast a smokescreen around the existence and activity of the devil and demons. The only answer to such deception is to pray for the person to receive a touch from the Lord which will open their eyes to see the spiritual prison they have fallen into.

8. Christian Deceptions

More difficult to identify are Christian doctrines and sects that are inspired by deceiving spirits. Here are a few possibilities:

- **Extreme healing doctrines**: many examples of this can be found in different countries. The basic idea is that medical help and taking medicine is considered as unbelief or even of the devil. This can lead to many premature deaths. False doctrines that challenge believers to display outstanding faith are difficult to discern, because they appeal to our hearts if we seek a deeper place with God. The point is that we must hear from the Holy Spirit, and no extreme doctrine can ever replace Him. To escape these deceiving spirits, there must be humility and a willingness to accept that we can get things wrong. Faith does not come from these claims, but from hearing the voice of God.

- **Extreme exclusivism**: the most extreme example of this in history is the Exclusive Brethren, who would not allow family members to eat with others who were not of the same denomination. To this day, women from this group have to wear head-covering at all times. This group had a deep love for God's word, but at some point things went into deception. Extreme exclusivism is a mark of a sect, and a starting point for deception. Once a group is cut off from fellowship with other Christians, they are open to further lies.

- **Extreme shepherding**: these movements take away all liberty from Church members to act according to their own consciences. The leadership will guide members on what clothing is acceptable, when to take holidays, who they can marry etc. If members are absent from meetings then this must be accounted for to the over-shepherds. This seems to produce zeal and holiness, but actually moves away from holiness by causing members to relate to man, not God, for their wisdom and discernment. Such doctrines must be renounced or there will be no escape from their power.

9. Demonically-inspired Music

Music is a means for mediating spirit into the hearers. Many musicians have openly acknowledged that they wrote some of their music under the influence of drugs. Music has the power to convey evil imaginations and rebellion against God, both by the lyrics and by the sheer force of the rhythm and form of the music. Music can also mediate sensuality. Certain venues aim to impact the soul with the careful use of lighting and sounds.

10. Eating Disorders

The human mind can be so distorted by the lies of the devil, that beautiful young girls see themselves as ugly. These deceptions can be very strong; some people stray into such self-hatred that they endanger their own lives. This is a more recent manifestation of deceiving spirits. While anorexia and bulimia were once unknown, they are quite common now. One of the keys here is to accept ourselves as loved by God and beautiful in His sight.

11. Hypnosis and Other Mind-control Activities

There are many avenues for Satan to enter and control the human spirit. Hypnosis involves the voluntary submission of the human will to the spirit and control of the hypnotist. This is a very dangerous thing to do since it involves the lowering of our inner guard. We should not agree to participate in any form of magic, however entertaining and innocent it may seem.

BIBLICAL DELIVERANCE — THE GADARENE DEMONIAC

The door is opened to demons through various activities, and many people are influenced by demonic powers without any exercise of personal choice. Some grow up in idolatrous societies, where witchcraft is practised from a young age. Others have rebelled against all the protective barriers of law, conscience and morality. Those who break the law find that they cannot reverse the process they have unleashed upon their soul. Jesus said that, *"whoever commits sin is a slave of sin"* [John 8:34]. Whatever the cause of bondage, the human soul cries out for liberty. At the deepest level, this cry is for liberty from the power of sin and freedom from the bondage of Satan. How can this be obtained?

We will consider the key Biblical example of the Gadarene demoniac. This story is recounted in Mark 5:1-20. It is described in great detail because of the importance the Bible attaches to this example of Jesus' saving power. The Gadarene demoniac was one of the worst examples of human depravity in the New Testament. The truth is plain. If he can be saved, then anyone can be saved. The key to deliverance is given in this chapter.

1. The Demoniac's Terrible State

- ➤ The man had an **'unclean spirit'**. This indicates that he was troubled with unclean thoughts, perhaps of a sexual nature.

- ➤ He lived **among the tombs.** The Greek word for tomb is 'mneimeion' which is based on the word for memory and corresponds to the

English word 'memorial'. The poor man lived under the power of memories. This means that he was dominated by past sins, guilt, shame, hurts caused and hurts felt. He was a bitter man, haunted by the past. One psychologist has said that: *"The past is not dead, it is not even past."* Time does not heal memories - only the love and forgiveness of God can heal the past. The most chilling part of this man's bondage was that he communed with the dead, whether in his imagination or through the spirit of demons is not clear. He lived among the tombs. This was a living death.

➢ He **broke chains** with supernatural strength. This indicates that he had power to break restrictions. He had doubtless broken God's moral laws, perhaps by worshipping idols, perhaps by sexual immorality. In breaking physical chains he did not find freedom, since there were invisible chains around his heart and mind.

➢ He **roamed the mountains**, the lonely desolate areas. Mountains are beautiful to the tourist; but to the outcast without a place to shelter, the mountains are a place of danger, loneliness, cold and hunger.

➢ He **cried** with a heart full of misery, loneliness and bondage. This great cry must have struck terror into the hearts of those who heard it. It was the great animal cry of the soul for deliverance, for someone to love him. God in heaven heard the cry. David Wilkerson tells the story of a drug addict in New York who filled his syringe with his own blood and wrote the word 'Help' on the ceiling above his bed. God heard that young man's cry and led him to Christians. God heard the cry of the demoniac and sent Jesus to him.

➢ **The pigs**! Pigs were unclean animals under Jewish law and it was against the will of God that these animals were being kept. Pigs typify the state of demon-possessed people because they have no discernment in what they eat. They will eat filth, even their own dung. People who are open to demons have no sense of right and wrong; they have no limits to what they will watch on TV; they have no standards as to what films are acceptable and what are not. The pigs also insanely ran down the hill and committed suicide. Suicide is unnatural and demons seem to drive their victims to suicide on all levels: intellectual suicide (by foolish deception), ministerial suicide (bringing shame on their own ministry), and actual suicide.

2. *God's Answer*

- **The man saw Jesus**. *Jesus* is God's answer. It is clear that the man was too far away to see Jesus' features, so there was no mere outward fascination or curiosity. The demoniac sensed the presence of Jesus. The presence of Jesus is the presence of Almighty God. It is the atmosphere of sinless holiness. There is total, absolute power in the hands of Jesus. He is God and can do what He pleases. All spirits and all things must bow to Him as Lord. The man sensed Jesus and *ran* to Him. This means that he was drawn magnetically to Him. Doubtless the demons screamed in protest, but it is clear that they could not stop the man.

- **He fell at Jesus' feet and worshipped Him**. The man recognised Jesus as God; by the deep instinct of his heart, he knew who Jesus was. The demons also recognised Jesus as the Son of the Most High God. They feared they would be tormented, and begged that He would not send them into the bottomless pit prematurely!

- **Jesus spoke words of majestic authority and grace**. These are the words of a King. *"Where the word of a king is, there is power; and who may say to Him, 'What are you doing?'"* [Eccl. 8:4].

- **The deliverance was instant**. It was not a process. The man was healed of madness in a moment of time. At no point in the Bible is it suggested that deliverance is a long drawn-out process. To get involved in such a process is to ascribe power and authority to the devil.

- **His wholeness was strong**, and not fragile. Jesus sent him to preach, confident in the permanence of the man's healing.

SUMMARY OF THE MAIN STEPS IN DELIVERANCE

1. Call on the Name of the Lord

"Whoever shall call on the name of the Lord shall be delivered." [Joel 2:32 KJV].

Rusty Woomer was born in West Virginia in 1954. He loved the outdoor life, probably because his life at home was filled with fear, abuse and poverty. His father was an alcoholic who frequently physically and mentally abused his family.

Rusty ran away from this life of abuse and began sleeping under bridges and in gas station restrooms to avoid going home. By around the age of 15, Rusty had left school and was a drug addict. By the age of 25 he had often been in prison for rape, violence and theft.

Everything culminated on 22 February 1979. Rusty, along with two other men, robbed and murdered shop owner John Turner. By the end of a day of violence, three more people were dead and a woman had been raped. Rusty was arrested and, the next day, confessed to the murders. He was given the death penalty for his crimes, and was sent to death row.

Some years later, a Christian named Bob McAlister was visiting the prison where Rusty was held. Bob had become accustomed to terrible sights. But what he found when he met Rusty was unlike anything he had ever seen before.

Rusty was sitting on the floor in his cell in a stupor of total despair. His face was the colour of chalk and all over him crawled dozens of cockroaches. His long blond hair was a greasy mass. His beard was matted. He stank horribly. The cell was covered with half-eaten sandwiches. As Bob looked into Rusty's face, Bob saw how low and thorough the work of evil can be.

"Rusty", Bob said. There was no response. Rusty stared into space as a roach crawled over his beard. "Rusty", said Bob, "say the name Jesus. Just say Jesus." For several minutes nothing happened. "Just say the name Jesus."

Very slowly, Rusty said: "Jesus." He continued to stare at the wall of his filthy cell. After about 5 minutes he repeated: "Jesus". Several more minutes passed, and then Rusty prayed: "Forgive me, Jesus. Forgive me". It was then that Rusty's heart cracked open and he wept from the deepest part of his soul as he said over and over "Jesus, forgive me".

When Bob returned to Rusty's cell 3 days later, he couldn't believe his eyes. The cell was immaculate. The smell of disinfectant hung in the air. Rusty himself was scrubbed. His hair was clean. The cockroaches were gone. His bed was made. Rusty looked directly into Bob's eyes and said: "I figured it was what Jesus wanted me to do." That was in October 1985.

Becoming a Christian washed the sin from Rusty's heart, but obviously could not make right what he had done in the past. The terrible crimes had had a devastating effect on many people, and Rusty had to face the consequences of his actions. At 1 a.m. on 27 April 1990, Rusty was executed for his crimes.

The key to deliverance is the realisation that the name of Jesus paralyses the powers of darkness. This name, spoken in brokenness, weakness, but yet in faith, will bring all the hosts of heaven to the aid of the possessed, the afflicted, the oppressed or the tempted.

To call on the name of the Lord is not a passive attitude of waiting for God to bless or to work. There is a reaching out, a pouring out of the soul in strong desire to be saved. Psalm 18 describes a man with a sense of the imminence of death [v4], in deepest sorrow [v5], in the grip of a strong enemy [v17]. David cries out with all his heart, and his cry ascends to God upon his throne [v6]. God's response is to *come down*. This is God's answer to the soul overwhelmed with bondage. He comes down and sets the captive free [v16-17]. Then God brings the captive to a broad place of safety [v19].

2. *Repent – Renounce – Forsake*

All known practices that opened the door to the powers of darkness need to be renounced and forsaken through repentance. It is meaningless to pray for deliverance without shutting the door to demonic activity. Sometimes the door may be open through cultural traditions. These may be hardest to renounce since such a course may lead to tension in the community, or even rejection. But the choice must be made between a life of freedom in Christ or bondage.

In the case of witchcraft it is vital to remove all objects that link a soul with superstitious beliefs. All charms, amulets, including good luck charms, horse-shoes, rabbits' feet, chains or leather strings around the neck, waist, legs or arms - all these things must be removed and destroyed.

In Ephesus the believers burnt their magic books which were worth 50,000 pieces of silver, which in modern money would be anything between one to ten million US dollars. It was a huge sum, and indicates the power and scope of the revival in Ephesus. Ultimately the local culture was threatened, as people stopped buying statues of Diana. (One of the Seven Wonders of the World was the huge statue of the goddess Diana in the temple in Ephesus.)

- o Freemasons will have to burn their special clothes, destroy the chains and other articles. Some will have to burn books that have reference to their occult beliefs.

- o In Africa, special protective magic plants will have to be cut down.

- o CDs and other recordings of demonically-inspired music must be destroyed.

- Those involved in drug or substance abuse must destroy their drugs and substances that have kept them prisoner.

- Pornography in all its forms must be destroyed. Those who are weak and unable to resist internet pornography will have to forsake the use of computers in their homes, and find some public place or office where they can be supervised.

- In the book of Joshua the key to the victory was in the words 'utter destruction'. The people of God had to utterly destroy all the idols and all avenues by which the powers of darkness could still exercise dominion. To pray for the kingdom to come while keeping a back door open for the devil is meaningless. First every link between the soul and the powers of darkness must be forsaken and destroyed.

3. *Believe on the Lord Jesus Christ*

It is vital to have a correct belief about the Lord Jesus Christ - this is the most essential foundation for this ministry. Jesus is the Creator of all *"thrones or dominions or principalities or powers"* [Colossians 1:16]. *"He is before all things, and in Him all things consist"* [Colossians 1:17]. The devil is a created and fallen being. To compare Jesus and the devil is comparing the Infinite with the finite; the Almighty with limited power; the All-Knowing with darkest ignorance and limited knowledge; Omnipresence with a spatially limited being.

Jesus created the angels and gave them their destiny and purpose. Lucifer has rebelled against Jesus, but he has lost much of what limited power he ever had. Satan is severely limited. He has no body. He has no power to override the human will or mind. He must lie, trick and deceive and get foolish human beings to speak for him, to act for him and yield their bodies to be used by him. Satan cannot kill directly, so he seeks to get human beings to do this for him. But even then he cannot overrule the sovereign will of God. There is one God, there is one sovereign Will to whom all must yield and give account. God is the One who rules and overrules. To call on the name of Jesus is to call on Him who rules the universe.

Here is a list of some of the matchless qualities of Jesus Christ:

- Creator of all things [Colossians 1:16]
- The exact image of God's character [Colossians 1:15; Hebrews 1:2]
- Divine! Jesus is the Son of God and God the Son [Hebrews 1:8; John 1:1]. Believers are sons of God, but we are not divine. Jesus is divine.

- He is worshipped by angels and human beings [Hebrews 1:6; Revelation 5:8-14].
- All power in heaven and earth is given to Him [Matthew 28:18].

4. Submit Entirely to Christ

Salvation and deliverance are through the power of the person of Christ. For this reason, the safest place is at the feet of Christ. This is true for all of us. The act of deliverance is the transfer of lordship from Satan to Christ. Satan is overcome and cast out, and the Lord Jesus Christ establishes His kingdom. The critical thing here is that many people want an end to the rule of Satan, since he is cruel and oppressive, but they do not want the Lordship of Christ. This is a very dangerous state, since while there may be deliverance, it will not be permanent.

Christ rules as King but He does not trick, dominate, lie, kill or steal! Satan does all these things [John 10:10]. Satan climbs up like a thief through the back door or the open window [John 10:1]. But Christ comes through the front door. He speaks honestly to the people, explaining the consequences of sin, and appealing to the person to voluntarily lay down their will to Him and receive Him as Lord and King. Christ seeks to win the love of people's hearts, He does not seek to bully or dominate. Heaven is not ruled by a tyrant, but by the King of love.

5. Receive His Word of Authority and Power

Jesus speaks with authority and power, and His Word must be received wholeheartedly. The parable of the sower can be applied to the whole ministry of salvation, including the ministry of deliverance. Hearts that receive His Word alongside other things are like the thorny ground. They will find that there is a choking of His Word and authority. Similarly, those who are superficial in heart, and living at the wayside, will find that the devil is quick to remove the Word of deliverance from their heart. Those who have stony, hard hearts will find that the Word will not penetrate.

There must be a wholehearted reception of the Word, as it cannot grow with competition. This is not a question of the power of the Word of God; it is a question of the will of the person receiving it. The Word of God is powerful, to those who will receive it as the Word of a King and not the suggestion of a mere man.

6. Practise Prayer with Fasting

Jesus said that there are certain kinds of bondage that need prayer with fasting [Matthew 17:21]. It is important to realise that any soul can be free through faith in Christ. Nevertheless, there is a difference in ministry according to the spiritual depth and maturity to which someone has attained. Jesus is here referring to the depth of spiritual life that is open to those who would enter in.

There are two ways in which prayer and fasting can lead to a manifestation of God's power to deliver souls:

- **Intensification of prayer in a specific crisis**: while there is no mention of fasting as a means for the release of souls in the book of Acts, there are two events that indicate the use of fasting as a deepening of spiritual life. Firstly, in Acts 13:1-3 the leaders were seeking God with prayer and fasting, which led to the launching of a new phase of missionary activity. The second event is the imprisonment of Peter. There is no mention of fasting in Acts 12 but there was clearly intense prayer for Peter's wellbeing and release from prison. There is a strong possibility that many were not eating simply because of their great desire for this. Whatever the case, this intense period of prayer led to the release of Peter from prison.

- **A deepening of the personal walk of the individual**: Jesus showed the pattern of ideal spiritual development for the believer. His period of prayer and fasting indicates that there is a deeper realm for the believer to attain of spiritual life and a deeper walk with God. This will be resisted by Satan but can lead to revival involving widespread healing and deliverance. It is important not to make the attaining of this deeper walk a mechanical thing by fasting and much prayer. The key to a deeper walk with God is love and desire; if these are present, then fasting will produce a deeper life and ministry. If they are practised by the merely religious or the fanatic then they will produce intensified religiousness and fanaticism but will bear no fruit for the Kingdom of God.

7. *Staying Free!*

The most important point to understand is that deliverance is *not* salvation, any more than healing is! In Luke 11:24-26 Jesus describes a demon leaving a man but then returning. The demon finds the house clean and swept, but there is no new occupier, there is no transfer of lordship and ownership. Salvation comes when a sinner bows in entire surrender and love to the Lordship of Christ.

The best way of staying free is to be filled with the Holy Spirit. It is vital that, when a person is delivered, the avenues for a return to bondage are completely sealed. Satan will not give up the battle easily and there may be fierce battles of temptation. Many have found they need a period of nurturing in a stable environment. Teen Challenge provided the ministry of deliverance from drugs, and provided homes to give a stable environment in which the new converts could rebuild their lives and be free from the atmosphere of temptation and sin.

There are several steps that are vital in staying free:

- **Be filled with the Spirit**. (Read the chapter on the baptism with the Spirit.) The fullness of the Spirit is vital to those who would know the true power of salvation. If the New Testament did not include the book of Acts then the disciples would have been left weak and vulnerable. The power of the Spirit brought the victory of Calvary, to give victory over sin and temptation [Romans 6].

- **Learn to use the gifts of the Spirit**. The gift of tongues will enable the delivered soul to stay free from any addiction to sinful habits of mind or body.

- **Join a Church**. This may be a difficult step for some converts, who find that their background is different from those of the average Church member. They will need to find a Church which has an open door to souls struggling to find their identity in Christ. This may be hard for some, but it is a vital step if the person is to stay free. Studying the Bible with others will produce a deeper understanding, and provoke a keener application to daily life.

- **Build friendships with those who will disciple and mentor by their lifestyle**. Prayer is a habit that can be learned by fellowship with other believers. Friendship that goes beyond meetings is one of the most important steps in staying free. Bad friends lead people to bondage, but good friends lead them to stronger faith and commitment. Many troubled souls have needed a sympathetic friend to turn to at any time of day or night. This is a challenge not just to the new convert, but mainly to the Church!

- **Learn the power of the Bible to resist temptation and overcome the devil**. When Jesus was tempted, even though He was the Son of God (and is the author of the Bible!), He used the Bible in overcoming every attack of the enemy. Young converts may not know much of the Bible, and it would be wise to ask an older Christian to guide them to portions that can be memorised and used in the warfare of the soul and times of temptation.

THE CHALLENGE OF LEADERSHIP

The great cry in so many places is for more leaders and preachers. There is no doubt that this is the great need throughout the Church. The question is, what can be done by the Church to aid the emergence of leaders and ministers? Jesus told the twelve to **pray** that the Lord of the Harvest would raise up more labourers and send them into the harvest. This is the main means by which leaders are raised up; but it also implies that those praying are seeking to bring in more leaders. Leaders must make it part of their ministry to raise up other leaders to take their place. It is significant that the Lord instructed those already labouring to pray. It is as they pray that understanding comes, and eagerness to recognise God's hand in sending out more people into the harvest field. The great questions facing the Church are:

- What is the true pattern of leadership in the New Testament?

- How did Jesus form leaders and how is this relevant to us today?

- What are the characteristics of leaders, as taught in the New Testament?

PRINCIPLES OF LEADERSHIP IN THE NEW TESTAMENT

1. Christ is Head

The first great foundation of leadership is the recognition that Christ is the supreme leader. He, and He alone, is the Head of the Church. Our role, whether as leaders or Church members, is to discern God's heart and mind. When God is not involved in the leading of His Church, the leaders begin to see the Church as an area for the development of their own plans and ideas. They feel free to experiment and do what they want. Conversely, Church members may begin to lobby and influence leaders in a carnal, even a political, way. This leads to spiritual death. Church politics and a party spirit are a cancer that will kill the Church.

Each member is directly connected to the Head, not through a pyramid structure. God leads His Church by being the Head of each individual member of His body. No leader should seek to replace Christ in the lives of the individual members of the Church. Every member of the Church is to learn the **principles** of true leadership, in order to be a leader to the part of the Church for which they are personally responsible. Every believer has some responsibility for others. Parents lead their families. Students in a school are responsible for leading others to faith and witnessing in the area under their influence. The same is true of all God's people. We do not all have to be dynamic leaders, but we must all learn to fulfil our calling.

2. Christ's Rule is through Glad Surrender

To say that Christ is the Head of the body, is a far more radical statement than to say He is the ruler of His kingdom. As King, Christ is over all powers in the universe. He is the King of Kings, setting up whom He will over the kingdoms of mankind. He rules over all, even granting the devil permission to pursue His evil ends. Christ is King over all, and is the final authority in everything that takes place. But Christ is not the head of the kings of the earth in the way that He is Head of His Church.

The great difference lies in that Christ's great power over the kingdoms is external. Whether people will it or not, He is Lord. Even some Christians submit to Christ as they would to an earthly ruler. They give Him outward respect, and yet keep the domain of their own hearts to themselves. In the same way, an individual may vote for a politician, and yet will not yield their affections and heart to him. That is entirely proper, but it is not how things should be in the Church.

The great qualification for any leader, elder, song leader, Sunday school teacher, etc. is that they have been introduced into this realm of the Headship of Christ; that they have become part of His mystical body. The mystical side of the Church is not to be confused with vague, other-worldly spiritual experiences. The mystical dimension of Church life refers simply to the fact that Christ is consciously known and discerned as the basis of all life. Without this dimension, the Church is no more than any worldly organisation - which is sadly so frequently the case.

It is also the case that all ministries must flow from the authority of the Head. He co-ordinates the various functions into a harmonious whole. Where people function in the body without knowing Christ as their individual Head, their ministry creates dissonance, and does not edify the body. Generally this problem can be swallowed up in the flow of Church life and ministry. But it is when people seek to promote themselves carnally to the centre of things that real problems arise, requiring the corrective action of elders.

3. Government is by the Holy Spirit

If the external pattern of worldly government was transferred to the Church, then the government of God would touch people's lives through God's representatives. This implies hierarchy. But this is not how the Church is governed. The Church is governed by the **activity of the Holy Spirit in the hearts and minds of those who have yielded all to Christ**.

It is at the point of yielding that a person is baptised with the Holy Spirit and made a member of His body. This whole transaction produces an immediate change in the tone of a person's life. They have passed from one kingdom to another, and it is discernible through inner assurance and an inner awareness of the eternal. It is in this state of heart that God Himself communicates His mind and will, as the individual abides in conscious communion with the triune God.

- **Leaders do not replace Christ** - this is a key for New Testament Church leadership. Without this, no system, no matter how biblical, will succeed. It is in this realm that patterns of leadership often fail. People are constantly tempted to trust in that which is outward and carnal. They trust in the systems they live in, or in their eldership, or in their charismatic leader. This is a great error, since none of these can give life to the Church.

- **Spiritual life is through the ministry of every member** - life is only maintained in the Church as God ministers through the individual members. Just as a body needs all the cells to be healthy, so the Church needs each member of the Church to be in healthy relationship with the rest of the body.

4. Spiritual Life is Maintained by Waiting on God

Waiting on God is the practical means by which the Headship of Christ is maintained, and by which also leadership and ministry emerge. Waiting on God can be defined as inner attentiveness to the indwelling Christ. The great enemy of faith is the ceaseless chatter and noise of the human heart. Many complain about the noise of the world, and yet it is inner noise that is the great enemy of our souls.

As people wait on God, they become conscious of a will and a desire that far exceeds their own. They realise the reality of Jesus' words, when He said that He did only those things that His Father showed Him [John 5:19]. The great power of Christ's life was that His inner life was undisturbed and clear. This should be true of the life of men and women in the Church, and also therefore of the whole Church.

This is the realm in which people emerge both as ministers and leaders in the Church of the Lord. It is also the realm in which ministry and leadership become weakened, for if people neglect their inner life, they have nothing to contribute to the life of the Church. No matter how clever, gifted or well-informed someone may be, the streams of living water must flow from an inner life of communion with God. It is in this realm that God's will and choice become clear. It is the Holy Spirit who sets people aside for apostleship [Acts. 13:2] and also for eldership [Acts 20:28].

5. Who Leads the Church under Christ?

This question goes right to the heart of leadership in the New Testament. The answer is that there are three dimensions in the government of the Church. These are:

- Apostolic leaders
- Elders
- The whole body of the Church

Many Churches run on a kind of pyramid government, with one supreme leader. This is an effective method but can lead to abuse. The truth is that we need all three dimensions to be strong in a mature, spiritual Church.

It is vital that all of us recognise our calling and ministry. There are pioneer leaders who can take the Church to another level, but this kind of leader is rare. There are administrators who run the Church well, but need to use other, more dynamic prophetic and apostolic ministries in order to feed forward movement into the Church. Such administrators must not try or pretend to be pioneering leaders, or they will fail.

The Church can be likened to a ship, forging its way through the waters. There are two distinct dimensions to leadership or government on board the ship. One is the internal administration of daily life. This must go on, whether the ship is docked for a few days or travelling at great speed. This is the dimension of caring for those on board, providing them with good food and clean accommodation. This is a vital ministry in Church life, and can be described as the ministry of **pastors and teachers**.

But no matter how well-oiled this internal administration is, it does not give the ship any forward movement. The second dimension of leadership/government is in steering the course, giving instructions to the engine room and the helmsman. This dimension is to do with **spiritual leadership**. The captain must know where he is going, he must be aware of hidden reefs. He must always be on the watch for the lighthouse and the buoys.

Through this ministry, all the members of the crew are kept alert and at their posts; their whole life takes on a wider dimension than the daily round of mere survival. Good management can keep the ship afloat and functioning well, but real leaders steer the course and fire the engines. To take the analogy one step further, a ship that is not used to moving forward may become unsteady as a result of even a slight swell in the sea. In the same way, a Church that lacks leadership will find itself experiencing severe problems which are not actually arising from outside, but rather from the vacuum which lies at the heart of things.

- **Leadership must have prophetic vision**

    It is vital for a Church to acknowledge apostolic or prophetic ministry. Not that it should waste time attaching labels to people, which have often led to the inflation of people's ego. But the need of the Church is to be aware of the kind of ministry that stirs movement and direction among God's people. The danger is to think that leadership involves introducing the latest ideas on Church growth. Undoubtedly, leaders do need to move with the times, and must seek to reach the world with means that are effective and relevant. Nevertheless, this is not the heart of leadership.

    The apostle Paul gives almost no instructions to the Churches on how to organise evangelism. He gives few hints as to how the Church is to multiply and grow. The thrust of apostolic ministry is to stir people up to discover the riches that lie in Christ Himself. This is by revelation of the unseen, heavenly realms, through the Holy Spirit. The apostolic leader is one who has entered into communion with the invisible God. He has been called to walk closely with Christ in order to become familiar with the foundations of the invisible Kingdom of God.

- **We need elders**

    Elders are believers who are older in the faith than others and show some maturity. The Church in the New Testament benefited from leadership through elders, and inspirational motivation and understanding from apostles and prophets. The Church does not just need apostles, it needs elders!

- **The Church must support the leadership**

    If the Church is not willing to follow its leaders then there will be a failure to fulfil the will of God in a specific locality. Moses was doubtless one of the greatest leaders a group of people could ever have. He is a pattern for leaders to study. He was close to God, humble, and yet full of faith. But Moses failed totally in that the generation he led out of Egypt simply would not follow his godly example. A Church that has no complaining is heading for revival!

How did Jesus form leaders and how is this relevant to us today?

We will now look at apostleship in the New Testament as a pattern for leadership. Clearly, not all leaders are apostles, but we can learn principles of leadership from the way that apostles were chosen and trained by Christ Himself.

1. Apostolic Ordination

(a) Apostles/Leaders are Ordained by God

There is only one apostle appointed by human beings in the New Testament, and that is Matthias in Acts 1. While the New Testament does not pour scorn on the procedure adopted for his election, the whole episode is quickly lost in the unfolding of a greater ordination, in the choice of the apostle Paul. The Scripture still refers to the twelve, thus including Matthias, but there is no evidence that his ordination introduced him into the true realms of spiritual apostleship. Paul, like the original twelve, and like Jesus Himself, was never ordained an apostle by anyone but God. He states this quite boldly: "Paul, an apostle, (not of men, neither by man, but by Jesus Christ and God the Father ...)" [Galatians 1:1].

Jesus spent the whole night in prayer and then in the morning chose the twelve [Luke 6:12-13]. Their ordination was founded on the fact that they were to be witnesses of Christ: "He appointed twelve, that they might be with Him" [Mark 3:14]. Closeness to Christ is the chief purpose of apostolic leadership. Without this there is no ministry. It is Christ who is to be the passion and centre of the leader's heart and vision.

(b) The Church Cannot Make Leaders

The Church can only recognise real leaders and praise God for them. There may be many elders in a Church, but it is a great error to therefore assume that they all have the same measure of leadership. Sometimes an eldership is referred to as a joint leadership. This can only be true if all the elders are leaders raised up by God for that purpose. The tragedy is that, when a leader moves on, the assumption is made that the remaining elders will be able to lead the Church forward. This can lead to deep tragedy, as the Church discovers the all too obvious fact that leaders are quite rare. When a Church loses a leader for whatever reason, it must look to God for a new one. It must not just look to the elders, nor must the elders look to themselves to provide something which they do not have. John the Baptist summed this up when he said: "A man can receive nothing unless it has been given him from heaven" [John 3:27]. No elder can go beyond what God has given him.

(c) Leaders are Fathers

At this point it is good to pause and state quite clearly that a Church finds leadership in ministries that have fathered life in the midst of it. This may be from a local man, but will often include men who are not resident in that locality. It will also include a changing group of men, as God introduces freshness into the Church through different ones. Some will visit the Church once; others will develop a deep and ongoing relationship with the Church for a considerable period of time. It is good for the Church to recognise these fathers in Christ, who are more than mere teachers, as Paul declared.

(d) There are More Than 12 Apostles in the New Testament

It is helpful to note the use of the word 'apostle' in the New Testament. There are, first of all, the twelve, followed by Matthias, and then the apostle Paul. In Acts 14:14 Barnabas is referred to as an apostle. Philippians 2:25 refers to Epaphroditus as "your apostle" (or 'messenger'). 2 Corinthians 8:23 refers to Titus and other brothers as the "apostles of the Churches" (or 'messengers').

So we can deduce that there was a general recognition of men in spiritual leadership. This does not mean that these men had any authority over local elderships beyond the influence that comes from mutual love and respect. Neither does it mean that these apostles were to remain dumb in the face of things going wrong in the Churches they were visiting. The force of their authority did not, however, lie in their position, but in the force of the truth that they shared.

It is also true that apostles and leaders are far from being infallible. In fact they are subject to many more temptations and snares, and need the prayers and the fellowship of believers in order to keep their hearts clear. The Churches are littered with examples of what can happen when people are lifted up with the pride of their office or ministry, and go beyond what God has called them to.

The need for fatherhood is not to be forgotten or minimised. Churches have roots that cannot be changed, and it can be dangerous for individuals or Churches to be cut off from the flow of spiritual truth as it has come to them from their 'fathers in Christ'. "Do not remove the ancient landmark which your fathers have set." [Proverbs 22:28].

2. The Apostolic Commission

The apostles were sent out to preach, teach and work miracles. They were endued with power for this ministry, and went out with the exhortation of the Lord as recorded in Matthew 10.

Call to preach in a location can change - the first thing to note is that they were commanded to go only to Israel [Matthew 10:5–6]. This specific commandment was altered by the Lord after His resurrection, when He commanded them to go and preach in all the world. People sometimes cling to a past calling, and miss what God has got for them in a new phase of life and ministry. Life does not develop in straight lines, but turns abrupt corners. George Muller was called to Bristol, and yet at the end of his life spent many years travelling the length and breadth of the world preaching the gospel.

They were also to work miracles [Matthew 10:7-8] - this calling was firmly accompanied by unusual signs and wonders accomplished at various times, taking the progress of the Church a whole leap forward. Paul declared to the Corinthians that the signs of an apostle had been fully worked among them [2 Corinthians 12:12]. But we must also understand that not all ministers are called to do miracles. If people try to go beyond their calling, this error will cause a sense of failure in their hearts. Paul says clearly that not all will work miracles, just as all are not apostles, prophets or teachers [1 Corinthians 12:29]. The best example of this is John the Baptist.

They were to trust God for His provision - they were at liberty to receive support for daily needs from those they ministered to [Matthew 10:9–10].
They were to expect dangers, from people most of all [Matthew 10:17] - but whatever the threatenings and dangers they would be subjected to,

they were not to fear [v26, 28 and 31]. Fear was therefore the chief enemy of the fulfilment of their calling, as conflict was inevitable. This exhortation to the apostles must of course be applied more widely to all ministers of the Lord, but chiefly those who have some prominent ministry such as prophets, evangelists, pastors and teachers. Peter declared in 1 Peter 5:1 that he was a 'fellow elder'. John also showed it was the title he preferred, never once in his writings referring to himself as an apostle.

3. Key Revelations for Apostles/Leaders

The apostles were called to be close to Jesus, which was the most important part of their apostleship. They were to walk with Him and continue with Him in His temptations [Luke 22:28]. This meant that they were to be witnesses of the great events of His life, including His miracles and His resurrection. But most of all they were to be witnesses of the inner secrets of His life and kingdom.

These inner secrets are the foundation of His Church. They are innumerable and unsearchable and yet the main characteristics can be discerned in three key Scriptures. These were events from which the Lord excluded the crowds, and even nine of the apostles. They were events in which He revealed something about Himself. In each event He expressly took only Peter, James and John with Him and on the first two occasions He made it clear that they were not to repeat what they had seen. We will consider each of these events.

4. Event 1: The Raising of Jairus's Daughter
[Mark 5:21-43]

This event shows us that the secret of true power is love. It came at the end of an incredibly busy phase of powerful ministry by Jesus. He had taught by Lake Galilee, crossed the lake, delivered the Gadarene, recrossed the lake to be met by huge crowds, and amongst them He had received Jairus's earnest request to come and heal his dying daughter. The Lord had not hesitated, but had immediately followed Jairus.

On their way, a woman with a haemorrhage lasting 12 years had touched Him. She had done this secretly as if she believed she could 'pick His pocket' and take away her healing without Him noticing. The reason for this was that she knew the Law, which declared that anyone touching a person defiled with blood would instantly become unclean. No Pharisee would have allowed her to approach him. Her tragedy was that her sickness separated her from all touch and affection. How true this is of sin - that by it our hearts become strangers to the inner awareness of God's love. The wonder of the whole event is that, when she was discovered, she heard the Lord's voice calling out, not with disgust or condemnation, but with love and kindness. His voice drew confession from her lips and she told Him everything in a few words. How great her delight and wonder, when she heard the blessed words of adoption from His lips: "Daughter, your faith has made you well. Go in peace and be healed of your affliction." [Mark 5:34].

And then the news came to Jairus: "Your daughter is dead." This was met by the quiet confidence of the Lord: "Only believe". The sight of the mourners was an offence to Jesus, knowing their hypocrisy, but this did not stop Him from seeking to win them. He declared the wonderful truth of faith, that death is not the cessation of life; it is only a temporary rest in the bosom of the Father at the end of life's day, whether that day be long or short. Death is sleep, and is just the prelude to the morning, when the dead in Christ shall awake and arise. But the mourners had no faith in God's word, which often spoke of death as sleep - as when "David slept (or rested) with his fathers" [1 Kings 2:10].

So Jesus drove the mourners away, and took the girl's parents and the three apostles in with Him. There He again defied the Law of uncleanness, which said that He could not touch a dead body without defilement. He took the girl by the hand and said the words: "Talitha Cumi", which means, "My little pet lamb, I say to you, arise." [Mark 5:41].

Here lie foundational principles of Church life; chiefly, that power does not lie in great noise, but in tender love. But further to this, that power lies in a word from God, spoken in a whisper. True leaders must lead the flock to such a saviour, for the tender lambs will not open to anyone else. God has not called leaders simply to lead for the sake of leading! They are called to lead men and women to the fountains of living waters.

5. Event 2: The Transfiguration
[Mark 9:2-10]

Here was a truly remarkable revelation. Christ led them up the mountain, and there His form was changed, and they saw unspeakable glory. They saw beyond the veil of Christ's human flesh into the glory of heaven itself - seeing even the glorified Moses and Elijah. Finally they heard the voice of the Father Himself speaking directly and audibly.

Here in this simple and direct confrontation with the invisible Kingdom of God lie the foundations of that kingdom. The first is in the brightness of the holiness and the glory. They witnessed a light and a purity, such as none on earth could ever equal, and this was the inner life of Christ shining through. All leaders must have some awareness of glory, of surpassing holiness. Without this they will falter in the face of the surpassing evil that is in the world. They will not keep going unless they know there is a sinless One, who can never be defiled, and who has lived in this world without defilement. His Church is glorious, because she is bone of His bone, flesh of His flesh, partaking of His glory by His indwelling in our hearts through the person of the Holy Spirit. The early Church did not have great programmes or detailed strategies. Their leaders were imprisoned, persecuted and executed - quite a pattern to follow! But through all the conflict came the blazing awareness of the reality of the unseen Christ glorified at the right hand of the Father. It is small wonder that Stephen's face also shone like that of an angel while beholding the glory of God, and Jesus standing at God's right hand [Acts 7:55-56].

The words of the Father to the three apostles are also an open window into the Godhead. The simple declaration was: "This is My beloved Son, hear him." [Mark 9:7]. This revealed to them what it means to be loved. The Church is to be a declaration to the world of what it is to be loved by God.

Insecurity is the most common cause of failure. A leader must know what it is to be loved by God. He will then not be filled with fears and insecurities. This is a revolutionary state of being, since the world does not know what it is like to be loved through and through, till there are no more fears and worries, till there is no more condemnation.

6. Event 3: The Agony in Gethsemane
[Mark 14:32-42]

In Gethsemane, the Lord again took only Peter, James and John with Him to witness the awful agony that came on His soul there in the garden.

Leaders must in some degree witness the soul-rending agony that crushed the soul of the Lord Jesus in the garden. This agony was the experience of the Son of Man, i.e. of Christ in His manhood. It is significantly absent from John's Gospel, which concentrates on Christ as the Son of God, and thus also does not describe the temptations in the wilderness. This does not mean that Christ was a divided personality, sometimes acting as God and sometimes as man. Christ was fully human and fully divine, and the love of God that burned in His heart caused the Man Christ Jesus to agonise over human sin with a sorrow that brought Him to the gates of death.
Such a physical state is quite rare and yet is not unknown in human hearts. The grief of bereavement has claimed people's lives, and Christ, there in the garden, declared that the sorrow He bore was crushing Him nearly to death. He prayed for strength, for he wanted to

prevail and persevere to the cross so that He might die not only of a broken heart, but also as the sacrifice for the sins of the whole world.

People guess at God's nature, but no-one really knows either the Father or the Son unless they are revealed. The Church is founded on the revelation of God in Christ. Jesus declared this to Peter, when he saw in a flash the truth beyond flesh and blood that the Son of God was here. Jesus said that He would build His Church on this revelation. He surely did not mean that He would build His Church on the mere doctrine of Christ's divinity, but that He would build it on the revelation to human hearts of Christ's true nature. This is apostolic mission - to know Him, and to declare Him in the midst of the Church, and also to a dying world, so that the invisible God might be fully known throughout the length and breadth of the earth.

This definition of apostolic ministry includes all the main ministries of the Church that operate in some measure of leadership in the Church. Prophets, evangelists, pastors and teachers must all, to some degree, be people who declare the unseen riches of Christ.

PAUL'S TEACHING ON APOSTLES'/LEADERS' ATTITUDE

The New Testament is full of lessons on leadership, especially from the writings of the great apostle Paul. Paul's teachings lie at the foundation of the whole subject.

1. The Apostle and Humility

A pattern emerged in the middle of the 20th century of leaders who became an elite. They kept themselves apart from the ordinary believers and encouraged the concept of a special group, living on a higher plane. There are elements of truth in this, and clearly leaders should be spiritual people. But Paul teaches an apostleship based not on elitism but on humility and service. The words he uses to describe leaders are very instructive:

Doulos: this is the Greek word for a slave and is used by Paul to describe himself frequently [Titus 1:1; Galatians 1:10; Romans 1:1]. Paul uses it to describe every servant of God [2 Timothy 2:24] and most importantly he says that Jesus Christ took on Himself the form of a slave. There are many implications:

A slave was owned by someone else! This means that Christ was owned by His Father, and Paul was owned by God. This is one of the key applications of the cross in our personal life. We are bought with a price and we no longer belong to ourselves.

THE CHALLENGE OF LEADERSHIP

A slave had no possessions of his own; he could not choose when he worked, when he had time off, what he wore, or where he lived. His whole life was an extension of his master's life.

A slave had no wages, no rights.

He was given all he needed for food, clothing and shelter. It was a secure life, but miserable unless he loved his master.

Paul describes himself as a bond slave of Jesus and he clearly enjoyed this position. Every leader must have the attitude of a love slave to Jesus. Note that it is Christ, not the Church, who is his master. The leader serves humbly in the Church, as a slave who does not seek primarily to please the people he is serving at dinner, but to please his master, who has given him the job to do and is watching how he does it. The slave may not even like some of the people he has to serve, but he does it well and gladly because he knows that his service will bring his master glory.

When Christ washed the disciples' feet in the upper room in John 13, he dressed Himself as a slave and did the job of the lowest slave. Other slaves would prepare the bowl and the towels, but it was the lowest slave who would wash the guests' feet. Christ said that this was the pattern for His kingdom and that His disciples must do as He did.

Diakonos: this is the simple Greek word for a servant; it indicates something like a waiter, and refers quite frequently to those who serve at tables. It is often thought that the seven men chosen in Acts 6 to serve at tables are the original pattern for the office of a deacon. Christ called Himself a 'deacon' in Matthew 20:26 and commanded His apostles to be servants to all. A waiter in a restaurant is the best picture. He is someone who attends to the needs of those who sit at table, watching for the moment that they will need him to serve them. Yet he does not intrude upon those he serves, but is self-effacing.

Uperetes: this is the Greek word for an 'under-rower', who was the lowest worker on a Roman ship. They were often despised criminals who were chained to their posts. They certainly had no choice where they sat, and their attention had to be given to the task in hand, or the whole movement of the ship was affected. The word is used by Paul in 1 Corinthians 4:1 of himself and other ministers.

Clearly Paul viewed his ministry in a very humble light. The underlying truth of all this is that a leader is dispensable, and able to take orders without fearing for his reputation. He is a slave of Christ and most delighted to do His will.

2. The Apostle and Money

Paul clearly believed that pastors were to be supported by the offerings of the local Church. In 1 Corinthians 9 he explains that soldiers, farm workers and shepherds must get some profit from their work, even if it is just the milk from the flock [v7]. He quotes the Old Testament that even the ox treading out the corn must eat, and is allowed to eat the corn it is walking on [v9].

There is little controversy in the concept of pastors and leaders being supported by the Church, and there will be different methods for that support according to how the Lord leads different ministries. However, the interesting thing is that Paul himself declined to accept financial support. 1 Corinthians 9 is Paul's account of his determination to remain free from the snares that can result from receiving pay from the Church. In a way, the snares are obvious, but they still need to be stated:

Paul was determined to make sure that the gospel was preached without charge. He did not want anyone to think that the gospel would be preached for financial reward.

Ministers must not be greedy for gain. Paul describes in Acts 20:33-35 that he worked to support others and himself. He had demonstrated generosity, and a willingness to work hard with his hands.

Ministers must be careful not to become servants of people. In Galatians 1:10 Paul states that if he were a people-pleaser he would cease to be the servant of Christ. Salaries can have this effect, and in some sad cases, Churches have withheld the salary of the pastor if they were unhappy with his preaching. Pastors and leaders must be accountable but they must also know that they are not preaching to please people, but God who called them.

The love of money can destroy a ministry. In 1 Timothy 6:6-10 Paul describes the danger of loving money. When blessing comes through a leader's ministry, people will offer him gifts - sometimes very large gifts. Paul says that the love of money is a root of all kinds of evil, but mainly that it produces all kinds of lusts, which in turn cause people to be pierced with sorrows.

The sin of Balaam. Balaam was invited to speak to Balak but God commanded him not to go [Numbers 22:12]. Then Balak renewed the invitation by sending important princes, to impress Balaam with a promise of great financial reward [Numbers 22:15-17]. God told Balaam to go with them if they invited him again in the morning. But Balaam was so filled with lust for the reward that he did not wait for the princes to invite him, but simply went with them. God was merciful to Balaam and did not slay him, and spoke faithfully through him.

THE CHALLENGE OF LEADERSHIP

But Balaam sold his soul to sinful men to co-operate with them for financial gain.

The doctrine of Balaam [Numbers 31:16]. The result was that, in the end, Balaam was completely corrupted; he advised Balak that the only way to defeat Israel was to entice the people to commit sin, by bowing down to the Midianite idols and committing fornication with the Midianite women [Numbers 25:1-2]. The result was that Israel lost its spiritual authority, until Phinehas put an end to the corruption by his act of executing a guilty couple. Jesus warned the Church at Pergamos that they were allowing this kind of ministry to continue in that Church. It would be characterised by:

- Indicating to believers that it is not a sin to sleep together before marriage, and that the occasional sexual transgression is normal!
- A seeking to 'smooth out' the difficulties for people to be Church members, by diluting the New Testament standards of righteousness and holiness.
- Omitting to preach strongly against sin in the Church; perhaps focusing on subjects such as the Second Coming or prosperity, but neglecting personal holiness.

The sin of Judas. Clearly Paul expected the highest standards from a leader of God in matters pertaining to money. The worst example in the whole Bible is that of Judas, who was clearly called to be an apostle. Some have speculated that, when Judas fell, Paul was ultimately given his ministry. Judas might have had the most prominent ministry of all the apostles if he had not fallen. Judas was simply a thief, and he saw that the position he was in could make him rich [John 12:6]. He stole from the bag of offerings that were given directly to Jesus by those He ministered to. Judas took from this money, and finally sold Jesus for 30 pieces of silver. It is possible he only thought that Jesus would exhibit further authority, and escape by some supernatural means. Whatever the case, he was blinded by the possibility of earning some money for nothing. He betrayed Jesus, but he also betrayed himself by selling his soul and his conscience in order to obtain money. All ministers must fear the thin end of the wedge. It is easy to exaggerate and even lie in order to impress congregations and obtain money.

A missionary once saw a prayer letter showing a 'missionary couple' standing in front of his own house and Church building. The prayer letter claimed that this was the couple's work in Africa; but the missionary had never seen the couple before! A fraudulent act like this is an offence of conscience and endangers the spiritual life of those who commit it.

---

3. The Apostle and Other Ministries

Paul had respect for other ministries. He always travelled with other ministers like Barnabas and Silas. He gave honour to the different ministries of people such as Peter and Apollos [1 Corinthians 3:3]. Leaders should promote other ministries, not just their own.

4. The Apostle and Suffering

Paul suffered terrible beatings, stoning, shipwrecks and other traumas for the sake of the gospel [2 Corinthians 11:23-33 and 12:1-10]. He saw a clear relationship between spiritual power and suffering. He believed that through weakness God would keep him in the attitude and position in which he could be used. This principle of ministry is brought out also in other verses in 2 Corinthians:

- 1:9 *"Yes, we had the sentence of death in ourselves, that we should not trust in ourselves but in God who raises the dead."*

- 4:10 *"...always carrying about in the body the dying of the Lord Jesus, that the life of Jesus also may be manifested in our body."* (See also verses 7-12 of the same chapter.)

Paul clearly saw suffering as an essential part of ministry. The deeper and greater the ministry, the more the suffering! In this light, it should provoke a deep humility in God's servants, and a realisation that the countries which suffer persecution may be streets ahead of the West spiritually.

LEADERSHIP IN ISRAEL

Eldership has been the pattern of government among God's people since the beginning. Abraham was the father of his household and the elder of all there with him, though he is only once referred to as an elder, in Hebrews 11:1. The same became true of Isaac and Jacob. Later in Exodus, Moses declared the word of God to the elders of Israel. There is no indication how many there were, nor how they were recognised. The inference is that the number was not fixed, and that there was no formal recognition - through maturity and wisdom, men natu-

THE CHALLENGE OF LEADERSHIP

rally became elders of the nation. It was the inevitable destiny of men who were responsible.

In Exodus 18, Moses took Jethro's common-sense advice and organised the whole nation so that the strain of leadership did not fall solely on him. This was good advice, but it seems to have been premature. It is easy to make elders because it seems a good idea, and yet, as in the case of Matthias in Acts 1, we are left with the sense that the whole process did no good either to the men appointed or to the nation. The process took on a different dimension with divine approval, when Moses was called up the mountain to receive further revelation. He was commanded in Exodus 24 to bring 70 of the elders of Israel with him. This indicates that these 70 were called to something higher than the other elders. One year later, in Numbers 11, Moses had reached the depths of despair. It seems that the men appointed in Exodus 18 had not helped bear the real burdens of leadership. Moses cried out to God to provide more men [Numbers 11:14-15]. God ordered him to gather 70 of the elders of Israel, and then the Lord anointed them with the spirit of prophecy, thus granting them power for the work to which they were called.

In this we can see the principle that human timing is often premature. We may see and feel the need, and act on the common-sense wisdom that is at our disposal. But this must fail. There must be a sense of the moving of God in the appointing of leaders, or else their ordination means nothing, and can even damage the flock. The elders of Israel were never to replace Moses. When Moses died, there was never a question of them taking up the leadership of Israel. God raised up a new leader - Joshua. Their role was to help in the administration of Israel and to assist God's chosen leader. This, of course, included their duty to admonish and correct that leader if he should need it.

Finally, the title of 'elder' in the Old Testament refers to the fact that they were older, probably grey-headed! This is sanctified common-sense.

CHURCH LEADERSHIP IN THE NEW TESTAMENT
1. The Tradition of the Elders: a Warning!

The first mention of eldership in the New Testament is in the context of Israel. Jesus foretells that he must suffer many things from the elders, the chief priests and the scribes [Matthew 16:21]. On another occasion, the Pharisees question Him because His disciples do not keep the 'tradition of the elders'. The Lord rebukes them for making the word of God of no effect by that very tradition, by exalting it above the word of God [Mark 7:1-9]. There can be little doubt that this is as great a danger for elders of the Church as it was for those of Israel. Elders must take note that, by their attitudes and actions, they will set traditions in process that may well outlive them!

> *When William Carey presented his paper on the need for missionary outreach at a Baptist ministers' conference, a Dr Rylands said: "Sit down young man; when God chooses to convert the heathen, He will do it without your aid or mine!"*
>
> *In fairness to Dr Rylands, however, when Carey did persist and founded the missionary society, Dr Rylands became one of his ardent supporters.*

2. Key References to Elders

The first mention of Church elders is in Acts 11:30, referring to the elders of the Church at Jerusalem. There is no clue as to how or when they were ordained. It is clear that the apostles themselves functioned as the first elders. But equally, by Acts 15:2, reference is made to the apostles and elders as distinct roles in the Church.

The first mention of the ordination of elders in local Churches is in Acts 14:23, where Paul and Barnabas are seen ordaining local elders in the new Churches that had sprung up only weeks beforehand. Doubtless then, all of these elders were spiritual novices, to say the least. This pattern of ordaining elders by outside help is confirmed in Titus, where Paul enjoins Titus to remember that he had been sent to Crete specifically to ordain men to this office.

A large eldership is implied in Acts 20, where Paul addresses the eldership of the Church at Ephesus in the port of Miletus. Here again, these men had become Christians just 3 years previously. The final mention of elders is in Revelation, where they are seen in heaven, glorified and crowned, surrounding the throne and worshipping.

3. Key Conclusions

We can draw several conclusions from these accounts:

- **Leaders/elders were vital** for the smooth running of local assemblies.

- **Leaders/elders were not necessarily spiritually mature.** That they were spiritually clear can be taken for granted, but their qualifications for eldership were not merely spiritual - they were also natural and to do with their maturity and stability as men.

- **Leaders or apostles ordained the first elders.** At the outset of a work, the elders must be recognised by those involved in founding the local assembly.

- **Subsequent leaders/elders are chosen by the Church.** We must not conclude that all elders are ordained or chosen by apostles. This is the pattern at the outset. But later the elders and the Church functioning together agree on further ordinations.

- **The role of leaders/elders** can be discerned in these New Testament chapters. They were not to be the only ministers in the Church, nor were they ordained as ministers primarily. They were ordained as those who would guide the Church through the difficult questions as they arose. Doubtless too, in the early Church, they would have to be fearless men, answering to the authorities for the activities of the Churches under their charge. Many of these first elders were to meet martyrdom, and thus were to be examples to the flock.

- **Elders around the throne.** The final lesson is from the scene around the throne [Revelation 4]. Here we can see that there are elders in heaven, recognised by God. This does not mean that all elders on earth will automatically have a place in that august assembly! Their number will probably include men of stature in the faith, like Moses and Elijah, and perhaps also Booth, Wesley etc. No-one can aspire to be among their number, for that is the choice of God alone. However, we can see the principle that elders have entered into an awareness of God on the throne, and their lives are filled with a sense of wonder. If a man loses the sense of awe and wonder about God, he has ceased to worship, and is no longer able to function as an elder.

THE ROLE OF LEADERS
1. To Give a Covering of Wisdom and Maturity

The appointment of elders is not merely about recognising someone's spiritual gift or ministry. Elders can be assumed to have gifting; they may be apostles or prophets, evangelists, pastors and teachers, and may possess a variety of gifts, from miracles, to discernment, to the gift of tongues. But eldership has also a natural role. Men must be **stable** in their personality and simply **mature**. Without these qualities, no amount of spiritual ministry is sufficient. But equally, no amount of natural maturity and wisdom are sufficient - there must be spiritual life too. Eldership, then, is a blend of the natural and the spiritual.

Eldership is defined by the most common word used for it in the New Testament – 'presbuteros' - an older one. This word occurs 61 times in the New Testament. (The second word for elder, 'episkopos' - overseer, occurs a mere 5 times.) The force of the word does not lie merely in being older. This can never in itself be a foundation for office in the Church. The word includes all the positive virtues associated with age - maturity, experience and wisdom, to name but a few. The opposite would be the term 'young man'. The qualities of youth that cannot bear office are impetuosity, inexperience, immaturity etc. Churches cannot be led by inexperienced or immature people. The Holy Spirit takes up the wisdom of years, and produces men of stature, able to lead and guide the Church.

The role of eldership, then, is first to offer the covering of spiritual and natural wisdom and maturity. The expectation of the Scripture is that all men will move steadily into the maturity of being fathers in Christ, and will begin to share in some measure in the leadership of the local assembly, taking responsibility seriously, in a sober manner. The body of elders in a growing congregation should be increasing. The key thing at this point is to distinguish between the call and anointing to lead, which makes a man a **leader** among elders, and the qualities of spiritual and natural maturity that make a man an elder.

2. Watchful Oversight

- **Watching for danger** - the word *episkopos* means an overseer. Elders are shepherds who must watch over their flocks. They are to be like the watchmen on the walls of Jerusalem, looking at the horizon for approaching danger.

In Krakow, in the 13th century, the Tatars surrounded the city in the middle of the night. One lone watchman became aware of them and sounded his trumpet at midnight, only to be shot by an arrow in the middle of his trumpet call. The tradition has been kept over centuries, and a trumpet blast is made, cut short right in the middle. That watchman saved the city, and his bravery is remembered as a warning to all to be vigilant.

- **Watching for God** - the elders on the watchtower, like Habakkuk, are there to hear what God will say to the flock, and to see what God wants to do among His people [Habakkuk 2:1].

- **Watching over people's souls** - *"Obey those who have the rule over you, and be submissive, for they watch out for your souls, as those who must give account. Let them do so with joy and not with grief, for that would be unprofitable for you."* [Hebrews 13:17]. Elders must be vigilant about the things that are happening in the lives of their flock. They must be aware of wrong doctrines coming in, and of people's carnal ambitions. They must watch to try and correct these things before they take a hold.

3. Going Ahead

In Romans 12:8 and 1 Thessalonians 5:12 the Greek word *proisteemi* is used, translated as to **rule** or **be over** others. The word literally means to **take the lead** or **stand before**. Elders must have overcome any self-conscious shyness about standing in front of people. They are not to be lost in the crowd when leadership is required. They *are* to be lost in the crowd at all other times though!

Elders must rule, which means that the Church must sense that there is someone in control who is safe and who is sensitive. This should mean that the Church has a deep sense of security, knowing that there are men aware of their responsibility for the ministry that is conducted in the meetings. In the Old Testament, the elders of the city sat in the gate, in public view, and were aware of who came into the city, and who left.

4. Steering the Course

In 1 Corinthians 12:28, Paul tells us of a spiritual gift of 'governments' (KJV). This does not mean that all elders have this gift; but it does mean that there is a gift of being able to see the answer for the present situation by a word or an insight from God, which brings light to the Church as it seeks guidance and direction. The Greek word for this gift, *kubernesis,* is the word for steering or piloting.

5. Ruling

This is perhaps the most difficult aspect of an elder's role to swallow in our modern age. But this word (Greek *haigoumenos*) is used of Jesus in Matthew 2:6, and of elders in Hebrews 13:7, 17 and 24. Elders are not policemen, and they have no police to enforce their rule. They can only have as much authority as the people recognise. Thus, Jeremiah had no authority in Israel.

This ruling of God's house should not be for selfish purposes or self-aggrandisement, though men can use it that way. The rule of elders involves the handing on of God's rule over people's souls. David gives the key: *"He who rules over men must be just, ruling in the fear of God. And he shall be like the light of the morning when the sun rises, a morning without clouds; like the tender grass springing out of the earth by clear shining after rain."* [2 Samuel 23:3-4].

There can be no doubt that elders must rule; sometimes they must enforce discipline, and they must correct, restrain or exhort. At times they will have to exclude those whose conduct is shameful to the Church. If elders will not rule, then other spirits and other people will wreak havoc in the Church.

6. Shepherding

The whole dimension of ruling is tempered by this word (Greek *poimaino*), used frequently of Christ and also of elders. The verb is used in Matthew 2:6, John 21:16 (only!), Acts 20:28 and 1 Peter 5:2. The word is often mistranslated 'feed'. A better translation is 'tend'. Shepherds are to **tend** their flock, which includes feeding, but is much more to do with overall care. All elders must have a shepherd's heart though not all will have the distinct pastoral ministry.

A key passage is John 21:15-17. Here Jesus draws Peter's attention to the fact that the key to tending His flock is to have a heart of love for Jesus, the Chief Shepherd, as Peter calls Him in 1 Peter 5:4. Jesus gives three commands to Peter. The first is the Greek word *bosko* (to feed), the second is the word 'tend' or 'shepherd' (Greek *poimaino*), the third is the word 'feed' again. This highlights the fact that shepherding the flock means they must be fed and watered. The food that the sheep require is love, but this must include the ministry of the word. This is because there must be a constant supply of the word from the heart of God to His people. If there is a vacuum in the realm of the word, then souls will become weak and dry, and a prey to other words. Error needs ground to abound. The most fertile ground for it is rebellion and pride. But it will also grow well where there is no preaching of the word of God.

7. Stewards of God [Titus 1:7]

This title was given to elders by Paul, and is perhaps the greatest role imaginable. It refers to the fact that elders are those who manage God's house and run His affairs. This may seem simple enough, but God's house is twofold - first it is God Himself, and secondly it is His people. To be the steward of His people is already a high calling, but to be a steward of God Himself is indescribable.

God is not known intimately outside of the Church. If there is no Church in a locality, then God remains unknown, along with all the riches that lie hidden in God. The great calling to be an elder is most of all to be immersed in the consciousness of God and to be aware of Him. As the world looks on the Church, they must see the revelation of God. Thus this must be true of elders. They must accurately reflect God, and be seen to be not masters of their own house, but stewards of the very person of God.

It must be said reverently, but it is nonetheless true, that those who hand out the communion bread and wine are symbolically serving God to the people. Elders are to handle, not the symbols alone, but the very person of God to men and women. They hand out His very presence, His substance, as they move among the people. This could, of course, easily turn into priest-craft. All the people are priests to God. But we should not miss the truth that those who minister are themselves called to be first the partakers of all the things that they minister. The Church itself is the pillar and the ground of the truth. God Himself dwells there, His presence is known there, and there too His stewards dwell with Him, full of faith and of the Holy Spirit.

THE ROLE OF DEACONS

The Greek word is *diakonos*, referring to a minister or servant. Unlike the word 'elder', there is no reference to age, nor to taking oversight of the flock. The emphasis here is not on authority and responsibility, but rather on ministry and a desire to serve the Lord in the midst of His people. This may include practical matters such as being a treasurer, but it is wrong to assume that this is the only realm in which deacons are to function. They have a heart to serve and to be available to help God's people wherever and whenever the need arises. It is abundantly clear that all elders must also be deacons. Jesus Himself said that He had come to serve (*diakoneo*). He said that he who would be greatest must be the deacon (servant) of all [Luke 22:26-27].

The emphasis here, then, is not on age; young people can be deacons - the seven men ordained in Acts 6 were probably young and eager to serve. Deaconhood is not a grade lower than an elder, it is a different grade. God's divisions are vertical, man's are horizontal. To be a deacon is to attain a high office - the highest - but it is distinct from eldership. Some deacons will never be able to bear the pressure of responsibility for the Church; they function best in joyful fulfilment of service.

A deacon's role also extends to spiritual ministry. There are many people who have gift and unction from God for some ministry, but lack all the wisdom and maturity to bear responsibility for the Church. To appoint people as deacons should mean including them in the leadership of the Church as pertains to ministry. Leaders' meetings can be dominated by needs and problems, but deacons can often be much more forward-looking, seeking opportunities for the work to grow through prayer and ministry. It should be a joy for a body of ordained elders and deacons to meet together to pray and plan. Such inclusive meetings will foster maturity and responsibility, giving every possibility that men may become elders - though it is unhelpful to think of deacons as trainee elders!

Qualifications are identical to those for elders. The one point of potential difference is the question of whether there should be deaconesses. The question of female elders does not arise, because that is distinctly a position of authority, and God has made it clear that women are not to rule over men [1 Timothy 2:12]. Phoebe was declared by Paul to be a servant of the Church at Cenchrea, and the word used here is 'deaconess' [Romans 16:1]. Since the office does not bear authority, but refers rather to service, there is no reason why women should be barred. In fact they will add a new dimension to the leadership meetings.

QUALIFICATIONS FOR LEADERSHIP/ELDERSHIP

Virtually all the qualifications are to do with a leader's personal life and character.

- **Blameless** - the first qualification in both 1Timothy 3:1-7 and Titus 1:6-9 is 'blameless'. This does not mean that the person must be perfect in every way. Peter was far from perfect, and denied the Lord three times under extreme pressure. He became embroiled in compromise while visiting the Church at Antioch [Galatians 2:11-21], but his eldership is not called into question. Elders must, however, be free from charges of misconduct as detailed by the apostle Paul. They must not be violent or rough, they must not be greedy for money or possessions. They must not be in trouble with people outside the

Church. They must not be given to drinking wine. These qualities are self-evident, lest he dishonour the name of the Lord and His people.

- **An ordered home** - the home reveals the true state of a person's heart. For this reason, a wife can easily disqualify her husband from office by indulging in gossip, or causing the home to be a place where believers do not feel comfortable for any reason. The state of the marriage is a key indicator as to whether a man can bear office, as is the manner in which he cares for and controls his children.

- **Vigilant, sober, patient** - these are qualities of positive proof of character. It is not enough to be free from grosser problems; there must be spiritual alertness, a serious demeanour, and an ability to listen and wait.

- **Apt to teach**, holding fast the faithful word - elders must not be silent. They must be able to express the mind of God and give clear expression to the truth of God on a regular basis. Some men regard silence as a great virtue, but there are moments when it is vital that an answer be given. At such moments, leaders must articulate what God is saying.

These qualifications are indicators as to whether a man should be ordained to the office of elder. They do not indicate the work he is to accomplish; they are the foundation on which he will do it. They can be summed up with the realisation that, as people observe elders, they must to some degree behold God in the flesh. This is also true of the whole Church, and must not be exaggerated - or no-one would dare to take on leadership responsibility. Nevertheless, in all areas of his life, an elder must consistently display the life and nature of God.

A quote from Spurgeon on the nature of true leadership:

"Labour to gather a Church alive for Jesus, every member energetic to the full, and the whole in incessant activity for the salvation of men. To this end there must be the best of preaching to feed the host into strength, continual prayer to bring down the power from on high, and the most heroic example on your own part to fire their zeal: then, under the divine blessing, a common-sense management of the entire force cannot fail to produce the most desirable issues. Who among you can grasp this idea and embody it in actual fact?"

10

THE PREACHING MINISTRY

THE NEED TO DECLARE GOD'S TRUTH

The preaching ministry is crucial because these are days where the prevailing philosophy is **existentialism** – that is, the belief that each individual must shape his or her own reality by his or her own choices. Existentialism rejects absolutes, whether religious or moral. People now do not wait to be told what to do; they wait to be engaged in discussion. The mind-set of the 21st century does not want to be instructed about the universe, but to help to form its own. This is the opposite of the preaching ministry, which declares the truth of God and demands response. No matter how unpopular, the Church must not compromise on the preaching ministry.

Paul says: *"For since, in the wisdom of God, the world through wisdom did not know God, it pleased God through the foolishness of the message preached to save those who believe."* [1 Corinthians 1:21].

God has decided that the gospel is to be preached. Jesus Himself was a preacher, and Paul declares that it was his calling [1 Corinthians 1:17]. Churches may have many programmes, but they cannot substitute anything for the preaching ministry. They may be involved in social action, and perhaps run hospitals or schools, but none of these can ever be a substitute for the Word of God being preached. Even counselling, Alpha courses, etc. cannot replace God's chosen method of having truth declared.

THE PREACHING MINISTRY

The Greek words for preaching are:

Evangelizo: To make known the good news about Jesus and salvation.

Kerusso: To herald the truth of the kingdom, the greatness of God, the power of the cross. The herald goes before the king and declares the imminent arrival of the king, who is following behind. John the Baptist was the King's herald – he opened the door for Jesus. The preacher is a herald who opens the door for Jesus to enter the lives and situations of the people.

ESSENTIAL FOUNDATIONS OF THE PREACHING MINISTRY
1. The Baptism with the Holy Spirit

The Lord commanded His apostles not to go into all the world until they were endued with power from on high [Luke 24:49; Acts 1:8]. The baptism with the Holy Spirit made the apostles witnesses of the supreme victory of the cross. It made them witnesses of Christ and of His death and resurrection, because it united them with the power of the cross. Many people have known the incredible transformation of their ministry through the baptism with the Holy Spirit.

The testimony of D.L. Moody

D.L. Moody was a successful minister but, by his own admission later, he lacked the power in his ministry. One day two women came up to him after a service. They said, "We have been praying for you." "Why don't you pray for the people?" he asked. "Because you need the power of the Spirit", they said. "I need the power! Why", said Moody, in relating the incident years after, "I thought I had power. I had the largest congregations in Chicago, and there were many conversions."

Moody also said that, in a sense, he was satisfied. He was in a comfort zone. But these two praying women rocked the boat. They told him that they were praying for an anointing by the Holy Spirit for him to have a special service to God. He could not get this off his mind and he said, "There came a great hunger in my soul. I did not know what it was and I began to cry out to God as never before. I felt I did not want to live if I could not have this power for service".

After the great fire of Chicago, Moody was working to raise money to rebuild a tabernacle. He said his heart was not in it because he kept crying out to God to fill him. During a visit to New York to raise money, he withdrew and prayed; he cried that God would fill him with His Spirit. He described it this way: "Well, one day, in the city of New York -- oh, what a day! -- I cannot describe it, I seldom refer to it; it is almost too sacred an experience to name. Paul had an experience of which he never spoke for 14 years. I can only say that God revealed Himself to me, and I had such an experience of His love that I had to ask Him to stay His hand. I went to preaching again. The sermons were not different; I did not present any new truths, and yet hundreds were converted. I would not now be placed back where I was before that blessed experience if you should give me all the world -- it would be as the small dust of the balance."

The baptism with the Holy Spirit makes us witnesses not just when we are preaching but also when we are living. Jesus said: *"You shall **be** witnesses to Me"* [Acts 1:8]. By the baptism with the Spirit, there is power without striving, because it is the grace and power of God at work.

2. The Messenger is also the Message

The preacher and the message must be one. The preacher is ministering concerning someone greater than himself, but he is a channel and he must be pure. Just as we want to drink pure water from a clean cup, so too we must hear the gospel through clean vessels. It is true that God can use even a donkey, but this is not His chosen method! The preacher will impart his own heart state; this impacts the hearers when they hear preaching. They can tell if the preacher is in faith, fear, unbelief or frustration. A congregation can soon tell if the preacher is a hard or a loving person. If the preacher talks about something he has not experienced, the congregation will soon realise this. If he is preaching about the baptism with the Holy Spirit, then obviously he must be full of the Holy Spirit.

Every voice is from a spirit: either God's, man's or Satan's. When we preach we minister the states of our own hearts in some measure. This is why we must make sure that we are in communion with God, and that we are speaking and ministering the knowledge of God. If we are in gross sin in our hearts, God will not allow us to continue in the ministry. He will not have hypocrites representing His kingdom.

3. Judgment Begins at the House of God...and with the Preachers

Peter explains that, when Christ returns, judgment must begin at the house of God [1 Peter 4:17]. Christ describes the Day of Judgment in Matthew 24:42–25:46. He begins by explaining that the first people to be judged will be the servants of His house.

The word He uses for His 'house' (in the Greek text of the KJV) is *therapeia*, which can be taken to mean 'house of healing' [Matthew 24:45]. The Church is intended to be a place of healing of wounds; but Jesus describes some servants as inflicting wounds on others [Matthew 24:49]. Preachers can inflict wounds on their hearers. Jesus said that the scribes (or lawyers) laid burdens on people that were heavy for them to bear [Matthew 23:4; Luke 11:46]. He also said that such servants who wound others will be dismembered or cut into pieces when He returns [Matthew 24:51]!

Clearly, Jesus views the preaching ministry as very importance. As James says: *"...let not many of you become teachers, knowing that we shall receive a stricter judgment"* [James 3:1]. Jesus said that if we break the least commandment and teach others to do so, we shall be called least in the Kingdom of Heaven [Matthew 5:19]. Clearly it is an awesome act to stand before people and teach them the ways of God, and His word.

Jesus said in Matthew 24:45 that faithful servants are those who feed His flock the right food in the right season. This means that preachers must discern the right food for the flock, and not repeat their favourite topics! On at least three occasions elders/pastors are exhorted to feed (or shepherd) the flock of God [John 21:15-17; Acts 20:28; 1 Peter 5:2]. The food of the flock is clearly the Word; but this cannot mean mere Bible knowledge, or professors would be the best pastors. Jesus reveals to Peter that the food of the flock is available when a pastor truly loves Him. Jesus did not want to know how much time Peter spent in prayer or how much of the Scriptures he read daily. He asked Peter if he loved Him. If we love Jesus, we will have food for the flock and we will minister healing to the flock as we feed them.

4. The Released Preacher Must First be Released in Prayer

Preaching is not a lecture. It is an interaction between God and people to declare the truth of God. There is of necessity a prophetic dimension to preaching. Not that the word 'prophecy' is the New Testament word for preaching - this would require a strained interpretation of the word 'prophecy'. But the prophetic element in preaching is the declaration of the hidden things of God and the secret thoughts of the hearers. When there is true preaching, congregations feel searched by the word, and exposed under the searching eye of God.

For this kind of preaching to take place, the preacher must be filled with the Holy Spirit and also released or abandoned to the Holy Spirit. Some preachers are too 'controlled' - they rely totally on their minds and are never prepared to be spontaneous. The preacher must be gripped by God if he is to lay hold of a congregation by his preaching. The place where this happens is in prayer. The preacher must let go of himself in worship. He does not become mindless, but he does not remain a slave to intellectualism. He knows the place of worship and of communion with God. Paul says that he knew what it was to be 'beside himself' and what it was to be sober or 'of sound mind' [2 Corinthians 5:13]. The faculty of reason must kneel humbly while the spirit soars in worship. There are aspects of preaching that are communicated when a preacher soars with the Holy Spirit. They cannot be manufactured, but they can be prepared by quiet waiting on God, and adoring worship.

5. The Call of God

The greatest calling that a person can ever have is the one God intended for them! It is possible for the preaching ministry to be exalted over all other gifts and ministries. However, it is not possible to *choose* to be a preacher, any more than it is possible to choose to have a prophetic ministry etc. This is God's choice. Martyn Lloyd-Jones said that if you ever meet a man who claims to be called to the ministry' do everything you can to make it hard for him! While few of us will unreservedly agree with Dr Jones on this point, it is nevertheless important to realise that true preachers have come through all discouragements and struggles, to the place where they can fulfil their ministry, overcoming obstacles in order to be a preacher.

- **Each person must know their calling**: Martyn Lloyd-Jones tells of a man who was a car mechanic but left his work to train as a pastor. He was happy until he went into the ministry, at which point he lost all his joy. He continued on for several years until he realised that God had not called him to the ministry. As soon as he realised this, he returned to his calling as a mechanic and found his joy again.

- **What is the call?** This is difficult to put into words, but it is not a natural gift, even though it does in some measure flow with natural gifts. Although someone with a stammer and a poor grasp of language may be used by God, it is nevertheless true that most preachers have good communication ability. This is the case in the examples of Peter, Stephen, Paul and others in the New Testament. Their ability to speak was not the call of God, but it enabled them to fulfil their calling. The call, then, is an inner compulsion. Paul said: *"For if I preach the gospel, I have nothing to boast of, for necessity is laid upon me; yes, woe is me if I do not preach the gospel! For if I do this willingly, I have a reward; but if against my will, I have been entrusted with a stewardship. What is my reward then? That* *when I preach the gospel, I may present the gospel of Christ without charge, that I may not abuse my authority in the gospel."* [1 Corinthians 9:16-18].

- **The call surpasses every other demand on our life**: when Peter and John heard the call, they left all and followed Jesus. The call was that if they would follow Him, He would make them fishers of men [Mark 1:17]. This does not mean that every called person must leave their employment. But it does mean that when someone is conscious of the call, they must let go of everything that competes with it. Paul said that he had suffered the loss of all things in pursuit of the call to know Christ [Philippians 3:7-14]. The call is not primarily to a ministry, but to a person, whom we are to love and enjoy.

- **We are called to minister to God first and to people second**: Jesus said that the first commandment is to love God and the second commandment is to love our neighbour as ourselves [Mark 12:29-31]. Often ministry is person-centred or need-centred. But Jesus did not minister to needs first; He ministered to Father first, and the outflow of His obedience to the Father was that people's needs were abundantly met. But Jesus did not follow the pressure of need; He followed the guidance of His Father. Even as He left the upper room to go to Gethsemane and the cross, He declared that He was doing it because He loved the Father.

When we get overwhelmed with need, as we surely must, if we concentrate on human problems, we become dry and unable to help anyone. We must concentrate on enjoying and pleasing God. Paul said that if he were a people-pleaser he would not be a servant of Christ [Galatians 1:10]. When Elijah went to the widow of Zarephath, he told her to make cakes for him first, and then for her son and herself [1 Kings 17:13]. This contradicted the obvious need that she had, but the result was that her needs were met in a much more glorious way than could ever have happened if she had put her own needs first. Ministers must take time to sit at the feet of Jesus, listening to Him and to His word, if they are to be effective.

6. Preach Christ and Him Crucified

When the New Testament speaks of the apostles' preaching ministry, it uses strange grammar. Paul says he had resolved to *"preach Christ crucified"* [1 Corinthians 1:23, 2:2]. The apostles did not cease *"teaching and preaching Jesus Christ"* [Acts 5:42]. The normal grammar would indicate that they taught 'about' Jesus Christ. But clearly it is not within the bounds of normal grammar to explain what happens during the act of preaching.

When a preacher declares the person and work of Christ, the person of Christ should be manifest during the preaching. Paul says in Titus 1:3 that God *"has manifested His word through preaching"*. Because Christ is risen from the dead and present everywhere, then during the true ministry of preaching, congregations should be conscious of God. They should sense the presence of Jesus. He should reach out through the preaching and touch the lives of people present. The preacher himself is to be invisible, as Christ is made manifest. For this to take place, the preacher must himself have fully embraced his own death, so that he is dead to self. It does not mean that he is always apologetic or embarrassed standing in front of people. The person who is truly free from self is free to be confident before congregations; he is not self-conscious at all. He is God-conscious and is liberated to flow in the Holy Spirit. Embarrassment is the sign that we are not free from self!

The preacher is then fully aware that, though there may be many important subjects to preach about - such as the Second Coming, marriage, the Tabernacle, marketplace ethics etc. yet there is only one theme that grips him as the supreme key to the problems that people face. That one subject is Christ and His cross. The Holy Spirit loves Jesus and is in holy awe about the cross. Therefore, when a preacher talks about these things, the Holy Spirit is filled with holy wonder, and applies them to the hearts of the hearers.

People have created audio and video recording equipment that can replay moments in history. But the greatest recorder of all is the Holy Spirit. He recorded the creation as it took place. He is the witness to the deep things of God, including the cross, and it is through Him alone that these things are made known [1 Corinthians 2:4-10]. It is through the preaching of Christ that He is made known.

THE SNARES OF THE PREACHING MINISTRY

The mark of the true ministry is holiness, and a lifestyle that demonstrates the fruit of the Spirit. Jesus said there would be false prophets, but that we would know them by their fruits [Matthew 7:15-23]. Similarly, the marks of the false prophets in Jude and 2 Peter 2, are that they do not resist temptation, but give in to sin.

There are many snares to the preaching ministry; here are the three main ones that are emphasised in the New Testament:

THE PREACHING MINISTRY

1. Pride and the Idolatry of the Ministry

Some preachers get a buzz from preaching. They enjoy the thrill of being the centre of attention; they enjoy holding the congregation in their control through the power of their preaching. It can become a drug that they cannot live without. Paul said: *"woe is me if I do not preach the gospel!"* [1 Corinthians 9:16], but he was not referring to his own enjoyment of the ministry, but to the divine compulsion to do the will of God. He said, *"for me to live is Christ"* - not preaching [Philippians 1:21]. He was content in prison because preaching was not his life, but knowing Jesus was. If we fall into this temptation we will become arrogant and proud, and may well fall into other equally serious sins.

2. The Love of Money – the Sin of Balaam and Gehazi
[2 Peter 2:15-16; Jude 11]

Balaam preached and prophesied hoping for financial reward [Numbers 22-24]. Gehazi took Naaman's money and contracted Naaman's leprosy [2 Kings 5:20-27]. Not all preachers will find big financial rewards in preaching, but this temptation can arise for all successful preachers. The preacher must not have an eye on the gift he is hoping to receive after the sermon. (Few treasurers will hand over a gift at the beginning of a service or weekend of ministry!) If our preaching is powerful, some people may be delivered or healed, and wish to express their gratitude by giving large gifts. If the preacher mentions his financial needs in the preaching, it is possible that wealthy members of the congregation will want to help him. The preacher must trust God for his support, and not manipulate congregations to give him money. This will require great self-control on occasions. When a rich person asks a preacher with no money in his pocket if there is anything he needs, the preacher must answer faithfully, and not exploit the generosity of the believers.

There is no such thing as a 'poor' preacher. Even if the preacher has no money, he must never complain that he is poor! Imagine telling someone, *"I'm poor, I only have Jesus!"* It would be like a billionaire's wife complaining that she had no money of her own, just her husband to rely on! The preacher has all the resources of Jesus Christ at his disposal, and Jesus will give him whatever he needs and never too late.

Kathryn Kuhlman gave generously to David Wilkerson, so he loved to go and minister at her services knowing that she would give generously to Teen Challenge. After some years, the Holy Spirit showed him that he had been relying on her and not on God, and he learned to go there only when he felt it was the will of God. Some people have made great sacrifices to be preachers, but if preachers have little money in their pocket, they can be tempted to give a false witness of their Master's faithfulness. Some may let it be known that they do not have enough money for a holiday or a car. While this may be true, it can be expressed in a way that dishonours God, who is their employer!

One English vicar took the Anglican Church to court, claiming that his pay was too low. The judge wisely dismissed the case, on the grounds that the man's employer was God and therefore beyond the competence of the court!

---

3. Immorality

Preachers are targets of the devil. If he can make preachers fall then he can ruin their ministry. Proverbs 6:26 teaches us that, *"the adulteress seeks the precious life"* [KJV]. There can be no doubt that the devil rejoices when precious servants of God fall into immorality. Proverbs 6:32–33 teaches that whoever commits adultery *"destroys his own soul"* and *"his shame will never be wiped away"* [KJV]. We may argue, *"Is there no forgiveness for such sins?"* Of course there is forgiveness, and restoration to salvation and fellowship with God and with His people. But the ministry of such men will be permanently damaged; never again will they be able to minister without someone remembering their sin.

Preachers (and ordinary believers) should resolve never to be alone in a compromising situation. They should refuse to be alone with a member of the opposite sex. They should refuse to counsel a member of the opposite sex alone, but should seek support from their spouse or other counsellors.

Churches, and particularly preachers, are **targets of the prince of darkness**. In the 1980s it was reported that a band of witches in South Africa had undertaken a 40-day fast to Satan with the intention of destroying Christian marriages. Similarly, in the late 1980s a Church in the UK was targeted by a spiritist, who lived opposite the Church. She hated it, and cursed the marriages in the Church. Sadly, the minister and his congregation were spiritually ill-equipped and inexperienced to deal with the attack. The spiritist sent her daughter to attend the Church and visit the homes of various couples. Every time she left a home, the husband and wife would be screaming at each other. Finally, the minister left his wife and his ministry to pursue an adulterous affair with a member of the congregation. The Church is in warfare, and pastors and preachers must be awake to the temptations that can arise at any time.

CONCLUSION: The Lord's servants must care for their own hearts, to make sure they are walking with the Lord in a healthy spiritual state, able to resist the temptations of the wicked one.

THE PREACHING MINISTRY

FIVE SPIRITUAL KEYS FOR PREACHERS

1. Pray as Much as You Read, in Preparation

It is a sad fact that many people trust in the reputation of the preacher, or in his gifts and experience or Bible knowledge. None of these can save anyone. It is only the Holy Spirit Who can take our preaching and make it powerful and effective. Read the following example about the conversion of Spurgeon, in his own words. When he went to a certain chapel, the preacher was unable to get there because of a heavy snowfall. The preacher who took his place was not naturally gifted, but God used him mightily.

I sometimes think I might have been in darkness and despair until now, had it not been for the goodness of God in sending a snowstorm one Sunday morning, while I was going to a certain place of worship. When I could go no further, I turned down a side street, and came to a little Primitive Methodist Chapel. In that chapel there may have been a dozen or fifteen people. I had heard of the Primitive Methodists, how they sang so loudly that they made people's heads ache; but that did not matter to me. I wanted to know how I might be saved, and if they could tell me that, I did not care how much they made my head ache. The minister did not come that morning; he was snowed up, I suppose. At last, a very thin-looking man, a shoemaker, or tailor, or something of that sort, went up into the pulpit to preach. Now, it is well that preachers should be instructed; but this man was really stupid. He was obliged to stick to his text, for the simple reason that he had little else to say. The text was:

"LOOK UNTO ME, AND BE YE SAVED, ALL THE ENDS OF THE EARTH."

He did not even pronounce the words rightly, but that did not matter. There was, I thought, a glimpse of hope for me in that text. The preacher began thus—"My dear friends, this is a very simple text indeed. It says, 'Look'. Now lookin' don't take a deal of pains. It ain't liftin' your foot or your finger; it is just, 'Look'.
Well, a man needn't go to College to learn to look. Anyone can look; even a child can look. But then the text says, 'Look unto Me'. Ay!" said he, in broad Essex, "many on ye are lookin' to yourselves, but it's no use lookin' there. You'll never find any comfort in yourselves. Some look to God the Father. No, look to Him by-and-by. Jesus Christ says, 'Look unto Me'. Some on ye say, 'We must wait for the

Spirit's workin'. You have no business with that just now. Look to Christ. The text says, 'Look unto Me'."

Then the good man followed up his text in this way: "Look unto Me; I am sweatin' great drops of blood. Look unto Me; I am hangin' on the cross. Look unto Me; I am dead and buried. Look unto Me; I rise again. Look unto Me; I ascend to Heaven. Look unto Me; I am sittin' at the Father's right hand. O poor sinner, look unto Me, look unto Me!"

When he had gone to about that length, and managed to spin out ten minutes or so, he was at the end of his tether. Then he looked at me under the gallery, and I daresay, with so few present, he knew me to be a stranger. Just fixing his eyes on me, as if he knew all my heart, he said, "Young man, you look very miserable." Well, I did; but I had not been accustomed to have remarks made from the pulpit on my personal appearance before. However, it was a good blow, struck right home. He continued, "and you always will be miserable—miserable in life, and miserable in death,—if you don't obey my text; but if you obey now, this moment, you will be saved." Then, lifting up his hands, he shouted, as only a Primitive Methodist could do, "Young man, look to Jesus Christ. Look! Look! Look! You have nothin' to do but to look and live."

I saw at once the way of salvation. I know not what else he said—I did not take much notice of it—I was so possessed with that one thought. Like as when the brazen serpent was lifted up, the people only looked and were healed, so it was with me. I had been waiting to do fifty things, but when I heard that word, "Look!" what a charming word it seemed to me! Oh! I looked until I could almost have looked my eyes away. There and then the cloud was gone, the darkness had rolled away, and that moment I saw the sun; and I could have risen that instant, and sung with the most enthusiastic of them, of the precious blood of Christ, and the simple faith which looks alone to Him. Oh, that somebody had told me this before, "Trust Christ, and you shall be saved."

The point of the story is that God uses a power that is wholly greater than us. If we rely on God, we will pray more and look to Him to work rather than to ourselves.

2. Be Bold in the Lord

After the lame beggar had been healed at the Beautiful Gate of the Temple, Peter was very bold when he was taken before the Sanhedrin [Acts 4:8-13]. He was not boastful about his gifts and abilities, but he was very bold in proclaiming the person of Jesus Christ.

3. Rely on the Holy Spirit

After the lame beggar was healed, Peter said to all the people who ran to him and John: *"...why (do you) look so intently at us, as though by our own power or godliness we had made this man walk?"* [Acts 3:12]. Peter was quick to let them know that it wasn't himself and John who had healed the man, but Jesus. He took it a step further, to say it wasn't even his faith, but the faith that comes from Jesus [Acts 3:16]. Peter was not afraid to let people know that he was weak without God.

4. Soak in the Bible Passage You Want to Preach from

Prayerfully read and re-read the text and context — both in English and in the original (use as many translations as possible). G. Campbell Morgan said that, before he preached from a passage in any book of the Bible, he read that entire book 50 times. If we give the true sense of the Bible we will be deep preachers, because the Bible is a deep book. It brings to light hidden truths about God and human beings. We will be the best psychologists, the best philosophers, the best counsellors, if we stick to what the Bible says.

5. Challenge the Hearts of the People

A preacher is not speaking to people's heads only, but also to their hearts. Peter had something to say that would change people's lives, so he said: *"... heed my words"* [Acts 2:14]. We must be challenging. Information is needed, but it must be given in a way that can be applied in people's lives. *"... we ought to give the more earnest heed to the things which we have heard, lest at any time we should let them slip"* [Hebrews 2:1, KJV]. If people don't heed the word preached, they could easily let the truth of God's word slip away from them.

"... faith by itself, if it does not have works, is dead" [James 2:17]. *"For indeed the gospel was preached to us as well as to them; but the word which they heard did not profit them, not being mixed with faith in those who heard it."* [Hebrews 4:2]. People will not profit from our ministry unless we get them to put the Word into practice. The Bible says we are to *"consider one another in order to stir up love and good works"* [Hebrews 10:24].

TEN PRACTICAL KEYS

(1) Know what you want the people to do after they have heard you preach.
Do you want the people:
- To repent, believe and be saved?
- To receive the baptism with the Holy Spirit?
- To be prayed with for healing or deliverance?
- To worship God?
- To receive greater understanding and take time to digest the new insights you have ministered to them?

You should have a clear object in mind if you want to be effective. You might change your objective during your preaching if the Holy Spirit leads you to do so. But you should have a clear objective in mind from the moment you start speaking.

(2) Be clear - don't keep big surprises till the end of your sermon.
Tell people what you are going to talk about, then talk about it, then tell them what you have talked about! Repetition is the art of the good communicator. Make sure you have communicated your main message. Ask yourself, *"What are the main things I want people to remember from this message?"*

(3) Don't use big words when you can use small ones
- that is spiritual pride. Speak so that a ten-year-old can understand you. That is what Billy Graham did! If you have been to Bible College and studied the Greek and the Hebrew, this is a great advantage in understanding the Bible. But it is no use trying to dazzle congregations with your great knowledge! Peter spoke Hebrew, Aramaic and Greek fluently, as they were his native languages. But he could not understand the Saviour because of his spiritual dullness, and needed to have things spelt out to him [Mark 8:14-21]. Most people need things to be expressed simply.

(4) Make a clear outline with:
- An introduction
- Your main points, with examples
- Your conclusion
- Your appeal

(5) Study
– *"Be diligent to present yourself approved to God, a worker who does not need to be ashamed, rightly dividing the word of truth"* [2 Timothy 2:15]. There are certain Bible tools that will help the preacher. They are not expensive, and are useful in widening our understanding of the Scriptures. (Here is a brief list: Halley's Bible Handbook, Unger's Bible Dictionary, Strong's Concordance, Vine's Dictionary, *Explore the Book* by Sidlow Baxter).

*(6) **Memorise the Scriptures*** - there is nothing more powerful than the Word of God. Peter, in his sermon on the Day of Pentecost, quoted large sections of Scripture. He knew them by heart. God has given the promise that His word will not return to Him void [Isaiah 55:10-11]. It is sharper than any two-edged sword [Hebrews 4:12]. The word will do more in the hearts of people than a preacher ever can.

*(7) **Use your voice to the full but don't scream*** - Peter *"raised his voice"* [Acts 2:14]. But this does not mean that he was screaming! Once, a small child asked, *"Why is the pastor so mad at us"*, referring to the preacher. Equally, we must not use a monotonous voice that will make people go to sleep. Once, a young preacher screamed at the congregation, *"We need sermons that will awaken the Church!"* A wise old pastor was sitting behind him and said, loud enough to be heard, *"What we first need are sermons that don't put people to sleep!"*

*(8) **Don't rely on tricks to get effect*** - you may use illustrations, but be careful not to undermine your ministry by play-acting. While we may be dramatic in our preaching, we must not pretend.

Campbell Morgan tells of an American businessman who went to hear a preacher in the Eastern USA. During his preaching, the preacher stopped and said: "I can't quite find the right word.... Perhaps it is... or ..." and then he found the right word. The businessman was impressed with the spontaneous manner in which the preacher spoke.

Three weeks later he was in the West Coast of USA and had the opportunity to hear the preacher again. During his preaching, the preacher stopped and said: "I can't quite find the right word... Perhaps it is... or..." The businessman suddenly realised that the man had not been spontaneous at all but had been play-acting! He left the meeting in disgust.

---

*(9) **Beware of humour*** - preachers are not to be comedians, especially if you want the congregation to take you seriously. Some preachers use humour to 'soften up' their congregation. This may sometimes be necessary if there is tension in the congregation. Humour may help you and the congregation relax, but beware! It will be hard to connect with the atmosphere of the Spirit and of heaven if we lose ourselves in carnal laughter. Jesus and the apostles did not tell jokes, though there is little doubt that God has a sense of humour.

Jesus would have laughed along with everybody else at life's humorous situations.

(10). Know when to stop - the truth is that few preachers know when to stop, especially when they really get warmed up to their subject.

A little boy went to Church with his father. When the preacher came in he placed a Bible, a notebook and a watch on the pulpit. "What are those for?", asked the little boy.

"Well", said the father, the Bible is the Word of God, the notebook is the outline of what the preacher wants to say to us, and the watch? Well, the watch doesn't mean anything at all!"

Sometimes the preacher is not connecting with the congregation, so he may talk on and on, trying to connect. Others have a great connection but do not know when to stop. Remember these guidelines:

- If you drill for oil and don't find it within 15 minutes, stop boring!

- Always leave a congregation wishing you had spoken longer, rather than wishing you had stopped sooner.

- Always remember that some of your congregation have been working hard all week and will be struggling to keep their concentration. You may not be tired, but they may be exhausted.

- Listening is sometimes a harder discipline than speaking!

- There will be a ripe moment to stop. If you miss it, the message of the Holy Spirit may be forgotten. People will be ready to respond, but if you miss the moment, they may be discouraged.

- Honour the congregation and the leaders, even if you are the leader of the Church! Remember that finishing on time will help Sunday School leaders.

11

CHURCH PLANTING AND EVANGELISM

METHODS, PRINCIPLES AND PASSION!

"*Methods* are many, ***principles*** are few;
Methods may change, but ***principles never do.***"

It is vital from the outset of this chapter to understand the difference between principles and methods.

- **Methods of Church planting will vary** according to the cultural and religious background of the society in which the evangelist is working. The evangelist must take great care to be sensitive to the culture. For example, in many cultures, including Moslem, Buddhist, Hindu and even communist societies, it is unlikely that large public meetings will be an appropriate method of evangelism. This method has worked in open societies such as America, and in some parts of Africa and India. But it is unlikely to work in Arab nations and could sometimes do more harm than good.

- **Principles of Church planting will never vary** - the principles of spiritual life will undergird all the activity of the Church planter. It is vital to get the principles right, since God will always bless the person who loves Him and loves sinners. Sadly, many have embraced methods as a substitute for principles. They have wanted to plant Churches with little or no love for people. The two must go hand in hand.

TEN PRINCIPLES OF SPIRITUAL LIFE FOR THE CHURCH PLANTER

The pattern for Church planting is found solely in the book of Acts, where the first Churches of the New Testament era were founded, first by Peter and then by Paul. In this section we will take Acts 16 - the founding of the Church at Philippi - as a pattern for Church planting, but we will also take other examples into consideration.

1. Leadership

Paul was the clear leader of various teams that went out of Antioch. He had the qualities of a leader which are vital if Churches are to be planted:

- **Pioneer spirit** - willingness to suffer the hardships of the pioneer lifestyle. C.T. Studd was a millionaire and national cricket champion in England, but he gave it all up to be a missionary, first in China and then in Central Africa. He wrote a booklet called 'The Chocolate Soldier', describing Christians who are made of 'chocolate' and melt at the first hint of hardship. Here is a quote from the booklet:

  > "Every true soldier is a hero! A SOLDIER WITHOUT HEROISM IS A **CHOCOLATE SOLDIER!** *Who has not been stirred to scorn and mirth at the very thought of a Chocolate Soldier? In peace true soldiers are captive lions, fretting in their cages. War gives them their liberty and sends them, like boys bounding out of school, to obtain their heart's desire or perish in the attempt. Battle is the soldier's vital breath! Peace turns him into a stooping asthmatic. War makes him a whole man again, and gives him the heart, strength, and vigour of a hero."*

  Paul was always advancing into areas where there were no Christians. He said that he was burdened to *"preach the gospel in regions beyond you"* and not to boast in what other men had accomplished [2 Corinthians 10:16]. Paul had the pioneer spirit, and was like Caleb and Joshua in his attitude to obstacles.

- **Not afraid of failure** - willingness to go into situations that have never been tried before, and that might succeed or fail. Some pastors/leaders are afraid of trying something in case it fails. The Church planter is not afraid of failure. Failure is when we know what to do and we do *not* do it through fear! Christ told us to shake the dust off our feet if people do not receive our message, and so we should expect that there will be such occasions. The Bible says that Christ was rejected by Israel [John 1:11].

- **Full of the Holy Spirit** - Paul was clearly baptised in the Holy Spirit and demonstrated the power and gifts that are so needed to show the glory of the Son of God. Paul frequently ministered to the sick and demon-possessed, as here in Acts 16:18. The baptism with the Holy Spirit is as essential in the Church planter as it is in the founding of a local assembly. The Church was formed when the Holy Spirit came upon the believers on the Day of Pentecost.

- **Full of faith** - Paul was not easily deterred from his purpose; he had the ability to hear the prophetic voice of God that gave him the faith to go on. He was no stranger to the supernatural, receiving visions [Acts 16:9] and prophetic insight into situations [Acts 18:9-10].

- **Humility** - Paul expected to benefit from fellowshipping with other believers [Romans 1:12] and he also realised that the gospel was greater than him and his ministry [Galatians 1:8].

2. Passion for the Lost

A love for lost people is vital. This is love for the unlovely and for those who are enemies of God. Normal human love and affection is love for our nation, our family and friends. But a*gape* love is the mark of the Church planter. It is sacrificial love that is poured out for people with whom we have nothing in common naturally. David Wilkerson went out to the drug addicts of New York although he had nothing in common with them at all. Jackie Pullinger left a comfortable life in England, to work among the drug addicts and Triad gangsters of Hong Kong.

Jonah is the example of a preacher who had no passion for the lost. Jonah disobeyed the call of God because he had no love for the Assyrian Empire and its capital city Nineveh. He fled to Tarshish, but God intervened and sent a storm to change his mind. Jonah was confronted with his disobedience through this, but he chose to die rather than repent! He was thrown into the sea, probably expecting death, but was swallowed by the whale (or big fish). There he cried out to God and had a change of heart.

The key lesson here is that we do not have a passion for the lost by natural virtue! It is imparted to us through Christ:

- **Through fellowship with Christ**, and catching the Shepherd heart of love that seeks the lost [Luke 19:10].

- **Through baptism with the Spirit** that unites us with Christ in His death and resurrection.

- **Through brokenness** and calling out to God to change our hard hearts. Jonah had to do this more than once!

- **Through understanding the awfulness of hell.** When Jonah went down into the belly of the whale he would have felt the horrors of hell itself and probably thought he had gone to hell. This experience must have made his preaching at Nineveh fervent and passionate.

Jonah preached with such passion that the whole city was converted. But Jonah himself needed God to do a deeper work in his heart. There was a deep inner hardness and racial prejudice in Jonah. When God spared the people, Jonah was disappointed! So, God took away Jonah's precious shade [Jonah 4:6-8]. Jonah was so angry and frustrated over his personal discomfort, that he cried out in anguish. God then rebuked his hardness and challenged him to repent. In the same way, believers can sometimes moan if their bus is late, if the air-conditioning breaks down, or the dinner is burnt! God is grieved when he sees His children care more for themselves than for the lost. We should be filled with deep sorrow that our colleagues, neighbours and relatives are lost and on the road to hell.

3. Strong Vision

The Church planter must have a vision in his heart of what God can do. Vision is what motivates the minister. Moses went up the mountain and received a vision of the Tabernacle [Exodus 25:8-9]. Then he came down and shared it with the people. Vision is the prophetic foresight of what God wants to do. It is seeing the Church in all its glorious power and heavenly life [Ephesians 3:3-7].

Hope is the seed-bed of faith. We need to hope for things before we can believe for them. *"Now faith is the substance of things hoped for"* [Hebrews 11:1]. Vision and hope are similar qualities. Without vision/hope the people perish [Proverbs 29:18 KJV]. What we are in our hearts is what we will become. The vision of our hearts will be produced through our ministry. If there is emptiness in our hearts then we will have a powerless, ineffective ministry. If, with the eye of faith, we see a powerful Church, full of the Holy Spirit and worshipping God in great abandonment, then we will produce such a Church as we teach and preach.

4. A Strong Team

God uses teams to plant and run Churches. Leadership is vital, but the best leader needs believers alongside him to implement his vision. The best results will be obtained when there is a strong team drawn together by the Holy Spirit to plant a local Church.

Paul had a very strong team with him in Philippi. Note the variety in the members of the team. Paul was the strong leader but did not see himself as more important than the other members. Luke writes that when Paul had the vision of the man of Macedonia [Acts 16:9-10], the whole team knew that God had called them *all*, not just Paul, to preach the gospel there. Sometimes one strong individual can so overshadow the team that there is no team spirit, and as a result less is achieved. Christ sent out the apostles two by two, and He would have paired people together who would learn from each other and complement each other's ministry.

- **Timothy** was a young convert from Lystra, the city where Paul had been stoned and then healed or raised from the dead (we are not sure whether Paul actually died through the stoning). So, as young as he was in the faith, Timothy knew the cost that was involved in working with Paul.

- **John Mark**, on the other hand, had earlier been a member of Paul's team, but had left the work when things got rough. Even the great miracles were not enough to make John Mark stick it out [Acts 13:13]. John Mark's fearfulness made Paul reject him as a team member later, and Paul and Barnabas had a severe disagreement about the matter, leading to a temporary split between the two. But later Paul was clearly reconciled with both Barnabas [see 1 Corinthians 9:6] and John Mark [2 Timothy 4:11].

- **Silas** had already proved a reliable brother, and had been chosen by the Jerusalem Church to carry a letter to Antioch [Acts 15:22, 27]. Silas was a Roman citizen [Acts 16:37-38]. Little is known about him; all we know is that he was a co-founder of the Churches with Paul and helped him to establish the Church in Corinth.

- **Luke 'the beloved physician'** [Colossians 4:14]. Luke was a companion on the journeys that Paul made from Acts 16 onwards. Paul clearly found him to be a dear friend and companion. Little is known about his ministry other than that he was a Gentile (the only Gentile writer of the New Testament). The great lesson here is that we are to make friends with our team members. The atmosphere among the team was one of family, not business! Most ministers and pastors often desperately need a close friend with whom they can share their conflicts and temptations in a discreet, loving atmosphere. The lesson is: be a friend to others!

The Antioch team - Acts 13:1 tells us that in the Church at Antioch there were certain prophets and teachers. The list of names is very instructive:

> **Barnabas** – a Jew from a wealthy background [Acts 4:36-37].

> **Simeon** – who was called Niger, which is Latin for a black man, perhaps from Africa?

> **Lucius** - from Cyrene, which is Libya in North Africa.

> **Manaen** - who was brought up with the tetrarch Herod. He was therefore from a privileged and wealthy background.

> **Saul** - who was from a strict Jewish background.

This team was remarkable for its variety in ethnic and class background. All good teams will have variety and will include a wide mix of people from different walks of life. This was one of the most powerful teams in history, and their prayer life and commitment to each other is a clear pattern for the planting of Churches. Some of this team stayed behind to take the work forward in Antioch. Two of the team were sent out, under prophetic guidance. The supporting Church did not send them money, it seems, and Paul used his skill in tent-making to support the ministry. Money, then, was neither the bond of the team, nor the main reason that Paul returned to Antioch. His visits there were to renew fellowship and to continue in the ministry that God had given him for the whole Church.

5. A Listening Ear – a Quiet Spirit

Paul and his team went out of the city on the Sabbath day to a riverside *"where prayer was customarily made"* [Acts 16:13]. This is a beautiful description of the place where believers are to live. Psalm 46:4 describes the river of God that makes the city of God glad. This psalm speaks of knowing God in and through a quiet/still heart [Psalm 46:10]. This state of heart is the atmosphere in which God is pleased to move. Christ kept a quiet heart and spirit before His Father. He was never worried or in unbelief. He was often burdened, but never fearful. He was never afraid of the devil, or disaster, or anything negative. The devil seeks to bring believers out of rest because then they will not be able to worship God, hear His voice or pray with faith.

The Sabbath speaks of ceasing from self-effort. God wants to build His Church through hearts that are at rest with Him. Such a state is one of faith. Later in the chapter, a demon-possessed girl met Paul and his team as they were on the way to the riverside to pray [Acts 16:16]. The devil sends his various agents to hinder us from what is vital. The devil is the enemy of a meek and quiet spirit, and the warfare of faith is specifically guarding our hearts from the panic and unbelief that threaten to engulf us when trouble comes.

6. An Attractive Life – a Clear Testimony

The most powerful evangelistic weapon is to have a life that makes others envious! This means that we need to have a faith and a life that are filled with serenity and love. Unbelievers should look at believers and wonder at the spiritual riches we possess. The richest people in the world do not know the joys that a believer has, for the best things in life are free! True, they cost Christ everything, but we cannot obtain salvation by money or works. All we have to do is repent and believe in Jesus Christ. Paul describes the gospel as spreading the fragrance of the knowledge of Christ [2 Corinthians 2:14-16]. Paul did not only denounce sin in his preaching, he glorified Christ and His work on the cross.

7. Agape Love

We have touched on this in discussing passion for the lost – agape love is the kind of love that is poured out for people with whom we have nothing in common. It is love for the humanly worthless and helpless. There is no economic return from caring for the dying in Calcutta's slums. When a journalist observed Mother Theresa wiping the filth from a dying beggar, he told her: *"I wouldn't do that for all the money in the world!"* She replied: *"Neither would I!"*

The motive for the one who has Calvary love in their hearts is not selfish advancement or profit, it is the glory of God at whatever cost. Here is an example of such love:

Two young Moravians heard of an island in the West Indies where an atheist British owner had 2,000 to 3,000 slaves. The owner had said: 'No preacher, no clergyman, will ever stay on this island. If he's shipwrecked we'll keep him in a separate house until he has to leave; but he's never going to talk to any of us about God. I'm through with all that nonsense.' The slaves had been brought from the jungles of Africa to this island to live and die without hearing of Christ.

The two young Moravians, in their early twenties, sold themselves to the British planter and used the money they received from their sale - for he paid no more than he would for any slave - to pay their passage out to his island, for he wouldn't even transport them. As the ship left its pier in the river at Hamburg and was going out into the North Sea, carried with the tide, the Moravians had come from Herrenhut to see these two lads off. They were never to return again, for this wasn't a four-year term; they sold themselves into lifetime slavery. It was simply that, as slaves, they could be Christians where these others were. The families were there weeping, for they knew they would never see them again. And they wondered why they were going, and questioned the wisdom of it.

As the gap widened and the ropes had been cast off and were being curled up on the pier, and the young boys saw the widening gap, one lad, with his arm linked through the arm of his fellow, raised his hand and shouted across the gap the last words that were heard from them; they were these: "MAY THE LAMB THAT WAS SLAIN RECEIVE THE REWARD OF HIS SUFFERING!"

This became the call of Moravian missions. And this is the only reason for being - that the Lamb that was slain may receive the reward of His suffering.

[From a sermon entitled 'Ten Shekels and a Shirt' by Paris Reidhead]

8. A Willingness to Suffer

Paul and Silas were arrested and beaten [Acts 16:23-24]. This is no more than Jesus Himself experienced, and we must arm ourselves with the same mind [1 Peter 4:1]. Paul bore in his body the scars that he received for his bold witness to the gospel and the person of Christ. He had been stoned at Lystra [Acts 14:19] and it is even possible that he had died and been raised from the dead. If he did not die, he was miraculously healed, since they had left him for dead. This meant that he would have been terribly scarred by the jagged pieces of rock that had been hurled at him. His back would have been deeply scarred by the frequent whippings he received.

In Acts 16 Paul was once more beaten, but he would not change his plans because of any personal danger. Such bravery is a requirement for true leadership in Church planting - often the reception in pioneer situations is hostile, to say the least. Ministers in some parts of the world can expect imprisonment and physical abuse as a common reaction to the gospel.

9. A Praising, Worshipping Heart

In the past Christians would go into the open air and preach, but more recently some groups have gone to public places to sing and praise God with a worshipping heart as well as to preach. While this is a matter for each team to decide before the Lord, it is nevertheless true that the leader and his team must keep a worshipping spirit.

Paul and Silas worshipped God in the darkest hour [Acts 16:25]. This was a very significant moment, and it represents the element of choice and faith in worship. Everything had gone wrong, and Paul and Silas had every right to complain and moan. But they made the conscious choice to praise and worship God. There was then a sound from another kingdom - which is precisely the power of worship. As they worshipped, God sent an earthquake. While not every prison story ends as powerfully as this one did, yet in spirit God moves when we praise Him. The lesson here is that things happen in the unseen world when we worship.

Note that the prisoners were listening to their singing before the earthquake came. Miraculously, none of them had the inclination to escape - they sat still and waited for the jailer to come and close the doors. God's power had subdued all the powers of darkness and changed these violent criminals into meek lambs!

10. Faith in the Power of the Gospel to Build a Lasting Church

Paul and Silas ordained elders from among young converts. It is vital to train new converts to spread the gospel and become new Church leaders. It is often mistakenly assumed that waiting for years will make men better candidates for leadership. This is true in terms of spiritual fatherhood, and it is also true that only time and experience can produce real depth and maturity. However, leadership is not the exclusive property of the spiritually aged! Many young converts have leadership ability.

It is remarkable that, when the Ethiopian eunuch was converted, the Holy Spirit caught Philip the evangelist away [Acts 8:39]! He was not led to disciple and teach the Ethiopian. This demonstrates the need **not to make methods out of experience**. Some people desperately need discipling, while others would suffer from it! God did not intend the African Church to be 'colonial'. He wanted them to develop with their own flavour! Too many missionaries have built a structure that has exalted the sending Church as superior to the receiving nation.

This has meant that the African Church was seen as 'needy and childlike'. The problem with treating people like children is that it becomes self-perpetuating. God clearly believed in His own power to keep the Ethiopian believer, and the Church should share God's faith in Himself! The Ethiopian Church grew and spread rapidly and was very successful, with very little outside input.

METHODS IN CHURCH PLANTING

So far we have looked at unchanging principles; here are some methods that will vary according to the context in which the Church planter is working.

The terms 'evangelism' and 'Church planting' are connected. Evangelism brings the gospel to those who do not have a relationship with Jesus Christ; and the fruit of our evangelism provides the foundation for a new congregation of believers. The primary goal is to make disciples, not simply to get people to attend Church meetings. But one outworking of discipleship is to have vision for a local Church, and personal commitment to gather with other believers.

1. Cell Groups

This method is found in the New Testament, though it would be wrong to say that the apostles used it as a conscious 'method', and it is nowhere advocated in the teaching of the apostles as the answer to Church growth. It has been developed in some Churches as a rigid method of Church growth - with rules, for example, that as soon as a group reaches a certain number, e.g. 20, then it must divide (or 'multiply'). Typically, these cells form and multiply via a network of people meeting in homes. In some cases, the individual cells are connected in a larger network that meets together periodically in a large group setting. The advantages of this relational model are that it focuses on personal development, care and small-group discipleship.

A cell group does not exist for mere social contact or to combat loneliness. This is a byproduct of cell groups, and not the primary goal. A cell group is part of the Church, and not different from a Church in its basic purpose.

The functions of the cell group include:

- **Worship/prayer: ONE OF** the main purposes of the Church is to worship God with love and praise. Therefore this is a main purpose of the cell group, as part of the Church. The presence of God is the life of the Church, and it is the life of the cell groups in the Church. The group will not grow through discussion, eating together etc. The group will grow because of the presence of Almighty God.

- **Bible teaching:** the Word of God is the life of the believer [Matthew 4:4] and therefore the teaching of the Bible is a chief activity of the cell group. At the level of small groups, believers can interact and ask questions in a way they cannot do in larger meetings. It is in the smaller meetings that timid souls can begin to share things they have learned, and so themselves find a context in which they can minister. Some will never progress beyond the smaller group in their ministry, but this is not because they have a lesser ministry. All of God's servants fulfil a vital role that no other can fulfil.

- **Fellowship:** the fellowship of the small group is very important, since in the modern world so many things have become impersonal, and individuals have become lonely and feel anonymous in a crowd. Some will attend a large Church where, beyond a handshake, they may never meet anyone in a meaningful way. God did not intend the human race to live in anonymity. For this reason it is good that cell groups do things that make people relax together and get to know each other. Members should watch over each other and help each other in practical ways. By this means the life of the Church will touch communities in ways that would not be possible without cell groups.

- **Evangelism:** as the cell group engages in these activities, friends and neighbours can be invited to participate at different levels. Sometimes newcomers will be invited to share a meal and listen to a short message. Sometimes there may be opportunities to help people with jobs, such as mending a leaking tap. Through small things like this, pre-believers can be drawn into contact with believers and begin to discover the living testimony of the people of God. This will create the context in which the gospel can be presented in a friendly way. Sometimes attending the main meetings of the Church may be too challenging for an individual; attending a small meeting with a free meal will often be much more attractive. (This is the pattern for the Alpha course.) Often, too, it may be possible to have cell groups, say, in the marketplace, perhaps over a lunchtime. In this way businessmen can welcome their colleagues to a more familiar setting at a time when there is no great competition with other activities.

2. Mother/Daughter Churches

An existing 'mother' Church can provide the vision and resources to plant a new 'daughter' Church. This may arise in a wide variety of ways:

- Sometimes a cell group will be in a geographically distinct area. The believers may have been travelling to the mother Church for several years, and develop a vision for their own local assembly.

- Sometimes one or more Church members may have a vision to move to a nearby or distant town, with the clear purpose of starting a Church, while receiving help and support from the sending Church.

- Sometimes people from an outlying location may join a Church. It is good for the leaders to be aware of the possibilities that present themselves when people come from outlying areas. Often it may be assumed that people will move closer to the Church they attend; but these people represent an opportunity to preach the gospel to new areas.

3. Parachute Drop

An evangelist/Church planter, perhaps with a family, may move into a new location - even a foreign country - to start a Church from scratch. The Church planter might have very little connection or existing support within the new area. He and his family are pioneering new territory. Where there is great risk, there is great reward, but this approach is not for the faint-hearted, and requires someone particularly gifted in personal evangelism. Pastors want their Churches to be big, but it is the will of God that believers spread the gospel. When Stephen was martyred, the believers were scattered as they fled from the subsequent persecution. God can use many things to send believers out, rather than huddling together and keeping the gospel to themselves.

If the Church is to be engaged in this type of Church planting, it is wise to consider the financial implications carefully. It should not immediately be assumed that 'missionaries' are supported by the sending Church. In some contexts it will be more successful if the missionary finds paid work among the people he is trying to reach. This will also raise money and enable him to help the people among whom he is working. Nevertheless, a wise pastor/eldership team will seek to support the ministry of such a brother, especially in the early stages.

4. Personal Evangelism/Discipling

The Scripture says, *"... he who wins souls is wise"* [Proverbs 11:30]. Here are some principles of personal evangelism from John 4:1-26 – the Samaritan woman at the well:

- **Evangelism will take place in ordinary social contact**: Jesus did not assume that the Samaritan woman would come to a meeting to hear Him preach! This is a very common error - many Christians think that 'Church' takes place only in the Church building. Jesus talked normally with the woman, approaching her on her level. Such opportunities will arise in the ordinary course of our lives, at our place of work, in our school, etc.

- **Build common interests:** it is an obvious point, but still true, that Jesus asked for water, thus creating a trivial point of common interest that opened a conversation [John 4:7]. It is very difficult to begin a spiritual conversation with someone, whether we have known them for a long time or just met them. Often a bridge for communication must be built. God can lead some people to meet others socially and then wait for the opportunities to arise later. When Paul preached in Athens, he began by mentioning the altar to the unknown God as a means of catching the people's interest [Acts 17:23].

- **Listen to the Holy Spirit as well as the person you are talking to!** Jesus' words were not just good ideas - He was not following a pamphlet on the ABC of personal evangelism. He was speaking words that were from God, and anyone who would share the gospel must pray and look to God throughout the whole conversation. Jesus probably spoke many words of knowledge to this woman, some clearly supernatural [John 4:17-18], others simply the truths that this woman most needed to hear [John 4:10].

- **Don't water the gospel down**: Jesus had the woman's interests at heart but He did not hesitate to show her the sins of her past and her need for repentance.

- **Don't condemn sinners unnecessarily**: remarkably, Jesus did not dwell on the woman's past sins, but moved on to God's great provision for her. While it is vital to listen to the Holy Spirit, who alone knows the hearts, it is also important not to try and do the work of the Holy Spirit. It is He who will convict of sin [John 16:8] and most sinners are already aware of their personal failure. Christ came to save, not to condemn [John 3:17].

- **Present truth clearly and boldly**: Christ told the woman His true identity - which was the key to salvation [John 4:26].

- **Don't despise the smallest of opportunities**: the result of Jesus' conversation with the Samaritan woman was the conversion of many people in the city of Sychar [John 4:39-42].

- **Believe that even hostile people may be desperate!** At first sight, the cultural and social distance between Jesus and the woman might have led us to believe that nothing would be achieved by this conversation. Jesus taught that we should constantly be aware that there are souls to be reaped into the kingdom, if we will believe and walk with God in personal evangelism. *"Do you not say, 'There are still four months and then comes the harvest'? Behold, I say to you, lift up your eyes and look at the fields, for they are already white for harvest!"* [John 4:35].

5. Campaigns

The true impact of gathering large crowds to hear the gospel can be difficult to assess. But often, in the Acts of the Apostles, large crowds gathered to hear the apostles even though this happened spontaneously. This then led the apostles to build relationships with individuals who were hungry for God, who then became the founding members of a new local assembly.

In recent years the 'Jesus film' has been shown publicly to great effect, and has provided a means of building bridges into a community - explaining who Jesus is, and enabling contact to be made with those who are seekers and are spiritually hungry. Reactions to the film can vary, though. One missionary in Tanzania showed the Jesus film to a crowd of Masai tribes-people. During the scene when Judas betrays Jesus, one warrior thought he was a real man, and hurled his spear at the screen in order to dispense instant justice!

Principles for organising a successful outreach meeting include the following:

- ▶ ***Organise well*** - it may be easy to set dates and invite a speaker, but time should be taken to involve other Churches, to make arrangements for practical needs such as toilets, car parking etc.

- ▶ ***Aim for excellence*** - there is no reason for the Church to do things in a slovenly or careless way. The testimony of the gospel begins in the way things are done. It would be tragic for sick or disabled people to attend a meeting and find that there is no preparation for their comfort. All of these things speak louder than the preaching. Some people may be put off and even leave before the preacher gets up to speak.

▶ **Pray** - the power of the message will be in proportion, not to the degree of organisation, but to the way in which believers have laid hold of God for the event. This means that at the heart of the event there are people who have made it their aim to walk with God and fellowship with Him through every step of the preparation.

▶ **Invite a gifted speaker** - many large evangelistic meetings fail because the speaker is not gifted for this purpose. It is wise to choose the speaker early and involve him in the organisation and decision-making process from as early a point as possible.

▶ **Prepare believers to give their testimony** - a clear testimony can be crucially important in presenting the gospel to people who have never heard it before. Some believers may not be able to speak clearly for, say, 10 minutes, and will perhaps do better being interviewed by a presenter.

▶ **Ensure the believers know how to lead a sinner to Christ** - some believers may not have given sufficient thought to this, and so will be confused at the last minute. Some may think they have to get the person to be filled with the Spirit in order to be saved. The key to salvation is simple and easy to understand. It centres on knowing:

1. Our need of a saviour – confession of sin and repentance.
2. The identity of Jesus - that He is the Son of God and that He lived in this world, and died for our sins. [Acts 8:37].
3. That through repentance and faith, God will accept us and give us an assurance of eternal life. [Luke 23:43].

6. Gifts of the Holy Spirit

It is vitally important that believers realise how original the Holy Spirit is in the way in which He works. None of Jesus' miracles and conversations can be used as a 'method', because He always was so unique in His methods. Human beings, on the other hand, love to see methods and patterns everywhere. But without the originality and life of the Holy Spirit, nothing will be achieved! We need to pray for gifts of the Holy Spirit [1 Corinthians 14:1]. We also need to be broken and renewed so that God can pour new wine into new vessels [Matthew 9:16-17].

By the second meeting of a new Church, traditions will have been formed. So often, even where there is no written liturgy, meetings will follow a rigid, predictable course. This is not completely wrong, but it does mean that believers can sometimes operate without looking to the Holy Spirit. Spurgeon occasionally reversed the order of his Sunday morning meeting and preached before the time of worship. He did this as some people were arriving later in the service because they just wanted to hear him speak!

7. Adapting to the Cultural Context

In some African cities it is possible to enter a Church building and be transported to 18th-century England! Some missionaries exported not only the gospel but also their culture and their way of doing things. The same thing can be seen today, in that many third-world Churches are given loudspeakers and keyboards and are taught songs that all make the Church identical to a western Church. While this may be attractive to some, it may grieve the Holy Spirit, for He seeks to speak in the context in which people have grown up. On the Day of Pentecost everyone heard the Holy Spirit speak in the dialect with which they were familiar.

When visiting Nigeria, T.L. Osborne asked the congregation what they thought Jesus looked like. Many thought He would look like a northern European, with long hair and blue eyes. Osborne called an African to step up, and he told them, *"Jesus looks like one of you!"* Jesus would surely have adapted His customs and His appearance as much as possible to the people He was visiting. This is the explanation for the success of Hudson Taylor and the China Inland Mission. He dressed as a local Chinese man, even adopting the same hairstyle of the day, so that he could blend in and be acceptable to the local people. Church planters must be willing to adapt their personal preferences to meet the people they are seeking to reach.

8. Processing Information -Being Aware of Unreached People Groups

It is possible to visit a country and think that it is evangelised because there are many big Churches. But this does not mean that there are no unreached people groups right on the doorstep. There may be many communities that have no witness available - there may be no-one reaching out to them. For this reason, it is right to ask God to open our eyes to the different people groups around the world, both far and near, that have never heard the gospel. Paul was burdened to preach to those who had never heard the gospel. So, too, we must be aware of the needs all around us.

CONCLUSION

The Church has been called to spread the gospel to all nations [Matthew 28:19-20]. It is interesting that Jesus did not tell His disciples to go and make Churches, but to make disciples. He said that He would build the Church, and that we should focus on making disciples. The truth is that Churches vary widely. There are strong ones, weak ones, rich and poor, big and small. But only Jesus is the true judge of the Church. He said that where two or three are gathered together in His name, there He would be in the midst, thus making it a Church [Matthew 18:20]. The apostle Paul expected that, as the gospel was preached, local Churches would be formed that would continue the work of the gospel. May this be our expectation and experience as we labour for the Lord.

12

CHURCH GROWTH

GROWTH WITH GOD'S APPROVAL

Church growth is one of the areas that most preoccupies the minds and hearts of God's servants. We all desire to see the Church grow; after all, growth is a sign of life. The issue goes to the heart of how a Church functions. One modern approach, especially in the USA, has been to analyse the 'market' that the Church is reaching. Hence, 'user-friendly' Churches have sprung up - some with burger restaurants which allow people to eat their breakfast or lunch while listening to the choir and the sermon! Pastors have used inventive methods to draw large congregations. One pastor has used wires so that he can fly around the altar area, and has obtained live kangaroos and elephants to use as visual aids. His reputation as a crowd-puller is considerable, and the growth of his Church numerically is phenomenal. Many such Churches grow from zero to thousands within weeks of opening. This is mega-church mentality. Is this the mind of the New Testament? Clearly, these were not the methods of Jesus and the apostles. But are these methods wrong?

Then there are sects such as the Jehovah's Witnesses which have achieved huge growth, but again, at what cost? Jehovah's Witnesses are motivated by a strong sense of guilt to share their 'gospel'. The result is a heavy atmosphere - certainly not an atmosphere of Christian liberty - apart from all the obviously wrong doctrines they believe. The Mormons use heavy investment and social aid as a method of drawing new members. These sects have used carnal methods very successfully. Some people have suggested we learn from their methods! Again, they do not reflect the methods of Jesus and the apostles, but are such methods totally wrong?

We need not only to examine in what ways these methods are wrong, but also to ask what the methods of Jesus and the apostles were. We will cover:

- How to obtain the outpouring of the Holy Spirit.
- How to maintain and promote Church growth.
- Identifying the false methods of Church growth.
- How to measure true success.

These are the key areas which will help leaders to address the question of Church growth.

KEYS TO OBTAINING OUTPOURING OF THE HOLY SPIRIT

The reason that this is so important is because the Church was born through an outpouring of the Holy Spirit and grew through it. Such an outpouring is sometimes labelled a **revival**. There are different degrees of outpouring.

1. Different Degrees of Outpouring

- ❖ ***Revival outpouring on a community:*** in the revival outpouring in Wales in 1904, the whole of Welsh society came under the power of the Holy Spirit. The same occurred in the Hebrides revival of the 1950s, under the ministry of Duncan Campbell. The island of Lewis, off the NW coast of Scotland, was so soaked in the presence of God that sinners visiting the island were instantly converted without even hearing any preaching! One businessman was visiting the island for the weekend and when he stepped off the ferry, as he walked up the road he fell to his knees under conviction of sin, asking God for forgiveness and salvation.

- ❖ ***Church-wide outpouring:*** when the Holy Spirit is poured out on a certain Church, the whole surrounding community may not feel or notice, but the atmosphere in the Church will be electrifying with God's presence. Spurgeon preached at the Metropolitan Tabernacle in London for 40 years, and throughout most of that period God was moving in a powerful way in this Church. The same is true of the ministry of many great men. Billy Graham preached in many cities, and occasionally his ministry was accompanied by city-wide revival and phenomenal Church growth. When he preached in London in the 1950s, thousands were genuinely converted; many pastors and leaders in the UK trace their conversion back to those crusades. The atmosphere was electrifying and crowds returning home filled the underground trains with hymn-singing. All of London knew that something was happening. Even the Prime Minister, Winston Churchill, met with Billy Graham and commented that Britain needed what this young man had. But on other occasions Billy Graham preached in British towns and cities with very little effect.

- ❖ **Personal outpouring:** it is a matter of great joy when an individual receives the baptism with the Holy Spirit, but he or she may be regarded as strange by fellow Christians. Finney describes how he worked in a lawyer's office as a young man. The senior lawyer was a Christian and attended the same Church as Finney. But Finney was not touched by the lives or prayers of those in that Church. When Finney was seeking God, the senior partner of the law firm asked if he would like them to pray for him. Finney replied, *"No thank you! None of your prayers is ever answered!"* Finney went into the woods to seek God, and at last he found peace. When returning to his office, he was suddenly engulfed in what he described as *"a mighty baptism with the Holy Spirit"*. This was a personal outpouring which made Finney stand out as different. It was, of course, not long before he was leading many others to Christ and to the fullness of the Spirit. Moody was also met in the same way, as he sought God to give him power in the ministry.

2. Outpouring is Vital for Church Growth

It is supremely important that leaders see the need for the outpouring of the Spirit. Our various Church activities must continue, including weekly meetings, evangelism, mission trips etc. But we must realise that there is an activity of God which must be working deeply in the hearts of people as we minister, and this is the outpouring of the Holy Spirit.

Finney realised that pastors and preachers are like farmers. They do not just wait for a harvest to appear, but will dig the ground, ploughing it up and then sowing and watering until the harvest appears. Often the processes of preparation are lonely - just as farmers often work long hours alone. But when harvest comes, the fields are full of labourers, and full of activity. Finney taught that an outpouring can be obtained if we co-operate with God in the same way that farmers co-operate with the seasons, the sun and the rain, to obtain a harvest. We will consider the keys to outpouring.

3. Key 1: Burdened Prayer – the Spirit of Intercession

Perhaps the greatest need is for burdened prayer. Joel describes in his prophecy the elements of true burdened prayer:

CHURCH GROWTH

- ♦ ***Awareness of the depth of the problem in the world*** [Joel 1:1-12] - the nation was under judgment because of the lack of godly living. The crops were destroyed and enemies were threatening to attack. In our day, there is the constant threat of terrorism, and the spread of diseases like AIDS. In many parts of the world there are famines or natural disasters. God is judging the nations for their sins, and the correct response of the Church is to cry to God for mercy.

- ♦ **Awareness of the depth of the problem in the Church** [Joel 1:13-20] - there was a neglect of the offerings to God. This demonstrates the need for the Church to attend to godly worship and to giving – both to the Church itself and to missions.

- ♦ **Call for special meetings** [Joel 1:13-14] - Churches may have to call for seasons of prayer and waiting on God for an outpouring of the Spirit.

- ♦ **The place of fasting** [Joel 2:12] - Joel describes the state of a man deeply convicted and burdened with prayer. There is fasting, there is weeping, there is a tearing of the heart and not the garments. There is pleading with God, with strong crying and self-humbling [Joel 2:17].

- ♦ **Blow the trumpet** [Joel 2:15] - this refers to the preaching and prophesying of God's word, to move men and women to prayer.

Joel then describes God's answer to such prayer:

- There will be a return to prosperity and blessing [Joel 2:18].

- There will be deliverance from attacking enemies [Joel 2:20].

- There will be an abundance of rain - the former and the latter rain [Joel 2:23]. Some have made a doctrine out of this called the Latter Rain Movement, that suggests there will be an outpouring greater than that in Acts 2 at the end of the age. While this may be appealing, there is little evidence that it is the true interpretation of this verse. Nevertheless, it does indicate that God has more than one outpouring for His people, and we are not to wait for the end of the age to receive it!

- There will be a great sense of God's presence [Joel 2:27].

- The Holy Spirit will be poured out on the whole congregation, from old to young, with supernatural revelation in dreams, visions and gifts of the Spirit, including prophecy [Joel 2:28-29].

Believers should seek the spirit of prayer, indicating that God has laid hold of them in a definite way to pray and seek Him. Jesus spent nights in prayer; in Gethsemane He prayed with such intensity that He sweated drops of blood [Luke 22:44]. David Brainerd, the missionary to the North American Indians, frequently spent long days and nights agonising in prayer, resulting in mass conversions among the Indians.

When believers are supernaturally burdened in prayer, then God is about to do something awesome. Sometimes it can be linked with a warning that God gives to His people. David Wilkerson tells how, for several weeks before 11th September 2001, the congregation in Times Square Church, New York were burdened in prayer - weeping and praying that God would help the city.

If believers do not have a burden to pray, then they should humble themselves and ask God to give them one. The Bible says that the *"the whole creation groans"* [Romans 8:22], and that *"the Spirit Himself makes intercession... with groanings which cannot be uttered"* [Romans 8:26]. Paul says that believers *"groan within ourselves"* [Romans 8:23]. These are the inner longings of the Holy Spirit for the *"revealing of the sons of God"* [Romans 8:19] and for the *"glorious liberty of the children of God"* [Romans 8:21]. The burdens that the Holy Spirit imparts are the foundation of a move of God. All of God's redemptive work flows through hearts yielded to co-operate with the longings of a loving God. This is the heart of intercession, and God seeks for intercessors who will stand in the gap and pray for nations and lost sinners. Paul said that he was burdened with great sorrow and continual grief in his heart [Romans 9]. This was a key part of Paul's ministry.

4. Key 2: Unity of Believers

In many cities of the world there has been a major leap forward in the growth of the Churches when they have began to meet together in united prayer.

Finney found that one town he went to was deeply divided on denominational lines.with a deep division between the Presbyterians and the Baptists over the subject of baptism. Interestingly, Finney sought to heal the division by preaching on baptism by immersion one evening, and on baptism by sprinkling the next evening. But he failed to persuade the two groups to overcome their prejudices and fellowship together for the sake of reaching the lost and reviving their Churches. The result was that there was no breakthrough, and Finney's ministry was largely ineffective in that town.

Believers should repent of speaking negatively, without sufficient Scriptural reason, of other denominations. ('Sufficient Scriptural reason' means that if a certain group of Churches denies a major foundation of the faith, such as the deity of Christ, then it would be the duty of believers to point out the faults and the dangers of that denomination.)

Pastors and leaders should promote unity by meeting together with other Church leaders to pray, and to attend each other's special meetings. In the individual Churches, believers should examine their hearts to make sure there is no bitterness or grudge that is hindering fellowship. There should be conscious effort to ensure that there are no jealousies or rivalries that divide the Church. Divisions should be healed through confession and forgiveness. Often there will be tears, and old divisions will be brought into the light and healed.

5. Key 3: Belief in the Inspiration of Scriptures

We have seen in an earlier chapter that there can be a danger, when Churches are seeking God for fresh moves of His Spirit, that the Scriptures are no longer consulted and seen as the sole guide. Only where the Bible is honoured will the Holy Spirit be poured out. Believers must be firmly anchored in the word of God, or there will be deceiving spirits at work in the midst of a move of the Holy Spirit. If there is to be lasting growth of the Church both in depth and numbers of truly converted people then there must be a deep dedication to preaching and teaching the word of God.

6. Key 4: The Preaching of the Cross

The outpouring of the Spirit was the great work that followed the cross. Christ died and by His sacrifice of Himself He removed every obstacle to the outpouring of the Holy Spirit. We may preach about blessing and the Holy Spirit, but we need to preach more about the cross. The blessing of the Holy Spirit will follow the preaching of the cross.

Read 1 Kings 18. The great picture of the cross linked with outpouring is in this chapter, where Elijah confronts Baal worship. The prophets of Baal had been allowed to dominate the country of Israel because King Ahab had married the daughter of Ethbaal, King of Tyre, who was a Baal worshipper. His daughter Jezebel had been extremely zealous for Baal and had persecuted all the true worshippers of Yahweh. The result was a complete collapse of all spiritual life in Israel.

God directs Elijah to repair the altar [v30-32], and to gather all Israel to witness this event. This historical event is a parable for all believers - the Church must return to the cross; and 'repair the altar'. If they have neglected the preaching of the cross, they must 'repair' the preaching and change the direction and flow of thought in the Church, to the place where God sacrificed everything in order that we may meet with Him.

The prophets of Baal build their altar but all their noise and prayers achieve nothing [1 Kings 18:26-29]. They serve a god who is dead and does not answer their prayers. Christians will find that, if they leave the cross, they may make a lot of noise, but the noise will be in vain - it is only through the cross that the Spirit is outpoured.

Elijah builds the altar of the Lord and orders water (probably seawater, since it had not rained for so long) to be poured on it. This was to indicate to everybody that the miracle they were to witness was not a mixture of human energy and the power of God; this was to be a pure miracle from God. Elijah takes twelve stones to make the altar. This indicates the apostolic preaching and teaching lying at the heart of all true moves of God, and which is the foundation of the Church [Ephesians 2:20]. Then he prays that God will reveal Himself by fire.

The fire falls! God comes to the altar built by Elijah, and to the twelve stones gathered. The Holy Spirit and fire fell, as a result of Jesus' sacrifice on the altar of the cross, on the twelve apostles gathered on the Day of Pentecost. The fire is a fire that burns with great zeal and devotion but does not exhaust. Like the burning bush, those indwelt by the fire of the Holy Spirit are full of zeal but not burnt out!

Finally comes the rain - the national outpouring of blessing and revival on the whole of Israel. This chapter is prophetic of our day, and teaches us how to obtain an outpouring of the Spirit and a move of God.

7. Key 5: Belief in, and Obedience to, the Holy Spirit

This is perhaps the greatest key of all in the pursuit of Church growth. We must trust completely in God and His plan to reach the nations. Sometimes God's guidance may defy logic, but it is vital that we obey. If we obey mere logic then we will work out strategies like ordinary businessmen. But if we obey the Holy Spirit, we will know that there is a mind at work behind the scenes Who knows more than any human being can ever see. Here success is measured by keeping the channels of communication open!

CHURCH GROWTH

In war there is often talk of the 'fog of war'. This means that, on the battleground, there may be total confusion. The individual soldier cannot see beyond his range of vision. So he may receive orders to attack a hill which seems to have no strategic value. He must obey orders and trust that the officers in charge are able to see more than he can. The army can only function if there is obedience to the chain of command. If this is true in fallible armies, how much more true is it when the Commander-in-Chief is none other than God Himself?

- **"He needed to go through Samaria"** [John 4:1]: Jesus obeyed an inner compulsion that led Him to an encounter with the woman of Samaria. There is no logic to the Holy Spirit's guidance and it will cross all barriers. This particular journey led Jesus from Judea into a hostile region. He crossed cultural barriers in the serenity of the Holy Spirit's guidance.

- **"...the Spirit said to Philip"** [Acts 8:29]: Philip left the scenes of revival in Samaria and went down to a desert region where no-one lived! There he met the Ethiopian eunuch, who by 'coincidence' was reading the prophet Isaiah, and by 'coincidence' he had reached the passage on the cross. By 'coincidence', when Philip had preached the gospel to him, they came across some water in the desert! Even more remarkable is the fact that the Spirit caught Philip away and did not leave him to disciple the man further, or instruct him on how to proceed after he returned to Ethiopia. So many of these things contradict our human planning skills. Truly we must be a Spirit-filled and Spirit-led people!

- **"...they were forbidden by the Holy Spirit to preach the word in Asia"** [Acts 16:6]: this is an astonishing verse, but it indicates that the Holy Spirit has an agenda which we cannot see. The small Roman province of Asia was in the western part of Turkey. Paul was directed to pass quickly through this region and go to Philippi, and bring the gospel to Europe. Later he returned to this region and established great Churches, including Ephesus. This then led to the establishment of the seven Churches of Asia [Revelation 2-3]. God has an agenda and, if we stick to it, we will see phenomenal Church growth from time to time. We must not have our eyes on numbers and programmes, but on the Lord of the harvest.

- **"We have not so much as heard whether there is a Holy Spirit."** [Acts 19:2]: most Churches, especially Pentecostal and Charismatic ones, claim expertise on the subject of the Holy Spirit. But this does not mean that they know the Holy Spirit in all His ways. Often it is the person who is prepared to step out of the pressure of conforming to their group, who is truly willing to obey the Holy Spirit. Many so-called 'experts' are only experts on a certain narrow line of the Holy Spirit's moving, and need to learn that the Holy Spirit is bigger and more present in the Churches than is often realised.

A Quaker preacher in America in the 19th century was commanded by the Spirit to go and preach in a loggers' camp. These loggers' camps were temporary, and made up of hardened men, who moved through the forests cutting wood. When the preacher got to the camp, it was deserted. He was puzzled but the Spirit told him to preach in an empty hall in the middle of the camp. He preached his heart out and then moved on.

Some years later he was in a Church where a man approached him and thanked him for leading him to Christ. He had been a hardened sinner working in the logging camps, and had been part of that deserted camp the Quaker preacher had visited. He explained that the loggers had moved out just two days before the preacher came, but that he had lost a tool and had returned to look for it. When he came back, he heard the Quaker preaching in the empty hall, and had listened through the window. He had been deeply convicted, and some days later had given his life to Christ, and had witnessed to the other loggers and led many of them to Christ also!

---

8. Key 6: The Need for Vision

Some Bible teachers have stressed the importance of having a vision, teaching that if we have a big vision we will eventually get a big Church. Is this true? It is true that if we have the expectation that our Church will always be small, such a mindset will not promote growth.

However, in certain countries, such as Saudi Arabia, small meetings are a miracle in themselves. Moreover, vision alone cannot deliver growth. Moses was a leader with great faith and vision, but he was unable to make the people of God spiritual by his gifts alone. It is important not to attribute growth and success to vision or any other methods. God is the author of growth.

The Bible clearly teaches the need to receive a vision from God so that it can then be outworked:

CHURCH GROWTH

- Moses went up the mountain and saw the Tabernacle laid out before him, and then came down and taught the craftsmen and laboured with them until the vision was fulfilled [Exodus 25:9].

- Solomon built the Temple according to a vision and pattern given to his father David by the Holy Spirit [1 Chronicles 28:11-13, 19].

- Paul spent three years in Arabia being given a revelation of the new covenant and the Church [Galatians 1: 17; Ephesians 3:3-10].

Without vision, pastors and leaders may give up under the weight of problems in their Churches. No Church is yet perfect, but sometimes there are huge problems confronting pastors, as in the case of the Corinthian Church. Without true vision, pastors will give up on the Biblical blueprint and settle for something less than Christ died for. The Church must be a victorious body of people confronting the evils of the day with faith and confidence. Even when persecuted, the Church must keep the vision of final triumph.

Leaders must walk closely with God in order to receive a vision that glorifies Him. Without a vision the people will perish [Proverbs 29:18 KJV], and there will be no forward movement. Vision is the bedrock of leadership. Vision is the seedbed of the future. Faith works to fulfil the vision which is imparted by the Holy Spirit.

Note however, the difference between visualisation and a vision imparted by the Holy Spirit. Visualisation implies that someone can go to God with their own 'vision' - they visualise what they want God to do. But this puts man in the driving seat. Only God imparts true vision, and we must run with it. If we do not have a vision from God, then we will have no future. If we do not see the Church going beyond its present size and effect, then it is possible that it will stagnate until a leader with vision is raised up by God.

In 1904 God laid it on Evan Roberts' heart to pray for the conversion of 100,000 souls. Within six months of tremendous revival, that was the number of people who were saved! Five years later almost all of the converts were still standing strong. Many became pastors and missionaries, affecting many nations throughout long years of ministry in the 20th century.

John Sung recorded in his diary that he prayed God would give him 100,000 souls in the coming year of evangelism. While the numbers cannot be counted, there is no doubt his vision was born of the Spirit and produced a tremendous harvest through his ministry.

9. Is Outpouring God's Main Method of Church Growth?

This question goes to the very heart of our understanding of Church growth. The principles of Church growth in the Scriptures are very different from human methods. We might tend to use methods that would result in gradual growth; but the Scriptures reveal that God sometimes works in sudden, unexpected ways. Jesus' ministry did not begin gradually, but suddenly. Jesus burst on the scene in an explosion of miracles and revelation that impacted the whole city of Capernaum. By the end of His first day of public ministry, the whole city was at the door of the house where He was staying [Mark 1:32-33].

Similarly, the Church grew from zero to 3,000 on its first day, and from 3,000 to 8,000 on its second day! Similar results were the mark of the revival in Samaria and other places. A large number were converted in Cornelius' house. This does not mean that God does not work in ones and twos - the Ethiopian eunuch was converted alone, as was the apostle Paul.

The Church cannot dictate to God how it will grow. We must obey the Holy Spirit and trust Him that He knows how best to reach the lost. This does not mean passivity, but faith and expectation that God will work as we seek Him.

PROMOTING GROWTH IN OLDER CHURCHES

Churches often grow very rapidly in the early stages of an outpouring, but later the growth may come to a halt. After the glow of the Welsh revival, the growth of the Churches there virtually stopped. At the start of a revival there are often few problems, but after, say, 20 years there may well be disagreements, rivalries and splits. Sins may have rocked the ministry, and there may be many problems that need solving. It is sometimes harder to get an older Church to grow than to start a new one! But this does not mean that we should abandon ship and jump onto another. God loves old Churches as well as new ones. After all, new Churches will become old one day.

The answer for older, stagnating Churches is to return to the first love of their early days. This will involve repentance and confession of sin. The letters of Jesus in Revelation to the seven Churches of Asia are keys to re-igniting Church growth. The seven letters indicate Jesus' intervention to revive and carry forward the work of older, established Churches. Five of the Churches had words of correction from the Lord; two had words of encouragement. Even Churches doing well need prophetic input! The seven Churches of Asia received these letters from the apostolic/prophetic ministry of the apostle John. This already indicates some important clues to the way forward:

- **Apostolic input from the wider Church** [Acts 16:4] - this verse indicates that there is a link between Church growth and connection with the wider apostolic vision and understanding. In practical terms, this means that Churches must guard against becoming cut off from the wider body of believers. Satan feeds in an isolationist tendency wherever and whenever the elders of a local assembly drop their guard. The Church can then become exclusive and self-sufficient. It was the sounding of the prophetic note, through John speaking forth the messages to the seven Churches, that led to the possibility of their renewal. Three examples from nature teach us important lessons in this context:

    a. **Cross-fertilisation** - if there is no cross-breeding in cattle or sheep, then the breed will become increasingly weaker as the generations pass. Fresh blood must be introduced into the stock for health to be maintained.

    b. **Fresh pastures** - if sheep are not moved to fresh pastures then they will nibble the grass down to its roots and even begin to eat the soil around the roots. The sheep will be poisoned, they will grow weak and some will even die. The shepherds must vary the diet of the sheep. If the 'sheep' listen to one man and one ministry alone, they will become strong for a while and then the growth will tail off.

    c. **Radical ploughing** - when a farmer ploughs a field with the same depth of plough, there will be a build-up over several years of a hard pan underneath the soil. This produces a barrier to deep root formation. The farmer will occasionally (around every five years) have to bring in a chisel plough, which cuts deeper and breaks up the underlying hardness. The point here is that listening to the same ministry year after year will produce underlying hardness. Fresh, cutting apostolic ministry must be introduced in order to break up the depths of believers.

- **Fresh reviving and renewal of the work** - starting a work can be easier than re-invigorating an older one, but God does not give up on people. Jesus' words to the seven Churches of Asia were prophetic utterances to expose sin and obstacles in the spiritual life of those Churches. If such prophetic ministry is allowed and welcomed, then there will be a deep repentance and fresh outpouring.

- **Fresh ministry and flexibility in ministry structures** - linked with the need for fresh reviving of the work, is the need to be open to correction and willing to repent when God speaks. This may mean that men who have had strong control over the Church need to lay down their office and position. A love of office has hindered many revivals; some leaders have guarded their position so jealously that they have grieved the Holy Spirit. Some pastors stay too long in a congregation - a pastor/leader can only take his flock so far. When a man's period of leadership has run its course, he will do well to lay down the mantle and acknowledge a younger man. This may mean that he should move away to fresh challenges. Then he will need to be humble in order to have the flexibility and faith to work with others.

THE SEVEN CHURCHES OF ASIA

The seven Churches in Revelation 2 and 3 are a picture of the Church throughout the Church age. Some people have suggested that they are symbolic of the successive states of the Church throughout history, but it seems more likely that all these seven kinds of Church can be found at any one time in Church history, whether in the 1st or the 21st centuries! What then are the main points exposed in these letters?

1. Ephesus – the Loveless Church

Ephesus was a 'successful' Church and here, again, it is important to recognise that not all that pleases people pleases God. The Church was hard-working, and had resisted false apostles - who will multiply in the last days [2 Timothy 3:1-9; 2 Peter 2]. It had not given in to weariness. The Church had been given the privilege of receiving the greatest ministry - being founded by Paul, pastored by Timothy and then probably having John in its eldership. The Church had been born in revival and was one of the most privileged among the early assemblies.

How sober, then, is the warning to even this great Church? Jesus said that it had 'fallen' and thus indicated that, as far as He was concerned, the condition of this Church was very perilous. The Church had slipped and fallen from its exalted position. Privilege always brings with it the danger of smug satisfaction and pride. We are blessed because God is good and gracious to sinners, not because we are great and worthy of blessing.

The Ephesus Church had continued on in the form of a successful Church, but was heading for disaster. They had lost their love for the Lord and for each other. Duty was the motive, not love. Outwardly, all was the same, but inwardly there was a coldness and distance from Christ and from each other. Their times of prayer would probably have been marked by fine-sounding prayers, but coldness. Their teaching would have been marked by great correctness, but no passion. Their worship would have been a shadow of former days, when zeal and love moved them to great acts of renunciation; Acts 19:19 tells of Ephesian belivers burning books worth 3 million US dollars.

Now the Church was cold and close to death. Though this may seem hard to believe, Paul describes the greatest sacrifice, knowledge and even faith as meaningless and empty if there is no love [1 Corinthians 13:1-3]. Clearly, the answer for this Church was to return to first love, and to seek God and a renewal of intimacy in prayer and devotion.

2. Smyrna – the Church in Times of Persecution

This Church needed words of affirmation and encouragement from the Lord. When we are in the right way, God seeks to affirm and strengthen us. This Church was passing through severe opposition and persecution. They seemed poor in their own sight but were rich in God's eyes. The key word of Jesus to this and to all Churches is, *"Be faithful until death, and I will give you the crown of life"*. This does not mean merely that we must be faithful all of our lives, but that we must be willing to give our lives for the Church, and for the Lord. The Lord Himself loved His Church and died for her [Ephesians 5:25]. Christians must have the lifestyle that chooses God above life itself.

3. Pergamos – False Teaching and Immorality

This Church had remained faithful to the Lord through days of persecution. Jesus uses the interesting name 'Antipas' to describe one of the early martyrs in this town. The name literally means *against everything*! This sums up the Christian's lot - we are strangers in every nation and opposers of every other religion and philosophy. Though we are kind, loving and generous to all, yet in our mind and philosophy we are in direct conflict with the world and the powers of darkness that lie behind the world's systems. [1 John 2:15-16]. All who would live faithful to Jesus will be persecuted [2 Timothy 3:12].

Jesus commends the Church at Pergamos but is grieved that, despite its many victories, there is impurity in the teaching. The teaching of Balaam led to idolatry and immorality, and was a ministry that was motivated by financial gain. These are serious warnings for the Church today, when there are so many scandals involving misuse of money and sexual immorality in the ministry. Once more the warning is chilling, since such impurities in a Church can of themselves draw great numbers - sinners do not want to renounce worldly, carnal pleasures. But the Church that would please God must live in purity, through faith and the power of the Holy Spirit.

4. Thyatira – False Teaching and Immorality

Thyatira was in a similar condition to Pergamos, and had works that were greater than in the early days of its existence. However, the false teaching here was even more evil, and involved a Jezebel spirit. Some commentators have assumed this to be an attack on the ministry of women, but this is surely a gross oversimplification. The Church is the bride of Christ, but this does not mean that it is only open to females! There are men with a Jezebel spirit - which here symbolises teaching that waters down the message of holiness in the Church and permits fornication, adultery, and divorce for trivial reasons.

While grace is needed in the Church in handling those who fail, yet there is to be a clear upholding of righteousness and holiness in the Churches, not by works of the law, but by grace through faith and empowered by the Holy Spirit. The Church must be holy, and no amount how much it may grow numerically, that will not change the Lord's mind on this essential foundation of spiritual life.

5. Sardis – the Church with a Great Name but a Dead Spirit

Sometimes people have tried to think of the best possible name or title for a Church or group of Churches, believing that it will make a significant difference – for instance, The True Church of God, or The True Apostolic Church of God, or The True Apostolic, Full Gospel, Pentecostal Four Square Assemblies of God. But in the end the title means nothing - it is the quality of the believers' lives that will make the reputation or 'name' of the Church. Jesus rebukes the Church at Sardis for having a great reputation but a poor life! He declares that their works are *"not perfect before God"*. What the Church was doing was not done out of undivided, heartfelt devotion to God. They were half-hearted. Perhaps they sometimes started a work but then gave up and did not see it through. Jesus tells them to repent and remember how God moved in the past; they must try somehow to regain that original freshness, by seeking God for a fresh outpouring of the Holy Spirit.

6. Philadelphia – the Church Distinguished by Great Love

This is the second of the seven Churches with no reproof from the Lord. Jesus declares that though the Church has little strength, yet it is very precious to Him, no doubt because of the brotherly love. This means that the Church has an open door in the Spirit - in prayer, in preaching, in evangelism, in all realms. Love will open the door, and love is the great key to growth. Love sinners, seek out people to help, take opportunities to love people. Such a Church will grow, and only such a Church deserves to grow!

7. Laodicea – the Lukewarm Church

The Laodicean Church has often been taken as a picture of the western Church in the 21st century. It has wealth but no zeal. It is a terrible condemnation that there is neither coldness nor zeal, and Jesus declares that He will vomit the Church - as tasteless - out of His mouth. Christ states that if there were coldness in the Church He could do something, because souls would realise their need, but lukewarmness produces just those sleepy conditions which allow the Christians to have enough religion not to fear eternity, but not enough to flee the world.

Jesus counsels this Church to be zealous! How can we find zeal if that is specifically what is lacking? The answer is, by obedience. Jesus is declaring that it lies within the response of His people to be zealous, rather than just waiting for something to happen. There are three aspects to His advice:

1. To buy gold - this is godly character and enduring faith.
2. To buy white clothing - this is purity and inner holiness.
3. To buy eye-salve to anoint their eyes - this is revelation from God.

The Church needs to transact with God on these things. But what is the currency of heaven - how can we buy them? The answer is, the currency of the heart - humility, faith, love and repentance. This is a currency that every person has to hand, but it cannot be used without giving up things that compete with the goal of faith.

KEY METHODS THAT CAN BE USED TO GROW THE CHURCH

Is it therefore wrong to use methods? Is it possible to miss God's will by being too bound by the need to be led by the Holy Spirit? The point is surely that the Holy Spirit does give wisdom to us on how to reach our generation. Once we become strait-jacketed to a system, we will not move out of the well-worn paths that others have used. But God is inventive and inspirational! Beyond this, it is also possible to recognise certain principles that will encourage growth in the Church.

1. Ministry at Every Level

The House Church movement may seem like a fairly recent phenomenon, but it is actually the pattern for New Testament Christianity. Acts 2:46 describes the Church as active in the larger meetings in the Temple areas, and then also in the smaller meetings from house to house. A sizeable Church cannot function with every member active in its main meetings. It is not possible for all to pray or prophesy or teach and preach in large meetings. Those meetings are more for people with particular gifting from God to minister.

A Church needs both large and small meetings in order to flourish. In larger meetings there is little intimacy, and in some of the mega-Churches, members have made few friends and have even remained largely unknown. They have not found the care and love that enables people to share their personal needs. But where smaller groups have functioned alongside the larger meetings, members have got to know each other intimately, and have been able to bring neighbours and friends along. The New Testament Church seems to have had larger meetings where gifted men taught the Word, and small house Churches where believers were nurtured.

Ephesians 4 tells of the gifts and ministries that all members have, and must exercise, if the Church is really to grow. If the Church is a one-man band then soon its growth will be stunted. An exceptionally gifted preacher or minister may attract crowds to hear him, but the believers in his Church may themselves not be very active in ministry, and this may ultimately lead to a loss of personal momentum among them. Pastors and elders must be careful to encourage others into ministry at all levels. It is very instructive that in the Ephesians 4:11 list of the fivefold ministries, none of them is in the singular. It is apostleS, prophetS, etc. It is the **whole** Church, empowered and released to the ministry, that will produce powerful growth [Ephesians 4:16].

2. Evangelistic Courses

Alpha and similar evangelistic courses are a 'method' but this does not mean that they are just human-centred or human-powered! God is able to give methods to His Church which are effective and powerful in reaching the lost. Alpha and similar courses are tools which many Churches have used to great effect. Churches should pray that God will show them how to use these tools, and where they should be adapted to fit the culture and circumstances in which they are being used. For example, it is a part of Alpha to have a special meal before the course. But if Alpha is used in prisons then it may well not be possible to have a special meal. It may, however, be possible to have something else that can be classified as special in a prison!

IDENTIFYING FALSE METHODS OF CHURCH GROWTH

...or how to grow the Church without God!!

1. Market Force Growth

Todd Rhoades has written an article entitled 'Ten Ways to Grow Your Church Without God'. To read his article in detail, see:

http://mondaymorninginsight.com/index.php/site/comments/ten_ways_to_grow_your_church_without_god/

The points that Rhoades identifies are not all negative. They include things like use of logos, creative designs, websites, advertising, and providing music and other meeting elements that are attractive to unbelievers. These are all aspectts that a wise pastor or board of elders will give close attention to.

However, the key question that we must ask is: can such methods lead to Church growth without the aid of the Holy Spirit? The scary answer is, of course, YES! None of these things is of itself a means of Church growth; for that, we need the Holy Spirit. The danger is that these, and other 'marketing' methods, may lead us to trust in our ability to build a large Church. The sad thing is that then the Church would not be the bride of Christ, created by God, but merely a religious organisation that is backing the cause of Christ. It is vital not to have a low view of the Church we are trying to grow.

George Barna - a statistician of Church trends and advocate of Church growth - says that the transition from the world to the Church should be as *"unnoticeable as possible"* for unbelievers. This may be interpreted positively to indicate that the Church should be relevant, and not require a cultural leap to join it. However, it could also be taken to mean that sinners should not be confronted with their sins, or with the need to deny themselves and carry their cross.

Much can be said about the need to make 'user-friendly' Churches. There is a great deal to learn about making the Church a happy and inviting place to be. But the Church must modernise without compromise. The real key is to have living and powerful prophetic words from God in the Church. Modernity and 'cultural relevance' must not replace the power and presence of God.

2. The Methods of Jehovah's Witnesses and Mormons

The two fastest-growing 'church bodies' in the USA and Canada, according to one report, are ones whose beliefs are known to conflict with traditional Christian teaching. Jehovah's Witnesses and the Mormons (the Church of Jesus Christ of Latter-day Saints) reported the largest membership increases in a year, according to the National Council of Churches' 2008 Yearbook of American and Canadian Churches. What are the elements we must avoid in the strategy of such organisations?

Guilt-driven evangelism - both Mormons and Jehovah's Witnesses make witnessing a central plank of salvation. Mormons are pressurised to engage in missionary work. Jehovah's Witnesses must witness to a certain number of people in order to fulfil the requirements of their faith. Guilt is a powerful evangelistic motive, and sadly it is also the motive of some Christians. But guilt must not be our motivating force, and preachers must be careful not to lay this burden on their flocks. The burden for the lost is a burden of love.

Money/aid as a missionary method - in Africa these two movements have distributed food and material aid to their members in a way that attracts people to join them. While this is a very crude method of growing in numbers, it is very effective in poor countries.

> Many Christian missions have large budgets for the aid of the people they serve. This is, of course, a noble and loving cause. Christ Himself told the rich young ruler to sell all he had and to give to the poor. However, it is a great mistake to link such aid with true conversions. Many mission schools in Africa would not admit pupils who had not been baptised. This led to multiple baptisms around the time of the new school intake! Aid must be given freely and without strings attached, or else the Church growth that results may be merely 'cupboard love'. There are many examples of believers (so-called 'rice Christians') moving from Church to Church in order to receive handouts from missionaries. One Church was discovered to have a series of signboards ready to

hang up on the front of its building, according to which western missionary group was visiting them. That Church probably figured in many different missions' statistics!

It is often best if local Christian leaders are directly involved in the distribution and use of mission aid that is donated. This elevates local leaders to equality with the donor nations, which grants them dignity, whereas this will be undermined by a 'colonial' type of control of the aid. It will reduce jealousy or rivalry, since the receiving Churches can handle the aid as a group. It will also reduce waste on unviable projects, and the possibility of deception, because local believers will know the credibility of the local people seeking help.

SNARES OF CHURCH GROWTH

There are dangers in the whole area of Church growth, which pastors and leaders must be aware of, or else they may become set on the wrong goals. What are these snares?

1. Snare 1: The Idol of Church Growth

The first epistle of John ends with the simple words: *"Little children, keep yourselves from idols. Amen."* [1 John 5:21]. These words may seem strange at first after such exalted truth as precedes them. Surely the Churches will not revert to making wooden images! But there are many other idols that believers can make. People can make 'idols' of their pastor or favourite preacher. And one of the most subtle forms of idolatry is success or Church growth. It is subtle because, of course, it is rightly desirable. Yet success in ministry or Church growth should not, in themselves, be our goal. The great goal is **faithfulness**.

Who among God's servants in the Old Testament was most faithful? Hebrews 3:2 tells us that Moses was faithful. Nevertheless, Moses did not succeed, through no fault of his own. Jeremiah faithfully prophesied to his generation, but his message was rejected. If Church growth is our master:

- We will be tempted to be faithful to what makes the Church grow rather than to the Lord.

- We will avoid offending the flock, with the danger that we may instead offend the Lord. We may cease to denounce sin, and seek to accommodate worldly and carnal practices.

- We will feed on the buzz of human applause, rather than on fellowship with Christ.

- We will be depressed when numbers go down and elated when they go up. This indicates that we are feeding on the success of our ministry rather than on Christ. If we feed on Christ then we will be full of faith whether things are going well or not.

2. Snare 2: The Sin of Numbering

In 1 Chronicles 21, David numbered Israel. Why did he do this? He wanted to measure his success, to see how well he was doing. He wanted to assure himself that he was king of a great nation, if not the greatest. He wanted to comfort himself with the sense of strength that numbers can give. But this temptation was from Satan. Even Joab, the commander of David's army, knew that it was a sin. Joab was a hard-hearted man, and lacked spiritual qualities such as gentleness and mercy, but he knew this was wrong [1 Chronicles 21:3].

This sin led to God's wrath being poured out on Israel – and, far from comforting David, the nation was punished and its numbers went down! David repented of this sin and returned to the altar, which speaks of a return to worship and the carrying of the cross, and allowing God to take His rightful place on the throne of our hearts.

3. Snare 3: Confusing Numbers with Success

The greatest danger of all in the area of Church growth is to assume that we are successful because we are big. Big does not mean successful in God's eyes. Jesus never challenged people to that kind of success; on many occasions Jesus' ministry seems to contradict the whole concept of drawing many people and counting that as success. Jesus was often followed by crowds, but He issued challenges that thinned the crowds down:

- Example 1: in Matthew 5:1 Jesus has drawn crowds through His miracles, but then he sets off up a mountain. When He has sat down, high up the mountain, His **disciples** draw near to Him. This suggests that Jesus is challenging His followers to more than mere decisions based on seeing miracles. He is challenging them to a life of discipleship that is willing to follow Him up mountains without being discouraged.

- Example 2: John chapter 6 begins with thousands following Jesus after the feeding of the 5,000. The crowds are so excited that they begin to proclaim Jesus as King [John 6:15]. We can even imagine a rousing praise meeting! But Jesus sends the crowds away, and when they find Him later He gives them some searching teaching on the need to follow Him for Himself, and not for bread or miracles. The crowds, and even some of His disciples, desert Him [John 6:66].

- Example 3: in Luke 14:25-33 great crowds follow Jesus, but He sifts the throng by giving them a searing challenge on discipleship. Jesus believed that it was vital for His followers to be true disciples.

WHAT IS SUCCESS?

It takes great courage for a minister to face up to the question of what makes for real success in God's eyes. Clearly, if the Church were a business, then we could measure its success by financial statistics. But it is not that simple.

1. Jeremiah – a Successful Prophet?

Jeremiah was a failure in terms of the outward success of his ministry. None of the kings he preached to appreciated or obeyed what he said. He saw his ministry fail to stir the hearts of the people to repentance. He was persecuted in many ways, and despite weeping and praying for the people, he was rejected and died - perhaps a martyr - during the period of the Babylonian captivity of Israel.

But Jeremiah was far from a failure. He had the great marks of success in his ministry.

o He loved the people: Love is the great foundation of success!

o He prayed with tears for the people and had a heart melted with compassion. Prayer from a melted heart is the source of success!

o He obeyed God's voice when all around him, even other priests, were rejecting and criticising his ministry. Fearless obedience is real success!

o He heard God's voice and maintained a close relationship with God throughout his ministry. Closeness to God, intimacy with God, is success in itself!

2. Moses – the Leader of a Lost Generation?

Moses saw almost the whole generation that he had led out of Egypt, perish in the wilderness. He had great failure in terms of the spiritual level of the nation he led. On many occasions Moses felt like giving up because of the awful carnality of the people. But he was successful because he knew God intimately. In Exodus 33:11, *"the Lord spoke to Moses face to face, as a man speaks to his friend"*. Moses saw the glory of the Lord and obeyed His voice.

3. Noah – Saved Only Seven People!

Noah cannot be termed a success in terms of numbers. One hundred years of preaching - and that with the huge visual aid of the ark - did not produce one single convert outside of his immediate family! Noah's success was not in the results, but in his faith and his willingness to go it alone with God against all that was happening in society around him. We need such courage today. **Abraham and the patriarchs** had a vision of God that carried them through lonely years of pioneering. This has been the lot of many missionaries and servants of God.

4. Conclusion

While success is not to be measured in numbers, the Church must avoid the 'bunker' mentality of a people who are not going to succeed in this lifetime. Success and victory are the Lord's promise to all who follow faithfully in His footsteps. He will give us personal victory, and will grant us to see people's lives changed and healed.

Christ gives power to His present-day disciples to preach the kingdom that has come with power, now, in this present age. There may be many difficulties, but we can expect great periods of expansion even in times of persecution and opposition. In the first century the gospel spread throughout the world like wild-fire under the tremendous power of a great outpouring of the Holy Spirit. Let us believe God to do the same in each of our lives and circumstances!

A GLORIOUS CHURCH IN A GLORIOUS KINGDOM

Jesus began His ministry proclaiming that the Kingdom of Heaven was at hand, and prophesying that He would build His Church. Yet the King was crucified, and He started no Churches during the 3½ years described in the Gospels. Then comes the wonderful book of Acts - the disciples' ministry is much the same as that of Jesus in the Gospels, but there is one huge difference. Now, the disciples are bearing the person of the King in their lives; they are continuing the incarnation, not by being God incarnate, but by allowing Christ to indwell them and make them into His body on the earth.

The New Testament teaches us that God's will for the Church, is that it should be a dynamic body, with every believer empowered to minister. In this chapter we will focus mainly on the pattern for Church life given in the books of Acts and Ephesians.

THE KEYS OF THE KINGDOM AND THE NEW TESTAMENT CHURCH

1. Keys in the New Testament

The keys of the Kingdom of Heaven are things which open the door for the kingdom to flood down and fill souls, changing lives, forming local Churches, and touching communities. Believers are swallowed up into the kingdom, and made into a Church which is in the kingdom. The kingdom itself is far greater. The Gospels never say that the Church is at hand, but that the kingdom is at hand. While Churches are to proclaim and manifest the kingdom, they must guard against the temptation to 'proclaim' their Church and to build a kingdom for themselves.

We will consider the keys of the kingdom in detail, but just note here other keys mentioned in the New Testament:

- The **key of knowledge** [Luke 11:52]. This is not only the Scriptures, since Jesus was talking to scribes who knew the Scriptures almost by heart, and yet He asserted that they had taken the key of knowledge away. The key of knowledge is the **way** in which we read, understand and interpret the Bible. The key is to read the Bible with faith, humility and spiritual thirst. Only then will it yield its truths, and impart life and salvation.

- The **key of David** [Revelation 3:7]. This key is in the hands of Jesus; it represents His authority to admit or exclude from God's kingdom - His power over the nations and over the future. Only He holds this key.

- The **keys of Hades and of Death** [Revelation 1:18]. This is the authority to decide the eternal destiny of every individual. Once more, these keys are in the hands of Jesus alone.

- The **key to the bottomless pit** [Revelation 9:1 and 20:1]. This is the power to imprison evil spirits in the dark abyss. It is not the final resting place of these spirits, but is a prison where they must await the final judgment. Some spirits are kept there until their time comes to play a role in world history.

2. What is a New Testament Church?

- A New Testament Church is a gathering of believers around the Person of Christ to discern and love Him. The believers gather to worship Him, to hear Him and to speak to one another His word, by preaching, by prophecy, by prayer for one another. The Church does not cease to be the Church when it is not meeting. The Church is the Church at all times and wherever the believers are found. The gifts of the Spirit can and should be used in all places: in the home [Mark 1:29-30], in public places [Luke 7:11-17], on journeys [Luke 18:35-43], at mealtimes [Luke 14:1-4]. The believers **are** the Church, and wherever believers are, there is the Church.

- A Church is only possible where the believers are baptised with the Holy Spirit. The living presence of Christ is grieved except where the Holy Spirit is allowed free reign. There is no contradiction between the centrality of Christ and the need for the Holy Spirit. Christ was full of the Holy Spirit [Luke 4:1] and so we would be rejecting part of Him if we rejected the fullness of the Spirit. 1

Corinthians 12:13 teaches that the baptism with the Holy Spirit is the act that unites us most deeply with Christ and with one another into one body. This truth is confirmed by the fact that there were no Churches in the Gospels - only in the book of Acts.

o Christ is the Head of the Church – so, in order to remain a living Church, each member must remain in living fellowship with Christ and submission to Him as Lord.

3. Biblical Images Used to Describe the Church

Various titles and metaphors are used for the Church in the New Testament:

- **Body of Christ** [1 Corinthians 12:27], indicating that the Church is to continue the ministry of Christ on earth.
- **Temple of the Holy Spirit** [Ephesians 2:21-22], indicating that God's presence is in the Church and that this body is meant to replace the physical Temple in Jerusalem.
- **The New Jerusalem** [Revelation 21:2], indicating the Church's place in God's kingdom.
- **Israel** [Galatians 6:16], indicating that the Church is the fulfilment of the spiritual promises of God to the Jews.
- **Pillar and ground of the truth** [1 Timothy 3:15], indicating that the Church is God's main means of self-revelation to the world.
- **Household of God** [Ephesians 2:19], indicating that the Church is God's personal home.
- **Bride of Christ** [Revelation 19:7 and 21:2], indicating the place of the Church in the affections of God.

4. Who is a Member of this Church?

Membership of the Church is known first and foremost by Christ alone [2 Timothy 2:19]. Local Churches and denominations may have many rules to determine who is allowed to be a member, and may publish lists of membership. However, none of these things guarantee that a person is truly a member of His body, the Church. That membership is based on personal union with Christ by the Holy Spirit [1 Corinthians 12:13]. It is obtained by repentance, faith and obedience in baptism.

5. Who Leads the Church?

As we've seen, local Church leadership is in the hands of elders, who are men chosen from mature, stable Church members. The gifts and calling of God are, however, independent of the office of eldership. So being in the office of elder does not guarantee that the man has vision and leadership ability as gifts from God. In its highest form, leadership is manifest in apostleship. Apostles are themselves to be subject to the local leadership (elders) of the Church. The apostle John was a member of the Church in Ephesus but refers to himself in that capacity as an elder [2 John 1]. Peter was an apostle, and present at the great council in Jerusalem in Acts 15, but was subject to James, the senior elder of the Church in Jerusalem.

WHAT ARE THE KEYS OF THE KINGDOM?

The keys of the kingdom are the vital elements necessary for outpouring of the Holy Spirit. Without them, living Churches cannot be formed or maintained, and in their place there will be gatherings of disciples in various levels of understanding, but without the essential elements that make a Church. These keys are vital in obtaining a living Church. (We considered some of them also in the previous chapter in the context of obtaining an outpouring of the Spirit for Church growth.)

1. Repentance

The Holy Spirit cannot be poured out and mixed with sin. Therefore sin is the most serious obstacle to a true New Testament Church, and to a true outpouring of the Holy Spirit. Sin must be confessed and utterly forsaken. People's heart's must be emptied of all uncleanness. All habits that weaken the heart must be renounced. Time must be taken so that repentance is deep and thorough. If repentance is not taken seriously, there is no reason why God should take us seriously when we pray for an outpouring of His Spirit.

The 'religious' person has more to fear than the worldly sinner in this respect. The worldly sinner has nothing to lose. Everyone knows that he was not a Christian, and did not profess to be one. Therefore when he confesses his sin, everyone approves and applauds. However, when the religious person confesses and repents, he has more to lose. He must lay down his reputation. This will be harder the longer a person has professed to be a Christian, and the higher their position in the Church.

God does not want to shame people – that is not the purpose of repentance - but there must be a broken, humble attitude, especially in the leadership of a Church, which indicates clearly that they are ready to acknowledge mistakes, or sins such as prayerlessness, pride or spiritual dryness. While public confession is not necessary, it might be appropriate to share with close brothers, in order to keep a spiritually refreshed life.

2. Faith

Believers must examine themselves, to ask how much they really believe and expect God to pour out His Spirit and form Churches that are like the one in Acts chapter 2. This kind of faith is matched by strong desire and determination to see God work. Jesus said in John 7:37: *"If anyone thirsts, let him come to Me and drink. He who believes in Me, as the Scripture has said, out of his heart will flow rivers of living water."* There is a deep work of the Holy Spirit that makes us one with God through the death of His Son. This work is the foundation of the Church, because it makes believers into a community of love. It takes the sin and awkwardness out of our souls and makes us bear with one another and wash each other's feet.

Do you believe this work is real? Do you believe that God can do this deep work in your heart? Can you ask in faith, believing that God will do it for you? Faith is a great key that allows the kingdom to come in power into our hearts.

3. Preaching the Cross

The apostles preached the death and resurrection of Jesus from the Day of Pentecost onwards. Really it was only from that day onwards that they understood the cross. The Holy Spirit brings the understanding of the cross. The cross, then, is the open door for the Holy Spirit to come. The fire and then the rain came on the altar that Elijah built on Mount Carmel after 3½ years of drought [1 Kings 18; Luke 4:25]. The fire and the Spirit were poured out as a result of the 'altar' of Calvary, ending the spiritual drought of Israel.

In order to secure an outpouring of the Spirit, we must preach the cross, and not only the Holy Spirit. A 'cross-less Pentecost' would be carnal, and not glorifying to God.

4. The Identity of Christ

In Matthew 16:13-19 Jesus gives Peter one of the keys, which is the truth that Jesus is the Messiah. The Church is built on the massive rock which is Christ. Peter is a stone, but not a solid rock. He wobbled several times! God strengthened him to make him stand, but Paul had to stand against him, as reported in Galatians 2:11-21.

The identity of Jesus Christ is the foundation of the Church. A Church is as strong as the degree to which it knows Him. Churches inevitably reveal what they really know of Christ. Thus some Churches reveal that they think Christ wears a gold cross round His neck, that He is surrounded by clouds of incense, and wears religious robes. Other Churches reveal a Christ who is more like a rock star, who is 'loud' and pleased with noise. The closer a Church (and its leaders) is to Christ, the stronger that Church will be. The Church is built on the revelation of the identity of Christ as to His Person and His character, including the following:

- **His person**:
  - Jesus is the exact image of God
  - Jesus is Almighty God
  - Jesus is eternal, from everlasting to everlasting
  - Jesus is the Creator

- **His character**:
  - Jesus is holy
  - Jesus is patient and loving
  - Jesus is gentle
  - Jesus is gracious, loving sinners
  - Jesus is full of joy
  - Jesus is full of sorrow over the state of people's hearts
  - Jesus is full of glory

As the Church knows Jesus in His essential identity, so it will be strong to do the work of God and build people up in faith.

5. Justification through Faith

Mankind is sinful and thus unworthy to receive the Holy Spirit. This is a legal barrier that makes it wrong for God to pour out His Spirit on sinners without a sacrifice for sin. There is also the barrier of guilt in the human heart, as every sinner knows that they are unworthy to receive such a gift from God. However, justification is the declaration that God has accepted Jesus' sacrifice. By this sacrifice, He has made us legally acceptable before God. This legal acceptance is the meaning of the word **justified**. However, it is not just a deliverance from the negative, it is also the imputing of the positive.

Imagine a man who is a debtor. He owes a million dollars. Christ, through His blood, has not only cancelled the debt, but in its place He has filled the account with a million dollars credit! Christ has forgiven our sins **and** imputed to us His virtues. Thus we are not just free from the guilt of past sins, we are positively worthy through Christ to receive the Holy Spirit [Colossians 1:12]. It is as if we had failed an exam, and God not only erases our failure, but gives us a pass with distinction! We are now fully reconciled to God, and so it is a righteous act for God to give the Holy Spirit. This realisation is a key since, without it, the human soul will strive endlessly, believing it must earn the gift of the Spirit by works. See Galatians 3:2-3.

Justification by faith is one of the great keys to outpouring of the Holy Spirit, since otherwise people are left to wallow in their sense of unworthiness. The only alternative to justification is works. The Holy Spirit is God's love gift, God's gift of grace. It is all of grace and there is nothing we can do to earn the Holy Spirit. This is equally true of mature believers as it is of new believers. None can earn the moving of the Holy Spirit. If we do not understand this, we will 'work' at prayer and faith, trying to build up some credit with God. But it is simply unattainable by human effort, and has already been attained by Jesus through His blood. For this reason it is vital that the truth of justification be preached to mature believers as well as to new converts.

6. The Scriptures

On the Day of Pentecost, Peter quoted from Joel and the Psalms. Use of the Scriptures is a powerful tool to release the presence and power of God, both in private devotion and in public speaking. The Holy Spirit will be poured out upon the Word of God.

The use of the Scriptures in prayer and ministry is a key to the inflow of the Holy Spirit. George Muller found that his prayer life was dry until he began to meditate on the Scriptures before praying.

7. Prayer

Prayer is the prelude to all the great moves of God's Spirit. In the book of Acts, we may ask who prayed. Certainly the apostles were praying in the upper room [Acts 1:14]. Their prayers were weak and yet sufficient. It is astonishing but true that prayer is based on an acknowledgment of weakness and dependence on God.

Who shows the way in prayer? Jesus! Jesus prayed for the outpouring of the Holy Spirit with prophetic insight all through His ministry. He prayed and the heavens were opened upon Him [Luke 3:21]. He prayed all through the night and God led Him to appoint the twelve apostles [Luke 6:12-13]. He prayed through the early hours of the morning prior to His arrest. His agonised praying opened the door for outpouring.

8. The Gifts of the Spirit

The 120 people in the upper room all prayed with tongues in response to the coming of the Holy Spirit [Acts 2:4]. This indicates an inner abandonment to the working of the Spirit, not filtering everything through our intellect. While it is open to abuse, and some people may make noises and claim that this is the manifestation of the Holy Spirit, nevertheless, the dangers should not rob us of the very real blessing of yielding our souls in entire abandonment to the Holy Spirit. This is a key in the release of the Spirit on a congregation, and in the work of the ministry. In other words, the Holy Spirit does not work through mere intellectual exercise. Our intellects should be thoroughly engaged in understanding the truth of God, but in the flow of worship, we must let go and allow the Holy Spirit to have free flow through our lives.

If the Holy Spirit can flow in us through the gift of tongues then it will not be long before He is flowing through us in prophecy. Paul clearly teaches that the gift of tongues will produce personal edification. It is not primarily for public use, and on the Day of Pentecost, it was not unknown tongues but known languages that were released by the Holy Spirit.

THE KING AND THE KINGDOM

Jesus came into the world as King over all, but also as heir to the throne of David. The genealogy in Matthew chapter 1 makes it clear that Jesus was no idle threat to Herod. He was in fact born to be King of the Jews. The genealogy of Jesus was through two avenues. First, he was the adopted son of Joseph, who was himself the rightful heir to the throne. Jesus was the legitimate heir to the throne by this means. Some may object that he was not directly a son of Joseph, but the adoption was by divine decree, and none may oppose that law! When Christ was born, all Jerusalem was troubled because of the wise men's search for the one *"born king of the Jews"* [Matthew 2:1-3].

The second genealogy of Jesus, given in Luke 3:23-38, identifies Jesus as the seed of David through Mary, and as the seed of Adam. (Mary was Heli's daughter, but, as head of the household, Joseph is named instead of Mary.) Luke's genealogy demonstrates that Christ was grafted, by physical descent, into the human race as well as into the royal line through His mother.

Jesus grew up as King, but without the trappings of worldly pomp and show. He was born in a manger - which suited the stamp of humility in His royal blood. His kingdom is truly not like the kingdoms of this world. It is in fact the opposite.

Jesus was anointed at Jordan [Luke 3:22], and so in one way He began to rule as King at that time. He began His Kingly rule at the same age as David [2 Samuel 5:4; Luke 3:23]. David had previously been anointed king by Samuel at around the age of 17; Jesus was anointed by His Father. From the moment of His anointing, Jesus ruled over all the dimensions of life. He did not rule in a merely political way, but He ruled absolutely in the spirit world, taking control over Satan, who tried to corrupt Him by the offer of worldly power. This offer of worldly power was a trap. Many fall into it and then progress in the financial or political empires of this world, only to find that they have lost their soul through compromise and disobedience. Some people have even achieved high office in Churches through lying and corruption. This is a grave offence and will be judged accordingly by the King.

Christ was patient and willing to wait for all to be given Him in due time. And so it proved. For 3½ years, Jesus ruled over Israel, scorning the emptiness of political power, and instead taking authority over demons, sickness, death, the weather and all of creation. He directed the path of shoals of fish and even individual fish. He cursed the fig tree. Christ reigned supreme. But the one area that He did not take authority was over the human heart. This He left to people's own deliberate choice and free will. He was no tyrant.

This dimension of the Kingdom of God is perhaps the most crucial. The multitudes of Israel received the blessings of the kingdom and then crucified the King. It is tragically the case that, even today, blessings are more spoken of than the One who blesses. If people are asked if they want to go to heaven, most will answer *"Yes!"* However, the gospel is not *"Do you want to go to heaven?"* but *"Will you receive Jesus as Saviour and Lord?"* It is possible to receive blessings rather than the Saviour, but it is not possible to be saved without Him.

PARABLES OF THE KINGDOM AND THE CHURCH

There are many parables of the kingdom, and they each have specific lessons to impart to the Church. They are prophetic in that they prophesy things that are to happen in the 'Church age', which is the age in which we are living. The following points relating to certain parables are grouped according to the lesson to be learned.

1. The Church is a Mixed Field in This Age

The parables of the sower and of the wheat and the tares [Matthew 13 1-30, 36-43] indicate that the Church in this age is not to expect perfection. This is a vital lesson, because without this awareness, believers will be grievously disappointed when they are confronted with serious problems in the Church, especially divisions. Many believers in their early years are so overwhelmed by the power of their own conversion that they expect the whole world to be converted as easily as they, and also expect the Church to be a wonderful place of perfect love. When the disappointments arise, some become cynical and give up hope of 'perfection'. The truth is very different, according to the prophetic teaching of Jesus.

He warns us that there are two sources of disappointment. First there is the varying response of 'believers'. Some are worldly, some respond superficially, and some do not have the depth of character to stand through a testing time. These problems should not discourage us from realising that a perfect response to God and His word is still possible. In other words, Jesus is teaching us not to become hardened or cynical, but rather to believe that God can make us good ground and produce a good harvest in our lives. While others face struggles, we learn from this to direct our own hearts into truly godly living. If we find this life, we will have abundance in our hearts, and will live to encourage others to find this place of fullness in the Kingdom of God. Churches will go through problems, but this does not mean that we give up believing in the abundant life of fullness – rather, the opposite. If there are problems, we know why. We seek God for deep fulfilment of His wonderful kingdom promises for ourselves and for all of God's people.

The second source of disappointment is because there are those in the Church who are not really at all converted, but instead have an affinity with the prince of darkness. This does not make them evil, but it does mean that their responses are not as the King would wish. Their responses may be bitter, selfish, petty, complaining and unbelieving. Jesus said these are things *"that offend"* [Matthew 13:41] and they will be removed at the end of the age when Jesus comes back. We are not able to deal with this problem before then. Churches can deal with immorality, and must discipline those who sin and refuse to repent; but they cannot remove difficult people from their midst. Some difficult people are very religious, some are very moral, and some very charismatic. Jesus said that some who cast out demons are not known by Him [Matthew 7:21-23]. Paul said that Satan has transformed himself into an angel of light and that his ministers sometimes appear as ministers of righteousness [2 Corinthians 11:14-15]. There is the genuine and there is the fake. We are not to become obsessed with finding out who is genuine, but we are to take the warnings to heart and make sure that we ourselves are genuine and are truly walking with God.

This second source of disappointment is when we sense that there is something deeply wrong about a person's life or ministry. We are not to try and sort these things out, but to be positive and loving, and commit these things to Christ to sort out. He is the Head of the Church, and He is not helped by our cynicism – rather, He is aided by our faith and love in the midst of confusion and difficulty.

2. The Church May Grow Huge and Become a Nesting Place for 'Strange Birds'

This lesson is particularly hard to swallow. But it is nevertheless true that the larger a Church organisation becomes, the more it is prone to compromising interference. This does not mean that large organisations are in themselves evil, but it does mean that big does not mean good, and it certainly does not mean trouble-free. Large organisations will inevitably attract career workers. This is a phenomenon not found in the New Testament. Once a pastor is in office to further a career, then there is huge danger. This can also be true of music writers, authors, preachers, and so on. Some Churches have built hospitals and universities, which again can offer career advancement. Jesus said that, when a 'tree' grows huge, *"birds of the air"* will come and roost [Matthew 13:31-32]. Some have taken this parable to mean that the gospel will grow in its influence until it is huge and dominant. Sadly, this is not the case. The gospel does grow in its influence, but wherever it becomes dominant, other things start to invade.

The image of the 'bird' may mean either individuals in the Church who are foreign to the true Spirit of Christ, or it may sometimes refer to evil spirits that actually roost in the branches of the Church. This is not difficult to understand in the context of pastors and theologians who believe the Bible is not inspired, and who promote or even practise alternative lifestyles such as extra-marital sex or homosexuality. These things are disturbing, but Jesus warned us. All over the world there are mission schools and hospitals, some of which are staffed by people who do not even profess to be Christians, and live worldly lives.

3. Corruption from Within Will Weaken the Church More Than Anything Else

Jesus taught that the Church is like unleavened bread that can be totally corrupted by unremoved 'leaven' or sin [Matthew 13:33]. Some have thought that in this parable it is the gospel which is like leaven, and that ultimately the gospel will transform the whole of society. But other teaching in the Bible points consistently away from this interpretation. The children of Israel were to remove all leaven from their homes and to keep the Feast of Unleavened Bread [Exodus 12:18-20]. Paul warns against the leaven of sin, which will affect the whole Church if not properly dealt with [1 Corinthians 5:6-8].

This teaching shows that the worst enemy of the Church is from within. Many have commented that with the 'conversion' of Constantine in AD 312, the Church was conquered by the world from within. The early Church had fought valiantly against terrible persecution and had remained pure. But when it became politically correct to be a Christian, then all motive for purity was lost.

The Church is like a plant, a living organism, which must be grown and nurtured and cannot be mass-produced like manufactured objects. This is a key, since otherwise the Church will seek to make converts through methods. While methods may be used in order to communicate the gospel, the Church must guard against reducing conversion to a method. There is a mystery and a power at work in true conversion that does not need propping up. None of the first converts were propped up by 'follow-up'. This does not mean that follow-up is wrong, but rather that the need for it is an indication that things are not yet right. In true conversion there is a joy and yieldedness to Christ that carries the person forward in the delight of salvation.

KEYS TO A HEALTHY CHURCH IN THE BOOK OF ACTS

- The primacy of prayer and the word in apostolic ministry - prayer was a central activity of the Church from the day of its birth.

- The centrality of Christ – He was preached and worshipped. The gospel is not a set of beliefs; it is the communication of a living Person and Presence.

- Belief in the need for the baptism with the Holy Spirit - the apostles were never satisfied by the conversion of sinners until there was an outpouring of the Holy Spirit to accompany it. Where this truth is neglected, the Church will soon wither and die. The rediscovery of this truth has nearly always been the key to a fresh wave of conversions and Church growth.

ATTACKS ON THE EARLY CHURCH

1. Intimidation by the Devil [Acts 3-4]

The first attack in Acts is against the public witness of the Church. The world does not oppose the ministry of miracles. Jesus did not get into trouble through his miracles. He got into trouble when He opened His mouth. The same is true of the apostles. If they had healed in the name of Abraham or even God in general, there would have been no problem. The offence was in the name of Jesus.

A group of street evangelists were doing a street drama in Leamington Spa, England. A man lay on the ground in chains, begging for help to gain freedom. A crowd gathered to watch. One actor represented philosophy, and quoted great philosophers, but the man was not set free. Another represented money, and again there was no freedom. Politics, education, all had their turn but failed to set the man free. The crowd laughed and applauded. Then one actor stepped forward and released the man. "What is your name?", cried the man. "Jesus!" came the answer. The laughter stopped and the crowd melted away

---

The rulers of the Jews were anxious to stop people talking about Jesus! Talk about the supernatural, bend spoons, do clever hypnosis tricks on audiences, and the result will be fame and money. But if we talk about Jesus, somehow there is great opposition to that name, and many people think that we should keep our faith to ourselves. Believers can be intimidated by either persecution or culture. When governments persecute Christians, this often has the effect of purifying the Church.

Ravi Zacharias tells of a believer who fled from Vietnam in the 1980s and was cornered by some security officers just hours before he was to board the boat. He lied to them, and denied it when they asked if he was trying to leave. Later, he was convicted of his sin, and sought them out, admitting that he was about to flee. The officers then asked if they could join him! They went with him in the boat and it was their skill in handling the boat that saved all their lives.

When governments persecute Christians, superficial believers give in quickly and deny their faith. Those that remain are forced to meet together at great personal risk, often in forests and secret locations.

In Russian communist days, a KGB officer stormed a Christian meeting and threatened the believers with death unless they recanted and denied their faith. Several admitted they were not believers and were allowed to leave. But the rest remained and were prepared to die rather than deny Christ. Then the KGB officer said, "You are real believers; please tell me, what must I do to be saved?"

The culture of a nation can also make it difficult for believers to share their faith. In western culture there is the general belief that all opinions are valid and that no-one should say to someone else, *"You are wrong in what you believe"*. People complain about Christians being too 'aggressive' in their evangelism. But in a dying world, while we must speak respectfully and politely, yet we must not keep silent. The world is perishing in lack of hope and faith, and the only answer is Christ. There is no other.

2. Sin in the Church

This is the most serious attack on the Church because it comes from 'within'. There are many Scriptures that warn of the danger of sin in the Church:

- ❖ Acts 5:1-11 tells how Ananias and Sapphira boasted that they had given all the money they had received from selling a piece of land, when in fact they had kept back part for their personal use. The sin was not in keeping back part of the money - it was in their pretence of total consecration, and in lying hypocrisy. The result was that they fell down dead in the presence of God's Holiness, which was ruling in the Church in those days.

- ❖ Paul says in 1 Corinthians 5:6 that *"a little leaven leavens the whole lump"* - indicating that sin in the Church will have an effect on the spiritual temperature of all the people of God.

- ❖ Joshua 6 and 7 records how Achan sinned secretly, and the result was that the whole nation was defeated by their enemies.

- ❖ In Revelation 2:14 Jesus warns the Church at Pergamos that there are teachers in the midst who *"hold the doctrine of Balaam"* and *"put a stumbling block"* in the way of God's people by teaching them to eat things sacrificed to idols and to commit fornication. Balaam was asked by Balak to curse the people of God, but God forbade him, so in the end he taught Balak the way to defeat them - by getting them to commit fornication with the Midianite women [Numbers 31:16].

The presence of sin in the Church will affect the whole body and will reduce the sense of God, and the joy in worship. God cannot be glorified by sin.

3. Murmurings and Cultural Differences

In Acts 6:1 there arose a dispute between the Jews of Greek culture and the Jews of stricter Judean culture. Somehow the Greek Jews were being discriminated against. It is at this point that the real target of Satan is revealed, and it is here that the apostles refused the temptation to *"leave the word of God and serve tables"* [Acts 6:2]. This was great wisdom on the part of the apostles, since it would have been easy for them to have become 'administrators'. This is often the fate of gifted men - they leave their true calling and become ineffective in soul-winning or in teaching God's people. The apostles, however, redoubled their efforts in the ministry of the word and prayer [Acts 6:4].

Notice that the cultural division was healed by wise handling of the problem. The Greeks had been discriminated against, so the distribution of the aid was put into the hands of Jews most of whom had Greek names, indicating that those who were formerly neglected were now given prominence. This is wisdom not unlike that of Solomon, and will always lead to healing and unity. God's ways are perfect.

4. Intensified Persecution

The threats mentioned in Acts 4:29 were then carried out, and first Stephen [Acts 7:59] and then James [Acts 12:1] were killed. The number of Christians martyred for their faith has risen over the centuries, and statistics show that more died for their faith in the 20th century than in any other. The numbers are in the millions. The Russian Revolution and the Cultural Revolution in China both involved the purging of millions of believers. The same is true in Vietnam, Cambodia and other places. Nevertheless, despite predictions that the Church would disappear in Russia and China, the Church there has seen phenomenal growth.

5. Doctrinal Divisions

In Acts 15 there was a very serious division over the question of circumcision. This was dealt with wisely and carefully, and the matter was solved with great wisdom. (See the detailed study of doctrinal division below.)

6. Personality Clashes

In Acts 15:39 Paul and Barnabas clashed so violently over Mark that they separated in the Lord's work. The rift between them was ultimately healed, and Paul mentions both Barnabas [1 Corinthians 9:6] and Mark [2 Timothy 4:11] with affection and obvious esteem. Personality is often the cause of division, but doctrine is often blamed! See below for further details.

CAUSES AND CURES OF DIVISIONS IN THE CHURCH

There are two main causes of divisions: doctrine and personality. Both are avoidable, and can be cured if identified before there is serious tearing of the body and damage to souls.

1. Divisions through Doctrinal Difference

In Acts 15 the New Testament Church faced its most serious test. The test was passed successfully, but sadly in the long history of the Church many divisions have not been healed in the same way. The Church has divided over many doctrines.

The issue in Acts 15 was over the foundations of salvation. How is a person saved? There was a group in the Church who held that believers had to be circumcised in order to be saved. This is the great doctrinal conflict that lies behind the book of Galatians. Similar conflicts have surfaced many times in the history of the Church, and the answers have not always been easy to discern! The process of divisions may be seen as inevitable, in order to recover truths that have been lost over the centuries. Thus, as truth has been rediscovered, believers have had to decide when the truth is worthy of dividing over.

There is no doubt that Paul would have divided the Church on this issue. He was the strongest voice in defence of the gospel. In doctrinal matters, there must be an examination of the issue at stake to see if it goes to the heart of the gospel. Paul was not ready to compromise; if there was no unity on this issue then there would be two Churches at the end. This does not mean that Paul was eager to divide. It is clear that he was at pains to please the Christians who were from a Jewish background. Right after this event, Paul had Timothy circumcised in order to make him acceptable to the Jews whom they were seeking to win [Acts 16:3]. But this willingness to adapt is different from allowing for a change in the means of salvation.

How was the potential split in the Church healed? There are six main steps. Any one step on its own is not sufficient, but the bringing together of these six factors is decisive. Sadly, there are few occasions when all come together at the same time.

(a) The Authority of the Apostle Peter [Acts 15:7-11]

The discussion was very heated, with *"much dispute"* [v7]. We can imagine that Paul's keen mind and personality made him argue vigorously for the gospel! But then Peter *"rose up"*. This marks a turning point in the narrative, and indicates that Peter had waited for this moment.

The phrase 'rose up' or 'stood up' occurs at several key moments in the book of Acts. Peter stood up with the eleven on the Day of Pentecost [Acts 2:14] and commanded the lame man to rise up in Acts 3:6. This indicates a rising up in faith and the prompting of the Holy Spirit. Unless men of God arise in faith and in the Spirit, the truth will be lost. The truth of the gospel must be contended for [Jude 3].

Peter was recognised by everyone as called and chosen by God to be an apostle. This recognition is key if truth is to prevail. The Church is not a democracy, and must recognise that there are men of specific and exceptional calling. (However, such men are neither infallible nor do they have absolute authority over the Church; the New Testament nowhere crowns Peter as a Pope!)

Peter claims a divine commission upon his life - that the Gentiles should hear the gospel through him [Acts 15:7]. Peter also claims the divine seal upon this ministry by a special outpouring of the Holy Spirit [v8]. He then states the fundamental elements of the gospel that God has entrusted him with:

- The gift of the Holy Spirit and the gift of a pure heart through that gift [v8-9].
- The bestowal of this gift by faith [v9].
- The impossibility of being pure by the Law [v10].
- The gift of salvation is through the grace of Jesus Christ [v11].

These elements are brought out through this conflict, and times of difficulty in the Church should make us all examine what are the true foundations of salvation. Churches are apt to add to these foundations, either consciously or unconsciously. People make value judgments on others according to the clothes they wear, their jewelry etc. Whatever our opinions on these things, we must be careful of effectively saying that, *"unless we do this or that we cannot be saved"*, if this is adding to the truth of the gospel.

(b) The Keeping of Silence in the Assembly [Acts 15:12]

Peter's words were authoritative and the effect was silence. This quietness of spirit is an effect of the Presence of God and should be deeply respected by God's people. Sadly, many congregations know nothing of the peace and solemn quiet of the Lord's Presence. When it comes upon a congregation, all should wait in anticipation of what the Lord will say and do. The noise of constant chatter and the eagerness to speak will often quench the Spirit and muffle the voice of God in the assembly. *'Be still and know'* is a spiritual principle. To violate this silence, unless prompted by the Holy

Spirit, is to risk grieving the Holy Spirit who is taking control of the assembly.

(c) The Authority and Testimony of the Apostles [Acts 15:13]

More testimony is then given, with apostolic authority. Paul and Barnabas were not just giving anecdotal evidence. They were recounting miracles and wonders that God had done among the Gentiles through their ministry. Such testimony is not to be taken lightly and is an indication of God's seal on a ministry.

(d) The Authority of the Scriptures [Acts 15:15-18]

James, the elder (the Lord's brother) then rises up to add the voice of the Scriptures to the debate. The key phrase here is *"as it is written"* [v15]. Decisions cannot be taken on the basis of human testimony, even that of an apostle, without the supporting wisdom of the Holy Scriptures. Some may say that the Bible alone is all that is needed. But we do well to remember that, when Jesus was opposed, it was by religious men who knew the Scriptures inside out! The Bible is the last word on all these matters and nothing must be done that contradicts the clear Word of God. But people must also be humble enough to acknowledge that they can be taught new things from the Word, and must be willing to let things go that are not based on the Word.

(e) A Word of Wisdom [Acts 15:19-29]

James then delivers a masterful word of wisdom through the Holy Spirit. The key here is that he picks out essential elements that can enable the Church to find unity. He knows that the Christians with Jewish background cannot have fellowship over a meal that includes blood. He also must clarify that fornication and idolatry are sins which will disqualify a soul from participation in Church life. Therefore, in just a few words, he gives guidelines around which the Church can unite and press forward. This is the wisdom of the Holy Spirit, and it cannot be over-emphasised how much the Church needs the gifts and utterance of the Holy Spirit to heal divisions. Often it is the lack of unction, or of prophetic clarity, that makes divisions inevitable.

(f) The Whole Church was Involved in the Process [Acts 15:22]

It was not a secret conclave. This is one of the indications of the spiritual maturity of the New Testament Church. Most Churches find a need to keep things quiet! Discretion is good when the issues of sin and discipline are being discussed, but the leaders should trust the Church, and also trust the discernment of the Church. No votes were taken! This was not democracy. But it is the moment when the Church is allowed to hear the discussion and discern the voice and authority of God in the midst. God is in control through His apostles, His Word and His Presence. If the people are not able to discern the voice of God, then there may be a more serious problem in the hearts of the people.

Doctrinal division is not always avoidable. The history of the Church is a history of truths lost and then rediscovered as God refreshes His people with revivals. When this happens, the result is often a new denomination, because the older Churches are unwilling to embrace the rediscovery of truth. The Greek word *paradosis* (tradition) has a number value of 666, and many have seen in this that the Spirit of Antichrist places human rules and traditions higher than God's word in the Churches. This is true of many denominations. Believers have fought hard for the truth of God, and in some generations the chief persecutor of the living Church has been the institutional Church. It has been calculated that over 30 million believers were martyred at the hands of the Spanish Inquisition and other bodies throughout the thousand years of medieval history.

2. Divisions through Clash of Personality

We have already mentioned the clash between Paul and Barnabas over Mark. The most common cause of Church divisions, especially in recent years, has been the clash of personalities. This is particularly grievous given the need of the Church to stand firm against enemies from outside. It is often ordinary members who suffer during such times, and it is vital that Churches learn to avoid these splits.

African proverb:
   "When elephants fight, the grass gets trampled!"

The Bible gives vital teaching on this subject through the lives of Saul and David. Their clash of personality was filled with all kinds of motives, including ambition, impatience, jealousy of each other's gifts, etc.

Saul, the first King of Israel, was given the kingdom but lost his position through carnality. The roots of Saul's carnality were in the fact that he neglected the ark and the presence of God. 1 Chron. 10:13 tells us that Saul did not enquire of the Lord. 1 Chron. 13:3 also tells of the fact that Saul did not enquire of the ark, which symbolises the presence of God. The result of this tragic neglect was that Saul slowly became deaf to God. He did not listen to God and therefore did not obey Him. The most stinging rebuke ever given to a man in the Bible is Samuel's rebuke of Saul in 1 Samuel 15:22-23. These verses speak of the Lord's displeasure in Saul because he would not listen or obey. Saul's attempt to sacrifice to the Lord was rejected because the Lord values 'obedience above sacrifice, and listening above the fat of rams'.

THE SIGNS OF SAUL'S CARNALITY:

- Saul disobeyed. He tried to sacrifice when forbidden to do so by the written word of God. Saul did not belong to the tribe of Levi - he was of Benjamin, and so committed a direct act of disobedience when he approached the altar of the Lord [1 Samuel 13:8-14].

- Saul was filled with fear in the face of his enemies [1 Samuel 17:11]. Saul was the tallest man in the army of Israel and the only soldier who had iron armour; but his heart was fearful because he had neglected the word and presence of the Lord. Fear drives out faith. Faith drives out fear. The choice is either to seek His word or be a victim of the spirit of fear.

- Saul was jealous of the success of men around him, especially David. This led him to be filled with murderous thoughts of destroying David [1 Samuel 18:8-9, 19:10].

- Saul was so consumed with this jealousy that he became irrational and close to madness, if not actually mad on occasions [1 Samuel 19:24].

- Saul became paranoid and believed there was a conspiracy against him involving everybody [1 Samuel 22:8]. This is paradoxical, since no-one was against him. Saul was chronically depressed and troubled by a demon; it is at this point that the Spirit of the Lord leaves him [1 Samuel 16:14]. But remember that this was not a hasty departure by the Spirit. The Spirit of the Lord had been grieved for years but had not left Saul, and it was only after many years that the Spirit finally left him.

- Saul murdered the priests of God, and commited a great sin against God Himself [1 Samuel 22:16-19].

- Saul was so isolated and cut off from God that God refused to speak to him [1 Sam. 28:6]. This is a very serious sign of carnality, and indicates someone in a serious state of spiritual decline.

- Saul knew he was a sinner, which he was able to confess. But he was not able to deeply repent or change [1 Samuel 26:21].

- Saul enquired of a witch [1 Sam. 28:8] - backsliding completely from a zeal that had filled his heart in earlier days [1 Sam. 28:3,9].

- Saul was driven to complete defeat and finally to suicide [1 Sam. 31:4].

David, the second King of Israel, was a spiritual man, and his spiritual life is presented to us in his prayer life in the Psalms. He meditated on God's word [Psalm 1:2-3]. He waited on God [Psalm 62:1]. He loved God's presence [Psalm 23]. He was filled with praises [Psalm 34:1]. David had an inner life that was filled with praises and love for God.

THE MARKS OF DAVID'S SPIRITUALITY:

- David could hear God's voice [1 Samuel 23:2-5]. Meditating on God's word, waiting quietly on God, loving God, all these things make our hearts sensitive to His voice.

- David was fearless in the face of opposition. He fearlessly attacked the bear, the lion and Goliath [1 Samuel 17:34-36].

- David loved his enemies, even after they had tried to kill him [2 Samuel 19:6]. This love for his enemies included Saul, whom he would not kill [1 Samuel 24 and 26].

- David was able to encourage himself in the face of disaster, and when all were against him [1 Samuel 30:6]. He did not give in to the depression that threatened his soul.

- David sinned with Bathsheba and his sin was very grievous; but he was able to find the place of repentance very quickly and completely. He did not become depressed and morose like Saul, but brought himself to God for cleansing [Psalm 51]. As a result, he was able to face the future with a sense of fresh cleansing and without condemnation.

- David was able to humble himself and submit to Saul's leadership even though he knew Saul was an unspiritual man. He honoured the Lord's anointed [1 Samuel 24:10, 26:9-10]. David saw himself as like a flea or dead dog [1 Samuel 24:14]. It is this ability to assess his life accurately despite his great successes in battle that caused David to bring peace to Israel and thus maintain unity.

The healing of divisions that result from personality clashes can be achieved through a self-humbling and dying to self, leading to love for those who sometimes seem to be our enemies. David could have pointed to the prophetic guidance of Samuel the man of God, who anointed him king [1 Samuel 16:1]. He could have pointed to his superiority over Saul in the battle with Goliath. But none of these things made him hurry or spoil God's plans by fighting carnally for himself. Dying to self, preferring others above ourselves, and loving our enemies - these are the simple keys to unity amongst God's servants.

EPHESIANS - GOD'S BLUEPRINT FOR A GLORIOUS CHURCH

Paul's letter to the Ephesians is a blueprint for the New Testament Church and is one of the most important documents on Church life. There are three phases of revelation in the letter to the Ephesians.

1. The Believer's Inheritance [Ephesians 1-3]

Paul teaches that the origins of the Church lie in the distant past, before the foundation of the world [1:4].

- It is rooted in the power that raised Christ from the dead [1:19-20].

- It is this power that has given believers the inestimable privilege of being seated with Christ in heavenly places [1:20 and 2:6].

- The Church, then, is a heavenly being, united with Christ who indwells it [2:22].

- The Church is a place of reconciliation and unity between races. Jew and Gentile both equally belong in the Church, although the Church is really the commonwealth of Israel, into which the Gentiles have now been introduced [2:11–20].

- God has freed believers from the power of darkness [2:1-5] and has made them a manifestation of His power to the principalities and powers in heavenly places [3:10].

- The mystery of the Church in its unity and love is the mystery of Christ indwelling the Church [3:8-19].

2. The Believer's Moral Standards [Ephesians 4:1-6:9]

- The unity of love is the guiding principle. Believers are to work in harmony in the spirit of humility and forbearance [4:1-3]. If believers cannot exhibit the unity of love within the Church, then they will automatically lose credibility before the world.

- The goal of the Church is to nurture each member into the perfect image of Christ [4:12-15]. Christ-like stature is the goal of the believer's moral standards.

- Given these underlying principles, members of the Church must not give way to anger [4:26] and must not indulge in former ways of life, e.g. stealing [4:28], or fornication [5:3-14].

- Our Christian life must be worked out in the home in the relationship between husband and wife [5:22-33].

- Children and their behaviour should also glorify Christ [6:1-4].

- Business or working relationships (here master and slaves) must also be marked by faithfulness and respect [6:5-9].

3. The Believer's Warfare [Ephesians 6:10-20]

The believer's warfare is not merely against natural temptations. There are powers that surround us in the spiritual world, against which we must wage war by the vital elements that make up the Christian's armour:

- ❖ **Truth** - this is biblical truth, but the Greek word means much more, and covers the whole realm of **reality**. In other words, Christians can wage war only as they acknowledge their failings. Without this there will be a spirit of hypocrisy and spiritual defeat in the believer. Biblical truth will gird the believer's mind to live according to what God has said, and not according to what they see or feel.

- ❖ **Righteousness** - truth is a belt that holds the armour in place; righteousness is the armour that covers the heart. Without this vital piece of armour, the heart is vulnerable to attack. A wound in the hand heals fairly easily, and life can be sustained without a hand, but a wound to the heart is fatal. The maintenance of righteousness is vital if we are to continue to have life itself in the Spirit.

- ❖ **Peace** - peace always follows righteousness and cannot precede it [see Romans 14:17]. There is no peace for the wicked [Isaiah 57:21]. The gospel is a gospel of peace through reconciliation. Peace is the mark of the gospel. There is nothing but false peace in the world, which is short-lived and evaporates in the face of evil and death. But the Christian has a peace that passes understanding, and this peace gives power to the gospel witness.

- ❖ **Faith** - which is the opposite of worry and fear. The believer does not fear the devil, but holds up the shield of confidence in God, and faith in God's power to defend those who trust in Him. This faith then extends to the tearing down of strongholds in the mind, just as Israel took the fortresses of Jericho, Ai, etc. [Joshua 6 and 8].

- ❖ **Salvation** - this is the helmet of the Christian, covering the realm of mental attacks which come in the form of condemnation by Satan. The believer must cling to the truth of reconciliation by the blood of Jesus. If Satan moves us off this ground, our head is suddenly defenceless against his attacks. We are perfectly right with God through Christ.

- ❖ **The Word** - the Word of God is the only weapon of attack in the Christian's armoury. We use it to attack the strongholds of the enemy. By this we mean that we trust the Word of the Spirit to penetrate the chinks in the armour of even the most hardened unbeliever. The Word of God imparts faith to unbelieving hearts. It speaks power into strengthless souls, and life into the spiritually dead.

- ❖ **Prayer** - Paul here mentions *"all prayer"*, indicating that there is more than one way of praying. The believer must learn all the different ways of praying as the Holy Spirit teaches him. Praying *"with all prayer"* and *"in the Spirit"* are the key factors here. The effect of prayer will be to empower the ministry of the Word preached. (See the chapter on prayer.)

SOLOMON'S TEMPLE – A TYPE OF THE CHURCH

Solomon's Temple is a type of the building of the Church. There are many lessons from this parallel, but here are a few of the essential ones, from 2 Chronicles 1-9:

- ♦ **Wisdom**: Solomon prayed for wisdom [2 Chronicles 1:10]. This is a key for all those who would lead God's people in the great work of Church planting and building. This is wisdom from above, and not merely following lines laid down in a book.

- ♦ **Determination**: Solomon determined to build a Temple for the Lord [2:1]. This determination is a reflection of the divine determination, which is unstoppable. Leaders must partake of this fire of God's will and purpose. It will make them strong against all opposition.

- ♦ **Built on Mount Moriah, the cross**: Solomon built the Temple on Mount Moriah [3:1], which is where Abraham offered Isaac [Genesis 22:2-14] and where David stopped the destroying angel by a sacrifice [1 Chronicles 21:15-28]. These are both pictures of Calvary (which was probably also at the same site), and indicate to us that the Church is built on the sacrifice of God's Son. This sacrifice must enter into the heart and sinew of the people of God, empowering us to live lives of selfless consecration and love for God and His people.

- **Built for the ark – God's holy presence**: the Temple was built to be the permanent resting place of the ark, the symbol of God's presence [5:7-14]. God's glory filled the Temple, and this is the purpose of the Church - that God's glory should fill His people. Without the manifest presence of God, the Church is powerless and meaningless.

- **Built to burn sacrifices to God**: Solomon's original vision was to build a house to offer burnt sacrifices to God [2:4-6]. The Temple was dedicated with an enormous number of animal sacrifices [7:4-5]. God said that the house was to be for sacrifice [7:12]. In the Church, this sacrifice is both worship, and also the giving of ourselves and our substance to God. The believers are to bring tithes and offerings to God as a willing offering of themselves, without condition. The concept of giving in order to receive is faulty since sacrifice does not come with conditions!

- **Built for prayer**: after the Temple was built, it was dedicated as a house of prayer. It was to be open to foreigners as well as to the people of Israel [6:29-33]. This was prophesied later in Isaiah 56:7, and confirmed by the Lord in Mark 11:17. The Temple, and the Church, are above all to be a house of prayer for all nations. For this reason, the chief study of the Church is to be the study of prayer.

- **Built for holiness**: Solomon's prayer of dedication [6:12-42] was a prayer that God would keep the people, even if they sinned, by bringing them back to this place of worship. The Temple, like the Tabernacle before it, was to be a most holy place [1 Kings 6:16]. Holiness was the watchword of the house, and the great condition for those who worshipped and approached God in that place. If God's people sinned, they would be cast out and the house destroyed; but if there was repentance, then there would be restoration [2 Chronicles 7:14].

EZRA – THE TEMPLE REBUILT – A TYPE OF THE CHURCH REDISCOVERED

The book of Ezra is about the rebuilding of the Temple. As such, it speaks to us about the rediscovery of the will of God for His Church in every generation. Over the centuries, the Church has frequently replaced the New Testament pattern with sacraments and traditions that are completely unbiblical. Special vestments, offices of pope, bishop, canon, vicar etc. are not found in the Bible. This does not mean that those who are members of such Churches are not saved; but it does mean that we must search again to find the true definition of Church. Our traditions, whether Anglican, Methodist, Pentecostal, charismatic, etc. can be a hindrance to the discovery of truth. We must come to the Bible with clear, open hearts.

In Ezra there is a clear parallel with New Testament truth:

- **The command from Cyrus** - a type of Christ. The command given by God from before the foundation of the world is that the Church will be built. Nothing can therefore stop this order from being fulfilled [Ezra 1:2].

- **The foundations dug** - repentance and faith, weeping and joy [Ezra 3:10-13; Haggai 2:3]. The digging refers to the need to get deep, to empty things out, before there can be infilling. Outpouring of the Spirit is the result of deep digging [see Luke 6:47-48]. Faith receives, and we can compare it with the pouring of concrete into foundations that have been dug.

- **Adversaries**:

    - **Compromise** [4:1-3]: the enemies of God will seek to overcome the Church at any cost, but especially through working alongside the Church.
    - **Counsellors** [4: 4-5]: these were to frustrate the people of God. The devil speaks negative, discouraging and frustrating things into the hearts of God's people. We must not listen, but must rebuke the tempter!
    - **Accusation** [4:6]: the 'accuser of the brethren' [Revelation 12:10] was cast down at Calvary and now there is no condemnation against the people of God, though this does not mean that the devil has stopped trying to accuse God's people to their face. But he is a liar.
    - **Force and power** [4:23-24]: the devil will use government, whether national or local, to seek to undermine God's work. In some cases the work of God has been hindered for a season through intense persecution. Believers must not be discouraged.

- **Ministry of prophets to make the people rise up** [5:1-2] - prophets speak words from God that cause people's heart to burn and stir. Without this direct speaking, the Church cannot fulfill her destiny.

- **Search made for the original command** [6:1-12]: the Church must seek to fellowship with God and to know His heart and find out the eternal calling which God has given to His people.

- **The house finished** [6:15]: the Church will be completed both in numbers and in spiritual perfection in every realm.

Ezra returns to Jerusalem and **brings the treasures back to the Temple** after his journey [8:24-34]. These treasures are a picture of the biblical truths, the hidden mysteries, that were once committed to the Church. The Church must not compromise or let go of anything that God has given her [Ephesians 3:8-13].

Ezra **intercedes for the fallen state of the nation** as a result of foreign wives [Ezra 9 and 10]. Intercession is the agony of soul that is deeply felt over the state of people's hearts. Only through intercession will waves of blessing be poured out and souls be saved. The Church is, above all, a house of prayer.

14

THE FUTURE

The Bible's teaching on the future has produced much controversy, and so it is important to draw out of the Bible the areas of greatest certainty, and then also to identify the areas where there are differences of interpretation.

FOUR MAIN METHODS OF INTERPRETING REVELATION

There are four main methods of interpreting the Book of Revelation and other biblical references to the 'last days' and the coming of Christ. These methods are simply four ways in which truth may be drawn from the book, and they show that it really does speak to all the ages of the Church, from the first century to the last years immediately preceding Christ's return.

1. Preterist

The preterist view interprets the Book of Revelation and other passages, such as Matthew 24, as referring to events that took place in the first century AD. Thus the 'Abomination of Desolation' [Matthew 24:15] occurred when the Roman armies desecrated and destroyed the Temple in AD 70. There is no doubt that many of Jesus' prophecies did refer to events that were to take place within a short period of time after He spoke them. This included most of the crises in Judea which led to the fall of Jerusalem. Jesus said that armies would surround Jerusalem [Luke 21:20]. The siege and fall of Jerusalem was a period of terrible tribulation for the Jews, which could be the meaning of the prophecy in Matthew 24:21.

The Christians heeded Jesus' warnings and fled from Judea to a town called Pella in Jordan in AD 67. There were false Messiahs in the siege, who claimed that God would deliver them. But Jesus had said that Jerusalem would fall and that it would be trodden underfoot until the time of the Gentiles was fulfilled [Luke 21:24].

It is important to recognise that some of the prophecies **were** fulfilled in the first century. However, Jesus also gave prophecies that were clearly **not** fulfilled in the first century. For example, He said that the angels would gather His elect from the four directions of the compass [Matthew 24:31]. This seems clearly to be a prophecy that relates to the end of the age, not merely to the first century. It becomes necessary to 'twist' such Scriptures in order to try and interpret them as having been fulfilled in the first century! John said that the prophecies of Revelation would *"shortly take place"* [Revelation 1:1], but it is clear that many of them still await fulfilment.

It is also important to recognise that there can be **cyclical** fulfilment of prophecy – that is, that there can be more than one fulfilment of a prophecy. Take, for example, the prophecy of the 'Abomination of Desolation'. This prophecy was originally given by Daniel [Daniel 8:11-14, 11:31]. It was fulfilled by the desecration of the Temple in 167-164 BC by Antiochus Epiphanes. But Jesus refers to it as something future, which was clearly fulfilled in AD 70 but also certainly has further fulfilments. These include the misuse of papal authority in the Middle Ages, and the Muslim occupation of Jerusalem - the Dome of the Rock on the Temple mount in Jerusalem is also a fulfilment of this prophecy, which continues to the present day. On the inside of the prayer area in the dome is an inscription stating that Mohammed is God's prophet and God has no Son. 1 John 2:22 states, *"He is antichrist who denies the Father and the Son."* There may yet be a further fulfilment of this prophecy, and of other prophecies. Jerusalem may yet again be surrounded by armies.

2. Historical

The historical method of interpreting the Book of Revelation is based on the belief that it concerns the unfolding of events over the whole of the Church age. According to this method, the seals of Revelation 6 are specific events in history. The discovery of the 'little book' in Revelation 10, and the death and resurrection of the two witnesses in Revelation 11 are, for example, understood as symbolising the Reformation.

This method of interpretation is fascinating and its proponents are convincing. But it requires a vast knowledge of history, which has only been available to a few of the generations of Bible readers since the Bible was written! The method has fewer proponents now, but was quite popular in the 19th century.

Whether or not the symbols of Revelation can be tied to specific events in world history, there is no doubt that the Book of Revelation does teach us about the ways of God in history. Hence, we know that changes occur in the course of history, not merely because people have made political decisions, but because Christ has opened a seal in heaven.

3. Symbolical

This method interprets the Book of Revelation by looking at the imagery in other parts of the Bible. Thus when 'Babylon' is mentioned in Revelation, a study of the origins of the earthly city reveals that it was the site where the Tower of Babel was built [Genesis 11:1-9]. It was also the city where Daniel was in exile for nearly the whole 70 years of Israel's captivity. The Babylonian Empire is the 'head of gold' in Nebuchadnezzar's vision in Daniel 2.

Most of the symbols used in the Book of Revelation can be found in other parts of the Bible. So this method helps us to understand the symbols used in Revelation, and the processes of the end times, and thus work out the meaning of the book.

4. Futurist

The futurist method interprets the Book of Revelation as referring to a very short period of time at the end of history. There are many variations of this interpretation, but the most common is that introduced by Scofield, through his Bible notes which were published at the end of the 19th century. According to this interpretation, the rapture of the Church (i.e. the taking up of Christians from earth into heaven) is described in Revelation 4:1, and the rest of the book describes the period of the tribulation, until chapter 19, when Christ's return to earth is described.

This is by far the most common interpretation today, but is not the only authoritative one in terms of principles of biblical interpretation. It makes many assumptions and speculations. These include a belief that the Temple will be rebuilt in Jerusalem and that sacrifices will again be made there. (The evidence for this is the mention of the daily sacrifices being taken away [Daniel 9:27]; if this is a future event, there must first be a re-establishment of the Temple.) There is also a belief that, at the rapture, there will be numerous accidents as Christian drivers and airline pilots, for instance, suddenly disappear. Again, this is speculation. The thought that believers will avoid tribulation is attractive to us all, but much of this interpretation is based on a very few selected Scriptures, which are not easy to interpret, including Daniel's 70th week [Daniel 9:27].

5. Is There a Right Method?

There is no doubt that some of the prophecies refer to the first century. There is also no doubt that the Book of Revelation teaches principles that can and must be applied to the whole 2,000 years of Church history. It is also clear that the Book of Revelation must be interpreted in the light of symbols and illustrations in the Old Testament Scriptures. Also, the fact that the book reveals the future is beyond doubt.

The only conclusion that can be reached by the serious Bible student is that the book speaks to us on several different levels and that we must seek to draw understanding from all four of these methods of studying it. The Bible throws light on human history. However, there are some views of the Book of Revelation that seem very weak. These tend to be based on current affairs. John Wesley was convinced that the Turkish Ottoman Empire was the Antichrist kingdom. During the cold war, many Christians believed that the USSR was the Antichrist. Such views have some contribution to make, but are often proved wrong by the progress of history.

THE PROPHETIC TIMETABLE

There are three timelines given in the Scripture for the end times:

(1) The statue seen by Nebuchadnezzar in Daniel chapter 2.
(2) The '70 weeks' prophecy of Daniel chapter 9.
(3) The Olivet prophecy given by Jesus in Matthew 24, Mark 13 and Luke 21.

1. The Statue Seen by Nebuchadnezzar in Daniel 2

In Daniel 2 Nebuchadnezzar had a dream in which he saw a statue with a head of gold, its chest and arms of silver, its belly and thighs of brass, its legs of iron, and its feet of iron mixed with clay. A stone is cut without hands, that strikes the statue on its feet and destroys it. The stone then becomes a great mountain which fills the earth. Daniel gives the interpretation, stretching from his day until the return of Christ, as follows:

- The *"head of gold"* is easy to understand - the Bible narrative itself clearly states that it represents the Babylonian kingdom under King Nebuchadnezzar, who conquered Jerusalem and carried the Jews, including the prophet Daniel himself, off into captivity [Daniel 2:36-38].

- After the Babylonian head of gold came the Persian Empire. The Persians under their various kings, including Cyrus (who allowed the people of Judah to return to Jerusalem – see Ezra and Nehemiah) swept away the Babylonian Empire in 536 B.C. They are the *"chest and arms of silver"* [v32].

- After about two centuries of dominance, the Persian Empire was swallowed up by the Greeks under Alexander the Great. Many consider Alexander to be the greatest military commander of all time, taking vast areas from southern Europe, across the Middle East and deep into southern Asia, all while a relatively young man. He died in his early thirties of natural causes. The Greeks became the *"belly and thighs of bronze"* [v32].

- After the Greeks came the Romans - the *"legs of iron"* [v33]. The Romans took the areas that the Greeks had, plus nearly all of the rest of Europe, including Britain. The Roman Empire was of course dominant during the time of the New Testament. The legs of iron represent the Roman Empire being divided into East and

West. History records that the Roman Empire fell in the 5th century AD – when it suffered a 'mortal wound' to its political empire, just as it suffered a 'mortal wound' to its religious empire in the time of Martin Luther 1,000 years later. But it obviously recovered from both, because verses 34-35 and 44 seem clearly to say that both will exist on the day of Christ's return. The Roman Empire continued in the form of the Orthodox Church in the East, with its capital in Constantinople, and the Catholic Church in the West, with its capital in Rome.

- The feet and toes of iron and clay represent more recent centuries of European history, with alliances that are made and then fail. Daniel's prophecy mentions the fact that the *"seed of men"* [v43] would also be mixed into these alliances, which was specifically fulfilled in the practice of intermarriage between the royal houses of Europe. The most powerful alliance is the recent European Union, founded on the Treaty of Rome. It is also arguably made of iron and clay, since there is economic strength (iron) and highly independent nations producing frequent divisions (clay). The empire represented by the feet and the toes corresponds with the ten horns of the Antichrist in Revelation 13.

- The stone which strikes the statue in the days of the final kingdom represents Christ's return and the setting up of the Millennial kingdom.

This timeline has proved so far to be so accurate that many liberal scholars believe the book of Daniel was written much more recently than it actually was. However, Daniel was translated into Greek in 250BC by the 70 scholars who translated the Septuagint in Alexandria, Egypt. Daniel was already an ancient text by that time.

2. The 70 Weeks Prophecy of Daniel 9

Many believers are convinced that the history of the last days can be best understood by interpreting Daniel's 70 weeks. Daniel prophesied in 9:24-27 that there would be a period of '70 weeks' covering the key events from the rebuilding of Jerusalem until the final consummation of everything at the return of Christ.

How can this be interpreted? Firstly, each day of the 70 weeks is taken to represent a year, based on the year/day scale found elsewhere in the Bible [see Numbers 14:34; Ezekiel 4:6]. This gives a total period of 7 x 70 = 490 years. Secondly, these years are not consecutive, but are interrupted, as follows:

(Note that there are other interpretations of this Scripture passage.)

- The start date - the command to restore and build Jerusalem - was around 458-457 BC [see Ezra 7:12-26].

- The appearing of Messiah: 62 + 7 = 69 x 7 = 483 years. This brings us to the public appearance of Christ in AD 26. (The modern calendar dates from Pope Gregory the Great, who made a mistake by 4 years in calculating the year of the birth of Christ. So Jesus was probably born in 4BC, began his ministry at the age of 30 in late AD26-early AD27, and was crucified at the age of 33 in AD30.)

There remains one final 'week' to account for, and it seems there is an intervening span of history between verses 26 and 27. The final 'week' refers to the resumption of Daniel's timetable at the end of time. This timetable requires a period of 7 years immediately preceding the final return of Christ.

Many people think that Daniel 9:26-27 indicates that the Prince of Rome who destroyed the Temple in AD 70 will be paralleled by a future Prince of Rome, who will be the Antichrist. Some think that the Treaty of Rome, which was made to found the European Union (EU), indicates that the EU is a revived Roman Empire. This would also fit in with Nebuchadnezzar's vision in Daniel 2, where a fragmented form of the Roman Empire is the form assumed by the Antichrist when Christ returns.

By this interpretation, the Antichrist will make a treaty which will lead to peace in the Middle East, but then he will break the treaty in the middle of the 'week' and great persecution will ensue. Most people who hold to this interpretation believe that the Church will be caught up to heaven in a 'secret rapture' at this point and that the second half of the week is the Great Tribulation, which will be *"the time of Jacob's trouble"* [Jeremiah 30:7]. This will culminate in a terrible war around Jerusalem, described in Zechariah 12-14 and Revelation 19. This is Armageddon.

This basic framework is the futurist interpretation of the last days. The numbers 1,260 days and 42 months (3½ years) appear and reappear in the Book of Revelation. This would fit in well with this interpretation.

While this interpretation may be basically correct, it is nevertheless wrong to try and build too detailed a picture based on it. Novels have been written speculating on the implications of a secret rapture, where all the Christians suddenly disappear. But this is just speculation. The Bible only says, *"One will be taken and the other left"* [Matthew 24:40].

THE FUTURE

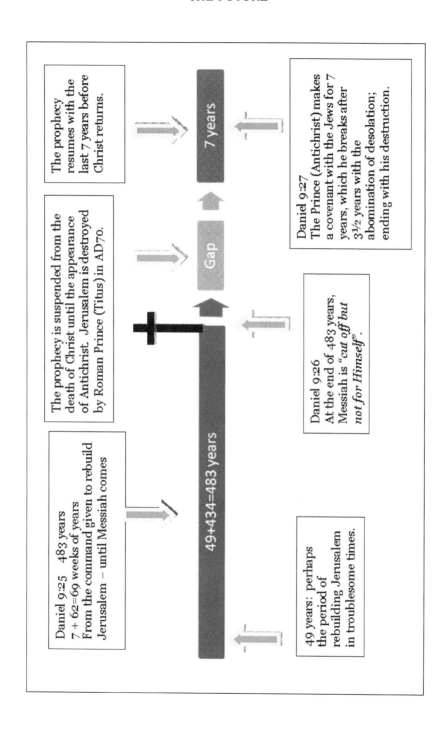

The secret rapture is assumed to be described in Revelation 4:1 when John is told to *"Come up here"*. The rest of the book is then interpreted as a description of events in the Great Tribulation, until the return of Christ in Revelation 19. So, almost all of Revelation is taken to fit into the 3½ years or so of the Great Tribulation, and thus to have no direct relevance to the majority of Christians. This does seem a weak interpretation of Revelation, as it relies almost entirely on the fact that the Church is not mentioned directly from after chapter 3 until chapter 19. This seems a weak principle by which to interpret the Bible. For example, the word 'disciple' does not occur in the New Testament after Acts, but this does not mean that Paul's epistles were not part of the Great Commission to go and make disciples of all nations! Nevertheless, that does not mean that the futurist interpretation is totally wrong. The important thing is to have an open mind and a humble, non-dogmatic attitude.

3. Jesus' Olivet Prophecy

Jesus Christ is the greatest of all the prophets in the Bible, and it is no wonder that His Olivet prophecy [Matthew 24, Mark 13 and Luke 21] provides us with a vital overview and key to understanding all Bible prophecy.

The disciples ask Jesus, in Matthew 24:3, *"Tell us, when will these things be? And what will be the sign of Your coming, and of the end of the age?"* Jesus then gives an outline of all the key events leading up to His return and to the end of all things. The diagram on the next page divides the Olivet prophecy into three sections - the events leading up to the end, the events fulfilled since the time of Jesus, and events still to come in the future.

(a) Events Leading Up to the End

- ❖ False Messiahs and false prophets will appear [Matthew 24:5, 11]. These will claim to be either the Son of God or equal in importance, re-interpreting all of the Scriptures in their own way. Mohammed himself may be included in this group, since he denies that Jesus is the Son of God, and re-interprets the whole of the Old Testament to suit his beliefs.

- ❖ Wars and rumours of wars [Matthew 24:6] will be continually on the earth. Jesus said that this was not a sign of the imminent return of Christ.

- ❖ There will be an increase of famines, earthquakes and diseases [Matthew 24:7] in the years preceding Christ's return; they will be like birth pangs that steadily increase in intensity until the end comes.

- ❖ Increasing persecution of the Church [Matthew 24:8]. Whether or not the Church goes through the Great Tribulation, there is no doubt at all that the Church often passes through some degree of tribulation.

- ❖ Increasing sin and iniquity resulting in a decrease of love and attitudes of compassion [Matthew 24:12].

- ❖ The gospel will be preached throughout the whole world. This is the final sign that the end has come [Matthew 24:14].

(b) Events Fulfilled Since the Time of Jesus

- ❖ Jerusalem was destroyed by the Romans in AD70. Not one stone was left upon another, as the fire which destroyed the Temple caused the gold to melt, and the Romans then literally took the stones apart in order to retrieve the gold. The Christians escaped the siege of Jerusalem, which lasted for 3 years, because they heeded the warning of Jesus in Luke 21:20.

- ❖ The fig tree shall blossom [Matthew 24:32]. This is understood to mean that Israel would be a nation once more and would return to its land. This was fulfilled in 1948. Many Christians had been predicting this.

- ❖ Jerusalem would be a Jewish city once more [Luke 21:24]. This was fulfilled in 1967 when, in the Six Day War, the Jews took control of Jerusalem and declared it the capital of Israel.

- ❖ Many small nations would regain their independence in the last days, not only Israel [Luke 21:29]. This is being fulfilled in our time as many small nations are reappearing, for example in the Balkans, and nations of the former USSR. Tibet may also regain nationhood, along with many others, such as the Kurds.

Leading up to the end

- False Messiahs and false prophets will appear: Matt 24:5, 11
- Wars and rumours of wars: Matt 24:6
- Famines, earthquakes and diseases: Matt 24:7
- Increasing persecution of the Church: Matt 24:8
- Increasing sin and iniquity resulting in a decrease of love and compassion: Matt 24:12
- The gospel will be preached throughout the whole world - and then the end will come: Matt 24:14

Events fulfilled since Jesus

- Jerusalem was destroyed by the Romans in AD 70: Luke 21:20
- The fig tree shall blossom: Matt 24:32. Israel became a nation once more in 1948.
- Jerusalem shall be a Jewish city once more: Luke 21:24. This was fulfilled in 1967.
- Many small nations will regain their independence in the last days, not only Israel: Luke 21:29

Events still to come

- The Abomination of Desolation shall be erected once more: Matt 24:15
- The Great Tribulation: Matt 24:21
- False Christs and prophets come to deceive: Matt 24:24
- The powers of heaven will be shaken: Matt 24:29
- Believers shall meet Christ in the air: Matt 24:31
- Christ shall return: Matt 24:27

The Olivet Prophecy

THE FUTURE

(c) Events Still to Come in the Future

- ❖ The Abomination of Desolation will be erected once more. The exact meaning of this is not clear. Some take it to mean that the Temple will be rebuilt and abused once more. Others see the Dome of the Rock as a fulfilment of this prophecy. Others see it as the perversion of Christianity in the liberal wing of the established Church.

- ❖ The Great Tribulation – this is the period of the most intense worldwide trouble and distress in the history of the world. Many premillennialists (those who believe that Christ will return to earth before the 1,000 years of the Millennium) believe that it will happen during the second half of Daniel's 70th 'week' and will be preceded by a 3½-year period of relative peace, through the political skill of the Antichrist. The Antichrist and his forces will then turn against the Jews, resulting in something like a second holocaust. It will last 3½ years, as did the first holocaust.

- ❖ False Messiahs and false prophets – throughout this period there will be a wave of false prophets, interpreting the Scriptures wrongly. Men will claim to be the Messiah and there will be spiritual and religious confusion.

- ❖ The powers of heaven will be shaken. It is only possible to speculate about this, but it may mean that there will be massive observable changes in the stars and planets, and in the earth's atmosphere. In these days of 'climate change', these concepts no longer seem unthinkable.

- ❖ Believers will meet Christ in the air. They will be gathered together to meet Christ at His return. This is the rapture [Matthew 24:31; 1 Thessalonians 4:16-18]. Some people hold the view that the rapture of the Christians will take place before the Great Tribulation, while others place it after this period. Strong views are held on both sides of this argument, but there is really insufficient evidence to be too dogmatic. This has not stopped thousands of preachers from being very forthright and even divisive on this issue.

- ❖ Christ will return [Matthew 24:27]! His coming will be like the lightning, so swift and clear. Light travels at 186,000 miles per second. If Christ returns as a flash of lightning in the sky, He could be seen all over the world in one second of time.

An Overview of the Book of Revelation

Revelation can be interpreted in the light of the symbolism and imagery of the Old Testament. This is in one way the most obvious method, since it harmonises the book with prophecies and events in the Old Testament.

The key message of Revelation is: GOD IS IN CONTROL. This message is of course contained in all the interpretations of Revelation, but the symbolical method interprets HOW God is in control. According to this method, the symbols explain how God rules from heaven. Activity on earth is because of things that happen in the unseen world.

Chapter 1: Christ revealed as Lord and God and in the midst of the Church.

Chapters 2-3: The seven types of Church throughout history. Christ addresses the Churches, correcting or commending and encouraging. The rest of the book is irrelevant unless the Churches are responding to their Lord. These are not types of Churches in historical succession, but seven types of Church that exist at any time in Church history.

Chapters 4-5: The scene in heaven before and during the cross. The song is a song of worship to the Creator in chapter 4, but turns in chapter 5 to the song of the redeemed. The slain Lamb of God appears on the throne, and the blood presented in heaven releases the song of the redeemed.

Chapters 6-11: The history of the world from the cross to the return of Christ is recounted. History is punctuated by the opening of seven seals. There is disagreement about what each seal represents, but here are some ideas:

The opening of the seven seals:

- **1st seal:** The white horse represents the Holy Spirit, who was sent forth immediately after the blood was presented in heaven. This act of God has changed the history of the world more than anything else.
- **2nd seal:** The red horse can be taken to represent war in general or perhaps the Muslim religion in particular.
- **3rd seal:** The black horse may represent great famines.
- **4th seal:** The grey horse represents death, and may mean something like the discovery of nuclear power and its ultimate use in destruction.

- **5th seal:** This indicates the outbreak of persecution throughout the centuries.
- **6th seal:** This indicates the shaking of the heavens and the earth at the end of the age, preceding judgment. In this period a great number of Jews are saved, as well as huge numbers of Gentiles [chapter 7]. Is this indicating a worldwide revival of huge proportions?
- **7th seal:** This indicates a period of judgments by God introduced by seven trumpets. God sends natural disasters to strike the earth.

The seven trumpet judgments:

- Disaster on earth [8:7]
- Disaster at sea [8:8]
- Disaster on water supplies [8:10-11]
- Disaster strikes the heavenly bodies - sun, moon and stars [8:12]
- A flood of demons is released on the earth, possibly through the drug culture of the 1960s onwards [9:1-11]
- Four demons are released that were bound in the River Euphrates, and these demons drag the world into another war - World War III – Armageddon [9:13-21]
- The return of Christ [11:15-19]

Chapter 10 is an interlude on the nature of John's prophetic ministry - a deepening of it through a rediscovery of the power of the Bible - the 'little book'.

Chapter 11:1-14 is a description of the end-times Church. There is an inner sanctuary of real Christians, and an outer court, a merely nominal Church which does not believe the Word or accept the Holy Spirit's movings. This end-time Church has the quality of being prophetic, but with great sorrow, symbolised by clothing of sackcloth. This Church has power and symbolises the two witnesses, who have the spiritual power of a Moses and an Elijah. As in history, there will probably be great leaders who will represent the Church with great testimony through signs and wonders. The Church is oppressed but always rises triumphant. The Church in China disappeared underground in the Communist revolution of 1949 and many pastors were imprisoned and some martyred. Many observers thought the Church was dead, but when the doors of China opened again, the Church had grown more under persecution than at any time in history.

Chapters 12-18 describe the main personalities that figure throughout Church history until the return of Christ. These figures take different forms in different ages, but they are present through the centuries.

Chapter 12: The Church, chosen (as Israel was before it) to be a vessel to bring forth the Christ in maturity and manifest Him to the world. The Church is opposed and persecuted, but is ultimately triumphant.

Chapter 13: The Antichrist and the False Prophet. These chameleon-like figures are manifested in Church history through the Catholic Church of the Middle Ages, the Muslim religion, Communism, Fascism etc. In each case there is an arm of propaganda to make the evil have an acceptable face.

Chapters 14-15: The end-time Church, holy for the Lord and before His throne above, praying and victorious.

Chapter 16: The disasters heralded by the seven last trumpets are repeated here.

Chapters 17-18: Babylon is the capital city of the beast, a great and terrible city like Rome, ancient Babylon and other great cities before and since. The evil power of Antichrist with his coalition of nations is the underlying evil behind this capital city. But the whole Antichrist system will collapse and destroy itself by internal conflict [17:17].

Chapter 19: The Antichrist will be finally annihilated by the King of Kings Himself at the height of the battle of Armageddon.

Chapter 20: The thousand-year rule of Christ on the earth, known as the Millennium, is followed by the universal judgment before the Great White Throne.

Chapters 21-22: The final separation of the just and the unjust takes place - the unjust to the Lake of Fire and the just to the New Creation.

THE MILLENNIUM

Perhaps the simplest interpretation of the Millennium is that there is to be a literal reign of 1,000 years on the earth by Jesus when He returns [Revelation 20:1-6]. This is known as the **Premillennial** view – i.e. Jesus returns before ('pre') the Millennium. There are some passages of the Old Testament that can be taken to support this view, such as Zechariah 14, which teaches that when Christ returns He will stand upon the Mount of Olives. The Mount will split in two. Water will flow out east from Jerusalem to the Dead Sea and west to the Mediterranean. The salt-laden seas will then be healed. The wolf will lie down with the lamb [Isaiah 11:6-9, 65:17-25] and there will be a 1,000-year period of the benign rule of Christ.

Why will God inaugurate the Millennium? There is no explicit reason given in Scripture. It may be that, by the Millennium, God will prove to mankind that the human race is not evil because of the devil, but because of the wrong exercise of personal moral choice. If the devil had not existed, mankind would still have had to prove itself by choosing the tree of life rather than the tree of the knowledge of good and evil.

Revelation 20:7-10 indicates that, at the end of the Millennium, the devil will be released from the bottomless pit and will once more deceive the nations. This is, of course, only possible for those who are unconverted. The point is that even the benign rule of Christ does not mean that He will force everyone to accept His rule through dictatorship, but rather through the force of His love. Mankind is free to choose; we are what we are by deliberate choice, not by force of circumstances.

There are many difficult questions to answer, such as:

Q: How will believers who have a new resurrection body live alongside sinners who still have a mortal body?
A: In the same way as Christ appeared to the disciples after the resurrection.

Q: How will Christ rule?
A: Through the agency of the Spirit in His followers and through His people who will administrate and rule with Him.

Q: Will He be constantly visible?
A: Probably not, as He will have no barrier stopping His free movement between earth and heaven.

The questions are innumerable and the answers are only possible through speculation since the Bible does not say much. Fortunately, the Bible does not make our understanding of the Millennium a key foundation or condition of salvation!

There are two other main views on the Millennium:

- **Post-millennialism** - in the 19th century some believers thought that evangelism would be so successful that the whole world would be converted and that the 1,000-year reign would happen before the final time of trouble and Armageddon. This is post (Latin for 'after') millennialism and means that Christ returns after the Millennium. Very few now believe this, especially after the awful traumas of world war in the 20th century.

- **Amillennialism** - according to this quite widely-held interpretation, the Millennium is not a literal 1,000-year period, but a symbol of the gospel age from Christ's first coming to His final return. Amillennialists think that Satan was bound as a result of Jesus' death and resurrection. Certainly, Satan is now bound in some crucial ways – he cannot either condemn God's people or ultimately stop Jesus' Great Commission being fulfilled. But, given the holocaust and other horrors of war, as well as increasing evil generally, it is perhaps hard to believe that Satan is fully bound.

THE DAY OF JUDGMENT

1. Key Scriptures

The main passages describing the Day of Judgment are found in Revelation 20 and Matthew 24 and 25, but there are also references elsewhere in the New Testament.

- Judgment begins with the Church or house of God **[1 Peter 4:17]**. Christ cleansed the Temple at the beginning of His ministry [John 2:13-17] and He will also cleanse His Church upon His return.

- The judgment will be severe against unfaithful stewards, especially pastors and Bible teachers [Matthew 24:43-51]. This is the first of three parables that Jesus gives, leading up to a description of His judgment of the nations. It is about the servant of the master of the house, who mistreats the other servants and eats and drinks with the worldly. That servant is dismembered and cast into hell with the unbelievers [v51]). The word used in this passage for 'household' (in the Greek text underlying the King James Version) is the Greek word *therapeia* and is based on the word for care or healing. It is the word used in Revelation 22:2 for the healing of the nations. God's intention is that the Church should be a house of care and healing, not of wounding. Christ received wounds in the house of his friends [Zechariah 13:6]. The true ministry will produce an atmosphere of healing, and those who disrupt this atmosphere will be judged severely.

- Judgment will be exercised against 'foolish virgins' who do not prepare for the return of the Bridegroom. This is the second parable given in the lead-up to Jesus' description of judgment day [Matthew 25:1-13]. Who are the foolish virgins? They are those who do not receive oil (a symbol of grace and of the Holy Spirit) to nourish a flame of love for Jesus. They are followers but not lovers of the Lord Jesus, and as such will be judged.

- The use of 'talents' will also be the basis of judgment in the house of God [Matthew 25:14-30]. The Lord has given to us grace, salvation, the Holy Spirit, the Bible, as well as countless natural blessings. The 'talents' that God has given us are many and we are to take advantage of them and multiply them. Note that the word *talent* here does **not** refer to a special ability, but to a huge gift that we don't deserve. God has sown into the earth through the death of His Son, and He expects a return - a harvest, a full reward. Believers must not hide the gospel or neglect to use the gifts that God has given us. These can be gifts of all kinds, but we are to live by faith and obedience and share what we have.

- Matthew 25:31-46 describes the division of the sheep from the goats. This is not a division based on race or nationality! The nations are gathered together, but when the Bible says the Judge will separate *them* [v32], this little word refers to individual people and not nations.

The judgment is based on **works**, not beliefs. This is perhaps the biggest shock for believers, because we know that we are saved through faith in Christ - so how can the judgment be based on a loving attitude to those less fortunate than ourselves? The answer is simple: we are saved by faith, but judged by works.

How can this be? The answer is that religious people do good works to please God and be accepted by Him. But believers believe and trust in God and, if this faith is genuine, there will be a change in our conduct. James says that faith which does not affect our actions is dead faith, and not living, justifying faith. God will not be deceived by religious hypocrites, and the final judgment will be perfect justice. This should produce the fear of the Lord in all who consider and believe these things.

- If believers are unfaithful, they will be judged with the unbelievers at the Great White Throne [Luke 12:46]. Otherwise, they will still appear before the judgment seat of Christ [2 Corinthians 5:10] to receive a reward for their faithfulness or some punishment for their neglect.

    - Differing degrees of punishment will be given for those who knew the Master's will, but did not obey. The servant in the parable in Luke 12:47 received many lashes.
    - There will be rewards of differing degrees for those who are faithful [Luke 19:16-19].

2. The Fact of Hell

One of the most fearful truths of the New Testament is the truth of hell. Believers as well as unbelievers may have difficulty grasping this terrible fact. Some believers have speculated that perhaps hell will annihilate the sinners so that they no longer exist. This doctrine is called **annihilationism**. Others have speculated that sinners in hell will be given the chance to repent, and that the pain of hell will produce this repentance. This doctrine is called **universal redemption**. Both doctrines conclude that there will be no hell after a period of time, and both appeal to the love of God as the reason that hell cannot last forever. These two ideas, however, are wrong for several reasons:

- The Bible teaches that hell will be an eternity of pain [Revelation 14:10-11].
- These views are based on rationalism and speculation, not on the Word of God. In other words, they are a blend of humanism rather than Christian teaching.
- They do not take into account the awfulness of evil and its destructive power.

The Bible does not tell us everything, and if these things are hard to understand, then rather than contradicting God's Word with speculation, believers should trust God for things that they find difficult. God has given us all that we need to know. We know that He is loving and merciful, and therefore we know that we will understand the bigger picture later in a fuller way. The key for us is to warn sinners of the awful danger that is hanging over them if they should die rejecting Christ and His offer of salvation.

3. What Does the Bible Teach about Hell?

- Sinners are raised from the dead and are sent to hell with a body [Revelation 20:13; John 5:28-29].
- There is destruction of the body and the soul in hell [Matthew 10:28].
- There will be wailing and gnashing of teeth in hell [Matthew 13:42].
- There is everlasting fire in hell [Matthew 18:8].
- Hell is a place of outer darkness [Matthew 22:13, 25:30].
- It is a place of torment and raging thirst, and yet with clear understanding and wakefulness [Luke 16:19-24].
- Hell is a place prepared, not for mankind, but for the devil and his angels [Matthew 25:41].
- Hell is a place where worms do not die [Mark 9:44]. The images of fire and worms are consistent with the valley of the son of Hinnom, or Gehenna. This was the rubbish dump of Jerusalem, where fires were constantly burning and there were heaps of rotting food swarming with maggots and worms.
- It is a place of final and eternal separation [Luke 16:26].

Note that most of this teaching was given by Christ Himself and that the warnings were addressed to His followers first, and then to the world.

THE FUTURE

THE NEW HEAVEN AND THE NEW EARTH

The last two chapters of the Bible mirror the first two chapters of Genesis; in that the first creation is replaced by the New Creation. There are, of course, huge contrasts and this indicates that there is not just a mere restoration of the condition of things before the Fall, but a progression. God has made something better in the New Creation. Here are some of the contrasts:

First Creation	New Creation
Seas and oceans	No sea
Day and night	No night
Sun and moon	No need of the sun

The implication is that divisions are abolished. There is no ocean separating people, and there is no darkness - either physical or spiritual. We can also conclude that there will be no barrier between heaven and earth, because God Himself will be living in this New Creation.

There is a wonderful list of things that will be **absent**:

- No sea (no geographical barriers separating the population) [Revelation 21:1]
- No more death [Revelation 21:4]
- No sorrow [Revelation 21:4]
- No crying [Revelation 21:4]
- No more pain [Revelation 21:4]
- No temple (no religious structures) [Revelation 21:22]
- No sun or moon [Revelation 21:23]
- No sinners [Revelation 21:27]
- No more curse [Revelation 22:3]
- No more night [Revelation 22:5]
- No devil or demons [Revelation 20:10]

The greatest promise is that the city will be illuminated by the direct presence of God [Revelation 22:5]

There are many questions we might ask, such as:

Q: Will the New Creation be made from the material of the old one?
A: Probably not, because Peter tells us that the elements will melt with great heat [2 Peter 3:10]. The point is, God is the Creator and He can produce unlimited materials and also dispose of old ones by the force of His word.

Q: Will there be different levels and groups of believers?
A: There will clearly be different levels of rewards, for Jesus spoke of this. Also there is an enigmatic phrase which says that the nations of those that are saved will walk in the light of the Bride, the New Jerusalem [Revelation 21:24]. These phrases provoke speculation but provide no answers!

THE PURPOSE OF TEACHING ABOUT THE END TIMES

There are many reasons why it is important to teach about the end times:

- The most obvious one – because the teaching is true and needs to be known!
- To instill in believers a healthy fear of God [Matthew 10:28].
- To give comfort and hope for the future [1 Thessalonians 4:13-18].
- To exhort believers to get ready by personal holiness [1 Thessalonians 5:23].
- To exhort believers to be ready by spiritual watchfulness and personal devotion to Christ [Matthew 24:1-13].

Jesus repeatedly taught that His believers should be constantly alert and ready for His return, both by love for Him and by personal holiness. He is the Beginning and the End. He was there at the Creation of the human race, and He is the Redeemer of sinful humanity. The Bible is a record of God's plan from the beginning to make each individual a willing partner with God in His life. This is the greatest story ever told and it is the personal invitation of God to every human being to turn to Him, and use the short life given to us on earth to prepare for the greatest adventure of all - eternal life with God.

~~~~~~~~~~~~~~~~~~~~~~~~~~~

The Christian's Compass

THE CHRISTIAN'S COMPASS STUDY GUIDE.

Chapter 1 - Who is God?

1. What is the main impact of the story of the King and the Shepherd?

2. Why do you think people do not recognise the hand of God in Creation?

3. How does the fact of having a conscience indicate a Creator?

4. Describe ways in which God has spoken to you directly.

5. List things that you believe about God's character and describe the way these things should affect the way you think and live.

6. List places in the Old Testament where the Trinity is revealed.

7. What does the fact of the Trinity tell you about the nature of God?

8. What miracles have you experienced in your own life? Do you know of anyone who has experienced healing or miraculous intervention in their lives? If miracles are signs, what are these sign-posts pointing to?

9. Jesus Christ is God, proved by miracles, prophecies and the uniqueness of His life and teaching. How should this change our attitude to His words, and most of all to His death and Resurrection?

Prayer suggestion: O Lord, lead me to the attitude of heart in which you can be revealed to me. I thirst to know you. Let me see you as you really are.

STUDY GUIDE

Chapter 2 - The Plan of Salvation

1. Discuss the implications of the theory of evolution on the moral and philosophical life of those who believe it. For example: If we are the product of chance, what does this tell us about our hope for the future?

2. Restate the three main ways in which we are in the image of God. How does this impact the way we value human life?

3. What was the main avenue by which Satan attacked the human race? Is it the same today? How can we learn from Jesus to repulse Satan's attacks?

4. Summarise 3 main things you have learned about sin from this chapter.

5. Why is knowledge about our problem of sin so important as a first step in coming to God?

6. Say in a few words how the power of the cross is able to remove our sins and defeat the power of darkness in our lives.

7. Describe the four elements of our response to God's offer of salvation.

Prayer suggestion: O Lord, I am a sinner and I have no power to make myself a better person. Please forgive me all my sins, wash my heart clean by the power of the Spirit and create in me a clean heart. Do this so that I may praise you aright and serve you with pure motives. Amen.

Chapter 3 - The Bible – the Word of God

1. What are the attitudes in the culture of the 21st century that weaken the authority of the Bible in the minds of men?

2. What are the proofs of the supernatural origin of the Bible?

3. What archaeological evidence do you know of, which has proved the accuracy of the Bible?

4. What are the blessings promised to us if we read the Bible?

5. What are the main keys to reading the Bible with a right heart and understanding?

6. What might we miss out on by not reading the Bible?

7. What does George Mueller's booklet teach us about the role of the Bible in our prayer life?

Prayer suggestion: Lord, open my mind and heart to understand your Word, and lead me through my reading of it into your presence.

Chapter 4 - Water Baptism and its meaning

1. What are the two key conditions for baptism?

2. What are the implications of these two conditions for infant baptism?

3. What does water baptism symbolise?

4. Trace the way the Church has developed a different method of baptism in the course of history?

5. God blessed people like John Wesley and Charles Finney who were practicing infant baptism. What does this teach you about the importance of the meaning of the symbol more than the symbol itself?

6. We should not reject people because of different views on baptism, but should this deter us from recognising the pattern of baptism in the Bible? What conclusions do you draw after reading the key texts about the biblical manner of baptism?

Prayer suggestion: Thank you Lord for going through baptism for me, both in water, and in your death and resurrection. Help me to follow in your footsteps in unconditional obedience and full surrender.

Chapter 5 - The Person and Work of the Holy Spirit

1. What do we learn from the words "Holy" and "Spirit" about Him?

2. The Holy Spirit is a person not a power: think of Bible verses which confirm this. Can you think of verses that describe what He feels?

3. What are the main things that the Holy Spirit does in our lives?

4. Give some of the key things that we must understand in order to receive the Holy Spirit?

STUDY GUIDE

5. Which of the 8 Old Testament pictures most helps you personally understand what the Holy Spirit wants to do in you?

6. Have you experienced the supernatural work of the Holy Spirit either through the gifts of the Spirit or through something that has changed in you which cannot be explained any other way?

Prayer suggestion: Lord, search me, show me anything in my life that hinders the free flowing of your Spirit, and fill me with your Holy Spirit.

Chapter 6 - The Price and Power of Discipleship

1. Why do you think it is most important to make disciples?

2. What do you learn from the fact that Jesus was a disciple of the Father?

3. What does it mean to carry one's cross?

4. Many true disciples have led the way on the mission field. Whose life and example has impacted you most?

5. What can a true disciple know and experience more than a casual Christian?

6. What are the three golden rules of discipleship?

7. In which key ways is Peter such an important example of a true disciple?

8. How should we treat 'failure' in our lives when trying to be a disciple?

Prayer suggestion: Lord, help me to embrace the cross, to take the humbler path, and to be empowered to live as a loving servant of Jesus.

Chapter 7 - The Ministry of Prayer and Intercession

1. What is prayer? Do any of the definitions particularly help you?

2. Why is insincerity such a poison to all of spiritual life but especially prayer?

3. What is meant by an 'inner room'? Jesus tells us to shut the door of this room and pray to our Father in secret. What do

we have to 'shut the door' to?

4. What is the order of prayer as taught by the Lord in the "Lord's Prayer"?

5. What are the main obstacles and hindrances in our prayer life?

6. What can we learn from the example of Jesus' own prayer life?

7. What does the victory of Jehoshaphat teach us about prayer?

8. As prayer is described as warfare, why is the armour of God vital?

9. What testimonies of answered prayer do you know? Can you learn anything from these events?

Prayer suggestion: Lord, lead me to a deeper place in prayer where I can fully know you and satisfy your heart's desire for my life.

Chapter 8 - Divine Healing and Deliverance

1. Most believers have heard about, or have experienced, God's healing power. Can you think of any examples?

2. Methods of healing don't work, but what are the most important keys to keep in mind when praying for healing?

3. What would you share with someone who is upset because they are suffering and have not been healed?

4. What are the two kinds of faith that we must encourage everyone to have?

5. What does the Old Testament tell us about the origins of Satan?

6. What are some of the most common avenues for Satan to trouble people?

7. What does the case of the Gadarene demoniac teach you about deliverance?

8. What are the key steps to obtaining and maintaining deliverance?

Prayer suggestion: Thank you Jesus, that at Your feet I find the power in Your presence to both set me free and keep me free. I praise You that you are Lord of all.

Chapter 9 - The Challenge of Leadership

1. What are the Christian qualities that allow the Headship of Christ to be a reality?

2. Who is to lead the Church under Christ's Headship?

3. Are there apostles in the Church today?

4. How are apostles made?

5. What are they key qualities of Christ's character that are fundamental in the life of leaders?

6. What words in the New Testament are used for leaders/ apostles and what does this teach us about their character?

7. How should apostles relate to money?

8. What is the function of elders?

9. What are the key qualities that are required in the life of elders?

10. How are elders made?

Prayer suggestion: Lord, bless our leaders, keep them close to you where they can hear your heartbeat and truly manifest your character in their lifestyle and through their ministry.

Chapter 10 - The Preaching Ministry

1. What are the essential foundations of the preaching ministry? Place them in the order of importance that you believe to be correct.

2. What strikes you about the testimonies of D.L. Moody and John Hyde?

3. What are the three great snares of the preaching ministry? Can you think of any ways in which congregations can help their ministers to overcome temptation?

4. What do you learn from the testimony of Spurgeon's conversion? What can we practically do to increase our effectiveness

in ministry?

5. Review the practical keys to preaching and think about which are the most important. Can you think of anything that might be added to this list?

Prayer suggestion: Lord, raise up preachers and teachers who love your truth, and preach it fearlessly without carnal ambition or pride. Be glorified in the midst of your people, and let your presence be known and felt in power.

Chapter 11 - Church Planting and Evangelism

1. The first section of this study is based on Acts 16. Read this chapter, and comment on what strikes you most about the unfolding purposes of God. Why is it so hard to make a method that can be imitated?

2. What are the qualities needed in a pioneer Church planter?

3. Why is team work so essential? Why is a good team in itself the foundation of a local Church?

4. Do you feel that you are part of a team? What can you do to encourage this?

5. What methods of Church planting have you been involved in? Is there a way of reaching out in your country and culture that has better access to people's needs and lives?

6. Do you think that many Church planting methods rely too little on the power of God to start and keep a work going?

Prayer suggestion: Lord, raise up new Churches in the land in situations where there is no testimony. Let there be fountains of worship opened in these places so that many will be harvested for the glory of God.

Chapter 12 - Church Growth

1. The outpouring of the Holy Spirit is the key to Church growth. What does this do to the pride of man?

2. What are the keys to obtaining fresh outpourings in our life, our Church and our community?

3. Identify areas where you think change needs come in your life,

STUDY GUIDE

in order to help your Church to grow.

4. Review the messages of Jesus to His Churches and reflect on the great need of the Church in your locality. Which of the great warnings seem most relevant to us today?

5. What methods might we use to promote Church growth? Have you got involved in something that brings you into contact with non Christians?

6. What are the wrong methods of Church growth?

7. What are the snares of Church growth?

8. What are the marks of true success?

Prayer suggestion: Teach me Lord to be encouraged by your smile of approval, whether others approve me or not. Lead your people to the attitude where you can pour out your Holy Spirit and so fulfil your heart's desire for the nations.

Chapter 13 - A Glorious Church in a Glorious Kingdom

1. Write down as many pictures or symbols of the Church that you can think of. What do they teach you?

2. Who is a member of the Church? What can we do to become members?

3. What are the keys of the Kingdom? Where are they used most commonly and by whom?

4. Why is it important to realise that the Church is not perfect in this age?

5. What are the dangers when Churches become big and old?

6. What are the attacks of Satan against the Church? What attacks can you identify in your own nation and culture?

7. What can we do to maintain unity in the face of serious doctrinal differences as in Acts 15?

8. What can we do to avoid personality clashes? How did David react to Saul's bad treatment and jealousy? How should we react to unspiritual behaviour?

Prayer suggestion: Lord, please refresh the Churches with fresh new prophetic ministry. Expose the root of problems and release us to know in fullness what you desire for your people. Let your kingdom come on earth as it is in heaven.

Chapter 14 - The Future

1. What are the different ways of looking at the book of Revelation? Which is the most obvious for people in situations like Africa, with little access to historical information?

2. What is the importance of interpreting symbols in Revelation from Old Testament accounts? For example: Babylon, the Lamb, lampstands, olive trees etc

3. Where are the 3 timelines found in the Bible? How does Nebuchadnezzar's image show world history? What does the destruction of the image signify?

4. From Matthew 24 what are the most striking prophecies that have been fulfilled?

5. What do you think are some of the big events still waiting to happen?

6. From your reading of the Bible do you think that Christians will pass through the great tribulation? Does it matter if we differ in beliefs over this? How can we personally ensure that doctrines do not divide us?

7. Write down in as short a form as possible the deciding factor on judgment day.

8. What are the essential elements of the condition of people in hell?

9. What are the essential elements of people in the New Creation.

10. How should knowing these things affect our life-style?

Prayer suggestion: Lord, help us to walk in white, and be worthy to stand before the Son of Man when you return to judge the nations. Help us to be ready and fully engaged in your will. Come quickly Lord Jesus! Amen

Made in the USA
Charleston, SC
24 April 2016